D0934464

ESOP: The Ultimate Instrument in Succession Planning

ESOP: The Ultimate Instrument in Succession Planning

SECOND EDITION

Robert A. Frisch

John Wiley & Sons, Inc.
New York • Chichester • Weinheim • Brisbane • Singapore • Toronto

This book is printed on acid-free paper. ∞

Copyright © 2001 by John Wiley & Sons, Inc., New York. All rights reserved.

Published simultaneously in Canada.

No part of this publication may be reproduced, stored in a retrieval system or transmitted in any form or by any means, electronic, mechanical, photocopying, recording, scanning or otherwise, except as permitted under Sections 107 or 108 of the 1976 United States Copyright Act, without either the prior written permission of the Publisher, or authorization through payment of the appropriate per-copy fee to the Copyright Clearance Center, 222 Rosewood Drive, Danvers, MA 01923, (978) 750-8400, fax (978) 750-4744. Requests to the Publisher for permission should be addressed to the Permissions Department, John Wiley & Sons, Inc., 605 Third Avenue, New York, NY 10158-0012, (212) 850-6011, fax (212) 850-6008, E-Mail: PERMREQ@WILEY.COM.

This publication is designed to provide accurate and authoritative information in regard to the subject matter covered. It is sold with the understanding that the publisher is not engaged in rendering legal, accounting, or other professional services. If legal advice or other expert assistance is required, the services of a competent professional person should be sought.

Library of Congress Cataloging-in-Publication Data:

Frisch, Robert A.
    ESOP : the ultimate instrument in succession planning / Robert A. Frisch.—2nd ed.
      p. cm.
    Rev. ed. of: ESOP handbook, c1995.
    Includes index.
    ISBN 0-471-43444-2 (cloth : alk. paper)
    1. Employee ownership—United States. I. Frisch, Robert A. ESOP handbook. II. Title.

HD5660.U5 F75 2001
658.15'22—dc21   2001026303

Printed in the United States of America.

10 9 8 7 6 5 4 3 2 1

About the Author

Robert A. Frisch

Robert A. Frisch is Chairman/CEO of The ESOT Group, Inc., headquartered nationally in Los Angeles. The firm, incorporated in 1975, specializes in the implementation and continued management of employee stock ownership plans (ESOPs) and has implemented hundreds of ESOPs throughout the country.

Frisch was a founder of a multistate financial corporation that was acquired by a conglomerate. He became vice president of a major Wall Street firm in charge of total financial planning for all their offices nationally.

Frisch consults extensively with owners of closely held companies on perpetuating the family business and with public and private companies on management buyouts.

The ESOT Group, Inc., known as the premier one-stop ESOP company, implements ESOPs and other equity-based compensation plans on a tailor made "turnkey" basis. The company's services include strategic planning, feasibility studies, ESOP plan design, obtaining IRS letters of determination, financing, repurchase liability studies, communicating the ownership culture to employees, and plan administration.

The firm maintains a free 24-hour ESOP information **hot line, 800-422-ESOP (3767).**

Frisch is author of seven definitive books on ESOPs and is a frequent lecturer to trade groups of CEOs, CPAs, and financial planning groups on ESOPs. He is considered one of the major figures in the ESOP movement.

FOR LEONA, DANA, RANDI, FRED, PAUL, LUCIE, AND LILY

The author would like to express his gratitude to his wife, Leona, for her patience, understanding, and wise counsel during the writing of seven books and eight updated editions on ESOPs and on succession planning since 1975.

Preface

An estimated 12,000 employee stock ownership plans (ESOPs) are in existence, representing companies of all different sizes and shapes. ESOPs have been implemented for virtually every rationale imaginable. The preponderance of ESOPs have been implemented for companies that were doing well with good prospects for the future. The vast majority of these have been created to foster succession planning for founders of privately held corporations who want to perpetuate their companies. Typically, they have between a 5- and 10-year retirement horizon.

Although some publicly traded corporations have ESOPs, most of the ESOPs that have been installed are for private companies with fewer than 300 employees. These companies are, with few exceptions, profitable; otherwise, the tax incentives would be of little or no value.

Leveraged ESOP buyouts (LBOs) of companies with thousands of employees have been newsworthy and, in most instances, praiseworthy. The alternative to an ESOP would have been the transfer of ownership to one individual or possibly a handful of investors rather than to the employees. Criticism that may have been levied on some of these transactions has been on relatively minor issues compared with the noble effect ESOPs have had in providing equity participation among the employees who would never, under any circumstances, have had the opportunity of owning a piece of the company that they have helped to build.

The more highly publicized ESOPs are those for corporations that were in the throes of economic chaos and facing the likelihood of going under. ESOPs in such instances were instituted in order to help save the company and preserve jobs for

Take 30% of stock — sell to ESOP — invest in
tax-deferred securities... to prepare for estate taxes.
w/i one year (stocks or bonds
U.S.

PREFACE

the employees. In spite of the publicity, these hard-luck scenarios represent less than one percent of the ESOPs in existence.

There have been a few instances in the past of flagrant abuses of ESOPs wherein unscrupulous owners have attempted, but generally not succeeded, in using ESOPs as a vehicle for bailing out a company that was on the verge of bankruptcy. Safeguards have since been instituted, which make this procedure a highly unlikely possibility. ESOPs must be valued by independent appraisal rather than by an internally prepared formula. This in itself is an effective obstacle to unconscionable bailouts.

Motives for Establishing ESOPs

Despite the suspicions of a very few legislators, a very large percentage of the ESOPs are in existence because of corporate owners who want to reward their employees for past and future loyalty by giving them equity in the corporation to which they are devoting a significant portion of their working careers and for succession planning. The ESOP advantages have made it feasible for the owners to fulfill these desires.

A large segment of ESOPs exist as the only viable alternative to selling the corporation to outsiders or liquidating the company when the owner is in need of retirement income to prepare for the eventuality of estate taxes. Either event would have triggered severe dislocations among the employees and a tax base loss to the community.

The initial loss of tax revenue to the government caused by an ESOP is quite minimal, since if a company did not have an ESOP it would generally have another form of tax qualified plan such as a pension, profit-sharing, or thrift plan, all of which are tax deductible and with none of the redeeming attributes of capital formation, which results in an immediate tax base expansion.

Were it not for the tax advantages, there is no reason to believe that owners of private business would share corporate ownership with employees any more than they have done in the past wherein such sharing has been virtually nonexistent. Legislators have continued to recognize this fact by continuing to broaden the availability of ESOPs. Until 1998, they were available only to C corporations. As of January 1, 1998, ESOPs have been able to be installed in Subchapter S corporations, although the rules are different for each.

A major portion of ESOPs are leveraged to enable the employees to have at least 30 percent of the equity of the corporation so that selling shareholders in C corporations can enjoy the tax deferment they are afforded upon sale of their securities described in Chapter 7. Corporate owners are often motivated to establish ESOPs in order to diversify their assets as a part of their succession planning strategy. The tax-deferred rollout into replacement securities offers an enticing opportunity to accomplish this end result.

Capital infusion for expansion or acquisitions is the motivating factor for a large block of ESOPs that have been effectuated because of the substantial tax advantages of these instruments of corporate finance.

Management buyouts of large and small corporations where the doability of the deal is doubtful have been turning to ESOPs as the enabling factor.

Venture capitalists who take an equity position in leveraged buyout situations have discovered ESOPs to be an ideal exit vehicle for cashing out their position. An escape hatch is a mandatory ingredient for an investor. Going public is not always a dependable means of recovering one's investment.

Surprisingly few companies have established ESOPs as a pure tax shelter. Of the hundreds of ESOPs that the writer has helped implement, none have been established with tax shelter as the primary motivation. The tax incentives have merely enhanced the feasibility of fulfilling an objective such as transferring equity ownership, increasing working capital, making acquisitions, or divesting a corporate subsidiary.

Leveraged buyouts that are not done in connection with ESOPs exacerbate the concentration of wealth. The fact that Congress recognizes this is evidenced by the fact that principal repayment is not tax deductible in LBOs but is deductible in ESOP buyouts.

A question that is asked frequently is, "If ESOPs are so good for businesses, owners, employees, and the economy, why aren't there more of them?" ESOPs are on the rise. They are being discovered in ever-widening circles. The fact that S corporations now can have them too is another impetus. They are complicated, and relatively few practitioners have made the effort to understand their workings.

In the author's view, nearly every profitable, growing corporation with an adequate payroll to make the plan worthwhile should consider implementing an ESOP as a means of succession planning. Hopefully, the contents of this book will confirm the rationale of this statement.

Though it focuses on the role ESOPs play in succession planning, this book details the rules by which they are governed and the many situations to which they can be applied. *ESOP: The Ultimate Instrument in Succession Planning* can really serve as an ESOP handbook.

This book is designed to be written in an easy-to-read yet comprehensive format, quite similar in style to the author's previous books. Because of this, it is hoped that the reader will be more likely to read the book from cover to cover. In this way, the full impact of the ESOP will blossom.

Contents

Chapter 1   Historical Background of ESOPs   **1**

Chapter 2   The Magic of ESOPs   **5**

2.1   Why ESOPs Are an Instrument of Succession Planning   5
2.2   How an ESOP Can Create a Market for a Stockholder's Stock   6
2.3   How a Corporation Can Cut the Cost of Borrowing Nearly in Half   7
2.4   ESOPs—What they Really Are   7
2.5   ESOP—The Ideal Financial Machine   8
2.6   Advantages—Generally   10
2.7   Congressional Backing   10
2.8   ESOP—A Misunderstood Program   11
2.9   Cost to Implement and Administer ESOPs   11

Chapter 3   The Environment for ESOPs   **13**

3.1   The ESOP Concept   13
3.2   Slow Early Days of ESOPs   14
3.3   Real Social Security through ESOPs   15
3.4   ESOPs and Motivation   15
3.5   The Use of ESOPs to Save Jobs   16

Chapter 4   Exit Alternatives for Owners of Private Corporations   **17**

4.1   The Preamble to Ownership Transition   17
4.2   Selling the Company to an Outside Buyer   18

4.3	The Initial Public Offering Alternative	19
4.4	The Management Buyout Alternative	20
4.5	The ESOP Alternative	20

Chapter 5 Planning for Succession   **23**

Chapter 6 ESOP versus Going Public versus Selling the Company   **27**

6.1	Going Public	27
6.2	Leveraged ESOP Loan versus Public Equity Financing	28
6.3	Selling to Outsiders	29
6.4	Selling to an ESOP	29

Chapter 7 How You Can Defer or Avoid All Taxes by Selling Some or All Your Private Company to Employees   **31**

7.1	The Tax-Deferred Stock Rollover	31
7.2	Stock That Is Eligible for the Nonrecognition Sale	32
7.3	ESOP Three-Year Holding Requirement	32
7.4	Qualified Replacement Property	33
7.5	Floating Rate Note	33
7.6	How to Create an Actively Traded Portfolio with a Floating Rate Note	34
7.7	How to Bootstrap a Seller-Financed ESOP	35
7.8	Allocation Eligibility	36
7.9	Procedures for Nontax Recognition on Stock Sale	37
7.10	The Corporation's Consent to the Nontax Recognition	37
7.11	How to Achieve Tax Nonrecognition with Less Bank Leverage	38
7.12	Tax Nonrecognition on an Installment Sale	39
7.13	Tax Requirements for the Tax-Deferred Rollout	39
7.14	Selling the Company to Outsiders	41

Chapter 8 How to Value the Stock of a Closely Held Company   **45**

8.1	Why Have a Valuation?	45
8.2	Independence of the Appraiser	45
8.3	Adequate Consideration	46
8.4	The Valuation Report Contents	47
8.5	Methods for Valuing Stock	48
8.6	Fairness Opinion	50
8.7	Control Premium, Minority Discounts, and Marketability Discounts	50

| 8.8 | Information the Appraiser Needs | 52 |
| 8.9 | Summary | 53 |

Chapter 9   Eligibility for ESOP Participation   **55**

| 9.1 | Eligibility | 55 |

Chapter 10   How to Fund an ESOP at Zero Net Outlay   **59**

Chapter 11   Contribution and Allocation Parameters of the ESOP   **61**

11.1	Employer Contribution Limits	61
11.2	Eligible Compensation	62
11.3	Employer Contribution Limits to a Nonleveraged ESOP	62
11.4	Combination ESOP	63
11.5	Leveraged ESOP	63
11.6	Dividends	64
11.7	Contribution Limits on ESOPs in Conjunction with Other Qualified Plans	65
11.8	Allocating the Benefits	65
11.9	Allocation Exclusions	67
11.10	Family Members Who Are Prohibited from Participation	67
11.11	Family Members Who Can Participate in the Allocation	67
11.12	Stockholders Who Own More Than 25 Percent of the Sponsor's Stock Directly or by Attribution	68
11.13	How to Determine if One Owns More Than 25 Percent	68

Chapter 12   ESOPs for Subchapter S Corporations   **71**

12.1	Introduction	71
12.2	Tax Flowthrough Attributes of S Corporations	71
12.3	Unavailability of the 1042 Tax-Deferred Rollover	72
12.4	Dividend Deductibility	72
12.5	Leveraged S Corporation ESOPs	72
12.6	Distributions to Terminated Participants	73
12.7	Prohibited Transaction Rules	73
12.8	Subchapter S Corporation ESOPs as an Employee Benefit	73
12.9	Conversion—S to C/C to S Corporation	74
12.10	Subchapter S Corporation ESOP Strategies	75

Chapter 13   How ESOPs Can Increase Working Capital and Cash Flow   **79**

Chapter 14   How to Increase Working Capital and Cash Flow by Converting a Profit-Sharing Plan or Pension Plan to an ESOP 81

14.1   Partial Conversion 81
14.2   Converting the Profit-Sharing Plan 82

Chapter 15   How to Convert or Terminate an ESOP 87

Chapter 16   Vesting Benefits 89

Chapter 17   Distributing the ESOP Benefits 91

17.1   Leveraged Distribution Rules 92
17.2   Distribution Methods 92
17.3   Nonleveraged Distribution Rules 92
17.4   Liberal Distribution Practice 93
17.5   Diversification Rules 93
17.6   How to Diversify the Accounts 94
17.7   Dividend Distribution 94
17.8   Withholding 95
17.9   Put Option 95
17.10 Buy–Sell Agreements 96
17.11 Distribution of Account Balances 96
17.12 Tax on Distributions and Rollovers 97
17.13 The Distribution Policy 98
17.14 The Asset Diversification Exemption 99
17.15 Withholding 99
17.16 Tax to the Participant 100

Chapter 18   Deductible Dividends—Only Through ESOPs 101

18.1   How Your Corporation Can Deduct Dividends to Service Debt 101
18.2   Passing the Dividend Through to Employees 102

Chapter 19   ESOP Account Diversification Rules 105

19.1   Introduction 105
19.2   The *De Minimis* Rule 106
19.3   Implementing the Diversification Elections 106

Chapter 20   Leveraged Buyouts and the ESOP   **109**

20.1   Leveraged Buyouts   109
20.2   Leveraging the Leveraged Buyout with an ESOP   111
20.3   Public Company Division Divestiture   111
20.4   Use of ESOPs in Corporate Divestitures   112
20.5   The MBO/ESOP Mechanics   113
20.6   Dilutionary Offsets   114

Chapter 21   The Leveraged ESOP for Business Succession   **115**

21.1   The Dilemma of Nonliquid Stock Ownership   115
21.2   How a Private Company Owner Can Provide for Successorship
       Through a Leveraged Buyout   117

**Chapter 22   How an ESOP Can Make a Leveraged Management
                Buyout Company Healthier**   **121**

22.1   How ESOPs Increase Corporate Value   122

**Chapter 23   ESOPs and Total Succession Planning™: Why Total
                Succession Planning™ Is a Must for Private Company
                Owners**   **123**

23.1   Hurdles of Transferring Ownership   123
23.2   The Loyalty Factor   124
23.3   The Need for a Successor   124
23.4   Preparing a Succession Plan   125
23.5   Succession and Exit Plan Components   125
23.6   What is a Total Succession Plan?   126
23.7   The ESOP as a Cornerstone for Total Succession Planning   126
23.8   Prefunding the ESOP   127
23.9   Moving Closer to Succession   128

Chapter 24   ESOP—A Practical Means to Succession Planning   **129**

24.1   Case Study   129
24.2   Using Minority and Marketability Discounts for a Gift   130
24.3   How to Maximize Net Investment Return   130
24.4   Wealth Replacement Trust   131
24.5   ESOP—The All-in-One Succession Planning Device   131

Chapter 25 The Amazing Leveraged ESOPs   **133**

25.1 The ABCs of a Leveraged ESOP Transaction   134
25.2 How a Leveraged ESOP Can Cash Out a Stockholder   135
25.3 Corporate Non-ESOP Loan Compared with a Leveraged
      ESOP Loan   136
25.4 The Cost Effective ESOP Loan   137

Chapter 26 The Management Leveraged ESOP Buyout   **139**

26.1 Selling a Division to the Employees through a Leveraged
      ESOP Buyout   139
26.2 Doing the Deal   140
26.3 How ESOP Divestitures Can Enhance Succession Planning   141
26.4 Management Groups as Acquirers   142
26.5 The Leveraged ESOP Divestiture   142

**Chapter 27 ESOP Techniques to Acquire Competitors, Suppliers, and
              Other Corporations with Tax Benefits to Buyer and Seller 145**

27.1 Acquisition Technique 1: Buying Target, Inc., Stock or Assets and
      Deducting the Cost   146
27.2 Acquisition Technique 2: Post-Transition ESOP   147
27.3 Acquisition Technique 3: How to Acquire the Target Company
      with Pretax Dollars and Give Tax Benefits to the Seller   149
27.4 The Loyalty Card   149
27.5 Steps to the Acquisition Strategy   149
27.6 Result of Transaction   150
27.7 Acquisition Technique 4: How a Selling Stockholder Can Acquire a
      Corporation with Tax-Free Dollars   151
27.8 Result of the Transaction   153

Chapter 28 How an ESOP Can Help You Create a Miniconglomerate   **155**

28.1 What to Look for in Selecting an ESOP Acquisition Target   156
28.2 What Prospective Lenders Look for in Financing an Acquisition   156
28.3 How to Structure Sequential ESOP Acquisitions   157
28.4 How to Sweeten the Acquisition for the Seller   159

Chapter 29 Strategies for Investing the ESOP Rollover   **161**

29.1 The Floating Rate Note   161
29.2 Selecting the Portfolio   162

29.3   Maximizing Income the Charitable Way   162
29.4   Summary   163

Chapter 30   Seven Practical ESOP Exit Strategies   **165**

30.1   Technique 1: Prefunding the ESOP   165
30.2   Technique 2: How to Sell Stock Under Section 1042 but Avoid
        Leverage   166
30.3   Technique 3: Self-Banking the Stock Sale   166
30.4   Technique 4: The Cashless Transaction   167
30.5   Technique 5: Corporation Wants Cashless Tax Deduction and
        Minimum Dilution   168
30.6   Technique 6: How Contribution of Redeemed Shares Can Minimize
        Dilution   169
30.7   Technique 7: How to Deduct Principal on an Existing Loan   169
30.8   The Flip Side of Antidilution   170

Chapter 31   How to Change Real Estate to Stock to Tax-Free Cash   **171**

Chapter 32   How Mr. Big Sold His Company Tax Free and Still Kept It **173**

32.1   The Locked-In Stock   173
32.2   How to Cash Out the Private Company Stock   174
32.3   The Cashing Out Procedure   174
32.4   Leveraging the Transaction   175
32.5   The Tax-Deferred (Possibly Tax-Free) Rollout   175

Chapter 33   What Lenders Look for in an ESOP Loan   **177**

33.1   Lender's Criteria   177
33.2   Analyze the Documents   179
33.3   Fraudulent Conveyance   179
33.4   Repurchase Liability Study   179

Chapter 34   How to Obtain Financing for the ESOP   **181**

34.1   Who Provides the Financing?   181
34.2   How a Lender Evaluates the Loan   182
34.3   Other Factors for Analysis   182
34.4   Real Value versus Cosmetic Effect   183

**Chapter 35   How to Recover Taxes Paid in Prior Years with No Cash
                Expenditures**   **185**

Chapter 36   Valuing Leveraged ESOP Stock   **187**

36.1   Valuation in a Management Buyout   187
36.2   Example   188
36.3   ESOP Transactions Involving Multi-Investors   189

Chapter 37   Issues in Selecting a Valuation Firm   **191**

37.1   Fiduciaries Select the Valuation Firm   191
37.2   Frequency of Appraisals   192
37.3   Multistock Transactions   192
37.4   Due Diligence in Selecting a Valuation Firm   192
37.5   What a Business Valuation Report Should Cover   193
37.6   Summary   194

Chapter 38   Cashing Out through a Nonleveraged ESOP   **195**

38.1   How Mr. Big Can Remove His Capital, Retain Control, and Perpetuate the Company   196
38.2   How to Feel Loved and Needed after Selling the Company— Keep Control   197

Chapter 39   Strategies for Selling an ESOP Company to Outsiders   **199**

Chapter 40   The Mature ESOP Company   **201**

40.1   Giving a Piece of the Pie to New Employees   202
40.2   Planning for Repurchase Liability   203
40.3   The Stagnating Company   203
40.4   Participative Management   204
40.5   Cooperative Governance Issues in ESOP Companies   204

Chapter 41   How and Why to Keep, Freeze, or Terminate an ESOP   **207**

41.1   Reasons to Keep the ESOP Active   208
41.2   Freezing the ESOP   208
41.3   Terminating the ESOP   209

Chapter 42   The Emerging Repurchase Liability   **211**

42.1   How the Put Option Affects Repurchase Liability   211
42.2   How the Repurchase Liability Affects Valuation   212
42.3   Repurchasing the Stock   212

42.4   Whether to Redeem or Recycle the Shares   213
42.5   A Funding Program That Won't Work   214
42.6   The Repurchase Liability Study   214
42.7   A Funding Program That Will Work   215
42.8   Methods of Funding the Repurchase Liability   215
42.9   Summary   216

**Chapter 43   The Charitable ESOP—How to Get a 200 Percent
Personal and Corporate Tax Deduction on Your
Charitable Gift and Other Strategies   217**

43.1   Tax Effect on the Donor   220
43.2   Tax Effect on the Corporation   220
43.3   The Charitable Remainder Trust CHESOP   221
43.4   Charitable Gift Annuity CHESOP   222
43.5   Pooled Income Fund Buyout Arrangement   222
43.6   Charitable Lead Trust ESOP Buyout   223

Chapter 44   Mixing and Matching ESOPs with Other Qualified Plans   225

44.1   Contribution Limits   225
44.2   Plan Characteristic Differences   226
44.3   How the 401(k) Works with an ESOP   227

**Chapter 45   ESOPs as an Executive Benefit in Combination with
Nonqualified Non-Equity Incentive Plans   231**

45.1   Designing the Incentive Plan   231
45.2   Providing the Cash to the Corporation for a SERP   236
45.3   The ESOP as a Compensation Plan   237

Chapter 46   Equity Participation Planning   239

46.1   Introduction   239
46.2   Stock Options   240
46.3   Incentive Stock Option Plan   241
46.4   ISO Tax Treatment   241
46.5   Nonqualified Stock Option Plan   242
46.6   NSO Tax Treatment   242
46.7   Stock Options—An Employee Win/No Lose Deal   242
46.8   Vesting of the Options   243
46.9   Stock Options for Employees of Closely Held Companies   243
46.10 Determining Stock Value for Private Company Options   243

46.11 Pros and Cons for Stock Options in Private Companies   244
46.12 Direct Stock Purchase Programs   244
46.13 Stock Purchase Plans under Code Section 423   245
46.14 Securities Issues   246
46.15 The Nonqualified Stock Bonus Plan   246
46.16 Restricted Stock Plan   247
46.17 Employee Stock Ownership Plans   248
46.18 Summary   248

Chapter 47   Profiles of Likely Candidates for ESOPs   249

Chapter 48   Security Law and the ESOP   251

48.1 Simplifying Securities Compliance   252
48.2 Antifraud Regulations   252
48.3 Registration Exemptions   252
48.4 Stock Offerings to Sophisticated or Accredited Investors   253
48.5 Public Company ESOPs   253
48.6 Blue Sky Laws   254

Chapter 49   Fiduciary Considerations   255

49.1 Those Who Are Not Fiduciaries   256
49.2 Investment Diversification and Fair Return Exemption   256
49.3 Exclusive Benefit of Participants   257
49.4 Trustee Selection   257
49.5 ESOP as a Takeover Defense   257
49.6 Multi-Investor Leveraged Buyouts   258
49.7 Adequate Consideration   258

**Chapter 50   How to Communicate ESOP Benefits to Employees
                for Greater Public Relations   259**

50.1 Building the Ownership Culture   261

Chapter 51   ESOPs for Lending Institutions   263

51.1 Why a Bank or a Savings and Loan Should Adopt an ESOP   263
51.2 ESOPs and Banks as Estate Trustees   265
51.3 ESOPs for Federal Savings and Loans   265
51.4 S&L as an Affiliated Person   266
51.5 Equity Commitment Notes as Regulatory Capital   266

Chapter 52   ESOP Disadvantages, Problems, and Solutions   **269**

52.1   Problems   269
52.2   Dilutionary Effect of Pensions and Profit-Sharing Plans   271

Chapter 53   The ESOP Implementation Procedure   **275**

53.1   Feasibility Study   275
53.2   Steps to Adopting an ESOP   276
53.3   The ESOP after Year One   277

Chapter 54   Accounting Basics   **279**

54.1   How Contributions to a Nonleveraged ESOP Are Treated   279
54.2   Accounting for Dividends   280
54.3   Reporting ESOP Loans on the Financial Statement   280
54.4   Recording the Purchase and Release of ESOP Stock   281
54.5   Earnings per Share   281

Chapter 55   Meet Some ESOP Companies   **283**

55.1   Case History Capsules   283

**Chapter 56   Driving Share Value for Small to Medium-Sized
                Companies**   **289**

56.1   Turning Turkeys into Improved Organizational Performance
       and Increased Share Value   289
56.2   Driving Share Value—an Example   290
56.3   Reviving the Mature ESOP   293

**Chapter 57   The Driving Share Value Program for Larger ESOP
                Companies**   **295**

57.1   The Larger Company   295
57.2   Employee Owner Driving Share Value Groups (DSVGs)   295
57.3   Establishing DSVGs   296
57.4   DSVGs—Not a Replacement for Management   296
57.5   Driving Share Value Groups Formation Checklist   297
57.6   The Senior Management/Employee Owner DSVG Committee
       Implementation Checklist   301
57.7   Summary   302

Chapter 58   Participative Management   **305**

58.1   The Transition to the Ownership Culture   306
58.2   Creating an Ownership Culture   307
58.3   Components of the Ownership Culture   308
58.4   Summary   309

Chapter 59   Governance Issues in ESOP Companies   **311**

59.1   Introduction   311
59.2   Impact on Employees of the First ESOP Transaction   311
59.3   How to Avoid Creating Two Classes of Employees   313

Chapter 60   Succession Planning Case Histories   **315**

60.1   Introduction   315
60.2   Case 1: The Parents Who Wanted to Be Fair   315
60.3   Case 2: Transition Plan for Owners with Different Goals   320
60.4   Case 3: Transition Using a CHESOP   323
60.5   Case 4: The Multistockholder Buyout   325
60.6   Case 5: The Management Buyout of a Division   327

Chapter 61   Companies That Should Not Have an ESOP   **331**

61.1   ESOP Noncandidates—Rules of Thumb   331

**Chapter 62   The Perfect Exit—Maximize Tax Benefit to Selling
                Shareholder and to the Corporation**   **333**

62.1   Exit Strategy   333
62.2   Floating Rate Note   334
62.3   How the Company Can Operate Tax-Free   335
62.4   Summary   335

**Chapter 63   Administration Policy Regarding Self-Correction—
                A Reprieve for Past Errors**   **337**

63.1   Introduction   337
63.2   Eligibility of Use APRSC   339
63.3   Summary   339

**Chapter 64   The Free ESOP Information Hotline
                800-422-ESOP (3767)**   **341**

Index   **343**

CHAPTER ONE

Historical Background of ESOPs

ESOPs can become the industrial equivalent to the Homestead Act, which was instrumental in giving this nation an identity as homeowners. Industrial wealth has been concentrated in the hands of a small percentage of the population. As this is being written, it is estimated that nearly 10 million employees of American corporations are covered under ESOPs and are experiencing the pride of owning equity in the company to which they are devoting their working careers.

The modern ESOP parallels the theory first put forth by a prominent German economist, Johann Henrich Von Thunen, during the early days of the industrial revolution. Von Thunen put an ESOP of sorts into being when he set aside a share of his farm's profits for his employees. He invested the profits in machinery that would enhance earnings. A portion of the profits was then put in each worker's name. Earnings that were invested in other than capital equipment spun off interest, which was allocated and distributed to the employees as a second income. The principal itself expanded and was distributed to the employee at retirement.

Von Thunen's concept was the antithesis of that set forth by his contemporary, Karl Marx, who felt that all capital should be owned by the government. Von Thunen wanted to spread the wealth among the people rather than let a handful of politicians control the productive capital. This would merely serve to substitute the politicians for the few nonpoliticians who at that time owned the vast portion of the capital.

In 1920, contributions to defined-benefit pension plans were given favored tax treatment by Congress. Legislation was passed in 1921 marking the birth of profit-sharing and stock bonus plans. The Tax Revision Act of 1942 served as the catalyst to induce industry to install these various tax-sheltered retirement plans.

Revenue Ruling 46, enacted in 1953, permitted any qualified retirement plan to borrow money for the purpose of purchasing stock. One year later, the nation's first leveraged ESOP was instituted. This was the well-known Peninsula Newspaper, Inc. ESOP. The company's owner wished to retire and transfer ownership to the employees. This was accomplished by means of a bank loan to the ESOP, in which all employees participated. The experiment was eminently successful, and today the paper is thriving and owned by its employees.

In 1973, the Regional Rail Reorganization Act became law, introducing legislation permitting ESOPs as a vehicle to enable corporations to finance their capital requirements.

The Employee Retirement Income Security Act of 1974 (ERISA) detailed the workings of the ESOP concept and added a certain precision to its implementation—coupled with some confusion.

The Trade Act of 1974 then added incentives for communities feeling the impact of trade competition from abroad. It structured a $500 million fund to be loaned in such situations, granting special favor to those companies having ESOPs.

The Tax Reduction Act of 1975 added impetus to the ESOP movement. In addition to increasing the investment tax credit (ITC) from 7 percent to 10 percent, it increased the ITC to 11 percent if the extra 1 percent was contributed to a tax credit ESOP or Tax Reduction Act ESOP (TRASOP).

The Tax Reform Act of 1976 extended TRASOP through 1980 and allowed corporations to claim an additional ITC of one-half percent if employees contributed that amount to the TRASOP. The conference report contained within this Act, along with Section 803(B) of the Act, stated that ESOPs are not to be treated as conventional retirement plans. They are to be treated as instruments of corporate finance.

The final Regulations, promulgated on September 2, 1977, recognized the function of the ESOP as a financing device that can benefit employees as well as the corporation and its stockholders. The Regulations reiterated congressional intent that the ESOP be treated as a valuable financial vehicle to create capital and to disseminate equity among the employees.

The Revenue Act of 1978, enacted on November 9, 1978, extended the TRASOP. The Regional Rail Reorganization Act Amendments of 1978 mandated that 15 percent of Conrail be owned by an ESOP. Funds were infused for this purpose. The U.S. Railway Association Authorization of 1979 created a mega-million-dollar loan account for the Delaware and Hudson Railroad, provided an ESOP was created for the railroad.

The Rock Island Transition and Employee Assistance Act authorized funds for the acquisition, lease, or rehabilitation of the Rock Island Railroad or the Milwaukee Railroad in conjunction with an ESOP.

The Final and Temporary IRS Regulations on Requirements for Electing 11 Percent Investment Tax Credit TRASOPs were issued on January 19, 1979. These regulations, along with the Technical Corrections Act of 1979, further clarified and liberalized the tax-credit ESOP.

1975: ESOPs were enacted into law. The Employee Retirement Income Security Act (ERISA). More than 20 legislative acts since have improved ESOPs.

HISTORICAL BACKGROUND OF ESOPs

ESOP → instrument of corporate finance / retirement vehicle

The Chrysler Corporation Loan Guarantee Act became effective in 1980 guaranteeing the loan, provided that Chrysler contribute $162.5 million (about 15 percent of the loan) of newly issued stock to an ESOP over a four-year period. This provision placed nearly a quarter of the corporate ownership in the employees' hands.

At the end of 1980, the Miscellaneous Revenue Act of 1980 became law. One of the more important aspects of the law was the extension of stock bonus plans (essentially nonleveraged ESOPs) of the right to make cash distributions to participants, subject to the participant's right to demand stock. This legislation, the first of the 1980s, led to new bills by congressional proponents of ESOPs. It became apparent that the Reagan administration was off and running in the direction of ESOPs as a means of capital formation for private enterprise.

In that same year, the Small Business Development Act was passed. Companies, 51 percent of whose stock was owned by at least 51 percent of the employees, would be granted preferential loan guarantee treatment.

The Economic Recovery Tax Act of 1981 was positive for ESOPs. It provided for a payroll-based tax-credit ESOP called the Payroll ESOP (PAYSOP) to replace the capital-related investment tax-credit TRASOP effective after 1982.

The 1981 Act also increased the allowable deductible contribution from 15 percent of covered payroll to 25 percent if used to repay principal of ESOP loans after 1981. Contributions for servicing interest could be made without limit. Greater employer flexibility was assured by the addition of what amounts to a call on a participant's stock under certain circumstances.

The Deficit Reduction Act of 1984 was a bonanza for ESOPs. It provided for a tax-free rollover, which lets stockholders sell stock to an ESOP without incurring capital gains tax so long as the proceeds of the sale are reinvested in domestic stocks or bonds within one year and the ESOP owns 30 percent or more of the company. The Act made dividends payable to ESOPs tax deductible if used to repay debt for the acquisition of stock of the sponsoring company or if passed through to the plan participants. It also excluded from tax 50 percent of the interest income received by banks or insurance companies for ESOP loans (Code Section 133). *was repealed*

While legislation has become more stringent for other forms of qualified plans, it has been increasingly benign for ESOPs.

The Tax Reform Act of 1986 added even more new incentives for corporations to establish ESOPs. Although it terminated PAYSOPs, it created new benefits. For example, the act made dividends deductible if used to service debt for the purpose of acquiring stock for the ESOP. It provided for a limited estate tax deduction on the sale of closely held stock to an ESOP with a phaseout provision effective after December 31, 1990. Numerous other beneficial provisions that are covered in this book were also part of the 1986 Act.

The Revenue Reconciliation Act of 1989 (RRA'89) modified the requirements of a tax-deferred sale of securities to an ESOP. The act also imposed new more stringent rules on the 50 percent interest exclusion on loans made by certain institutions

1997: S-Corps eligible for ESOPs.

to an ESOP. RRA'89 also repealed the provision that had permitted limited exclusion from estate tax of stock sold or transferred to an ESOP.

The Small Business Job Protection Act of 1996 (SBJPA'96) repealed Code Section 133, the 50 percent interest rate exclusion for lenders effective on loans made after August 20, 1996. Because of the restrictions, Section 133 loans were seldom used for private corporations but were used primarily in conjunction with large public company ESOPs.

The Taxpayer Relief Act of 1997 (TRA'97) made it possible and practical for Subchapter S corporations to have ESOPs. The rules governing S corporations are quite different from those of C corporations and will be discussed in Chapter 12 of this book.

The Economic Growth and Tax Relief Reconciliation Act of 2001 broadly improved ESOPs and other defined contribution plans.

The tax reduction that took place in 2001 made major changes in the amounts that could be contributed to ESOPs alone or in combination with other tax qualified plans.

CHAPTER TWO

The Magic of ESOPs

2.1 WHY ESOPS ARE AN INSTRUMENT OF SUCCESSION PLANNING

What if there were a way that would let the owner of a private company:

- Sell stock of the company, pay no tax on the proceeds, and still keep control?

- Increase the company's working capital and cash flow with no cash expenditure and no additional productive effort?

- Buy out minority or majority stockholders with pretax dollars?

- Cut the cost of borrowing loan principal nearly in half by deducting principal payments as well as interest?

- Recover taxes paid in prior years with no cash expenditure?

- Possibly transform the assets of the corporation's profit sharing plan into working capital?

- Make acquisitions with pretax dollars and tax free to the seller?

- Make life insurance premiums tax deductible?

- Provide the employees with equity at no cash outlay on their part or the owner's part?

- Deduct the payment of dividends from taxes?

- Increase productivity, profitability, and company value with no cash outlay?

- Improve employee benefits dramatically with no cash outlay?

- And what if employees or executives with little or no cash could buy a division, a subsidiary, or a corporation with other people's money (OPM), with the government paying nearly half the cost of the loan principal and the business paying the rest?

- Allow the corporation to operate in a totally tax-free environment.

Too good to be true? An ESOP makes it all happen and does so with the sanction and encouragement of the United States Congress. ESOPs and employee stock ownership trusts (ESOTs), which are interchangeable, are tax-qualified plans and trusts, respectively, which are created by corporations for the benefit of their employees. Because of the unique nature of these plans, they benefit both the corporation and stockholders. This is why they are so ideally suited as the ultimate instrument of succession planning.

Unlike typical pension and profit-sharing plans, an ESOP is mandated to invest its assets primarily in stock of the employer. It is a seeker of stock and can obtain it from the corporation in the form of newly issued stock or treasury stock contributions. The company gets a tax deduction based on the value of the stock or cash it contributes. Another source of stock is from stockholders who are willing to sell some or all of their holdings.

2.2 HOW AN ESOP CAN CREATE A MARKET FOR A STOCKHOLDER'S STOCK

In lieu of contributing stock to the ESOP, a corporation can make deductible contributions of cash. The cash can be used to acquire stock of shareholders who wish to divest themselves of some or all of their stockholdings. It is difficult for holders of private company stock to sell their stock. A sale of part of one's stock to the corporation is treated like a dividend for tax purposes. A sale to others generally means giving up control. Finding a buyer for minority shares of a private non–dividend-paying company is like searching for the Holy Grail. A majority owner or a minority stockholder can sell stock to an ESOP and defer taxes or possibly eliminate them.

This is a great way for an owner to transform paper into cash and diversify his or her estate while at the same time pass the company down to heirs or a second-line management team. By so doing, the owner can enjoy the spendability of his or her equity, assure perpetuation of the company, cash out minority stockholders, and still control the assets that are not in the ESOP. As we will see, this will enable the owner to continue to effectively control the corporation.

An ESOP is a defined contribution plan (stock bonus or combined stock bonus + money purchase pension plan).— Qualified Employee Retirement Plan (1975) (ERISA)

2.3 HOW A CORPORATION CAN CUT THE COST OF BORROWING NEARLY IN HALF

Neither pensions nor profit-sharing plans can borrow, but ESOPs are permitted to do so if the proceeds of the loan are used to purchase employer stock. Tax-deductible corporate cash contributions to the ESOP are employed by the plan trustee to buy stock from the corporation or from stockholders. The deductibility of the amount needed to service principal payments in addition to interest reduces the cost for repaying the loan by the taxes saved. This should accelerate the debt amortization and save ongoing interest payments as well. One dollar of cash flow can, therefore, go nearly twice as far in retiring debt principal.

ESOPs may borrow $ if it is used to purchase employer stock.

2.4 ESOPs—WHAT THEY REALLY ARE

An ESOP is a defined-contribution plan that is a stock bonus plan or a combination of a stock bonus plan and money-purchase pension plan designed to invest primarily in qualifying employer securities. ESOPs must meet the requirements of Code Section 4975(e)(7). ESOPs were enacted into law by the Employee Retirement Income Security Act of 1975 (ERISA). All qualified employee retirement plans are governed by this federal law.

In a company whose stock is not readily traded, qualifying employer securities denotes common stock of the employer corporation that has voting power and dividend rights equal to or greater than that of any stock in the company that has the greatest voting power and dividend rates. Noncallable preferred stock, whether voting or nonvoting, that may be converted to such common stock is also a form of qualifying employer security so long as the conversion price is a reasonable one. ESOPs of public companies may, of course, invest in the tradeable securities of that company.

With a defined-contribution plan, the company can vary its tax-deductible contribution and make no commitment to the employee as to a precise retirement benefit. This is in contrast to a money-purchase plan in which the plan's formula determines the contribution. A defined-benefit pension plan promises a specific benefit and adjusts contributions in an amount needed to achieve the benefit promised.

Stock bonus plans, profit-sharing plans, thrift plans, and money-purchase plans fall into the general category of defined-contribution plans. An ESOP must invest primarily in qualifying employer securities, which it can obtain from the corporation or from stockholders who are willing to sell their stock. The corporation can make tax-deductible contributions of authorized but unissued stock, treasury stock, or cash to the ESOP.

7

The company's contributions to the ESOP are tax deductible & may vary as desired.

2.5 ESOP—THE IDEAL FINANCIAL MACHINE

One of the most unusual attributes of ESOPs is their ability to create a corporate environment that is at one time beneficial to the sponsoring corporation, the stockholders, the employees, and the economy.

(a) For the Corporation

ESOP benefits to the sponsoring corporation include these profitable benefits:

- Increased capital (see Exhibit 2.1)

- Increased productivity

- Increased net profit

- Improved market share

- Increased stock value

- Improved public relations

Exhibit 2.1

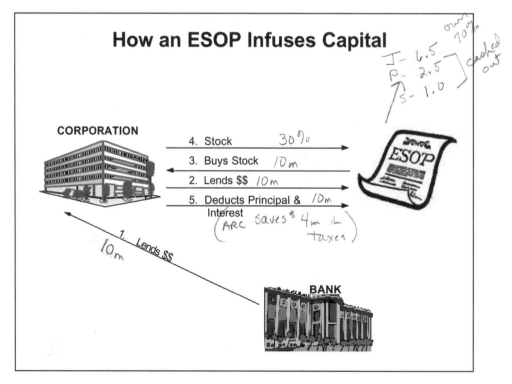

- Increased expansion
- Faster debt reduction because of ability to deduct contributions and dividends for repaying principal
- Improved employee morale
- Greater employee involvement toward the common goal
- A vehicle for succession planning
- An ideal recruiting tool
- Reduced turnover
- Reduced unemployment insurance premiums
- A vehicle for the orderly transition of management and employees
- An alternate to selling the company to outsiders
- An efficient, low-cost employee benefit program that can replace other costly plans
- A means to reward loyalty with equity without creating additional stockholders

(b) For the Stockholders

ESOP benefits to the stockholders include:

- Increased share value
- Tax-deferred or tax-free exit from a private corporation
- Others share the responsibility and stress load
- A vehicle for succession planning
- A means to step down gradually per the owner's own timetable
- What is good for the corporation is good for the stockholders
- Continued voting control in a private corporation
- Facilitates charitable gifts

(c) For the Employees

ESOP benefits to the employees include:

- Lower likelihood the company will be sold to outsiders
- Greater financial security for retirement

- Greater involvement and pride in their vocation through a sense of ownership

- Greater ability to affect their own wealth

- Ability to feel like owners

- Potential for current FICA-free dividends

- Fairness determined by independent valuation or, for public companies, the market pricing

(d) For the Economy

ESOP benefits to the economy include:

- Greater corporate profits mean more taxes

- Greater corporate growth creates more employment of those who will become taxpayers

- Reduced turnover reduces unemployment insurance compensation and welfare payments

- At retirement, less reliance on the Social Security and welfare systems

- No need for an expensive government agency to dole out retirement payments

- Retirees will spend their retirement income, thereby funding the economic chain, each segment of which will pay local, state, and federal taxes

2.6 ADVANTAGES—GENERALLY

Can one imagine a more perfect financial machine for a company? No machine is perfect, but the ESOP provides the means for company owners to determine the extent to which the vehicle will be used to achieve their corporate and personal objectives.

The ESOP makes it much easier to achieve corporate growth and increased profitability while repaying loyalty to the employees and an incentive for them to create greater wealth for themselves and for the stockholders.

2.7 CONGRESSIONAL BACKING

Congressional leaders have recognized the benefits ESOPs can bring to the economy by increasing the tax base. They have passed many pieces of legislation over

Company should be profitable before considering an ESOP.

the years to make ESOPs even more advantageous to the parties to the transaction, namely, the corporation, the stockholders, the employees, and the U.S. government.

2.8 ESOP—A MISUNDERSTOOD PROGRAM

The use of ESOPs should be expanded even further by the government because of the obvious stimulus to the economy. Moreover, if a profitable, growing corporation has an adequate payroll and does not have an ESOP, there is a strong likelihood that the owners do not have an adequate understanding of the advantages of ESOPs and may even harbor some misperceptions about them.

ESOPs are truly a win–win instrument of corporate finance. It is important that more information be disseminated about the true nature of ESOPs.

2.9 COST TO IMPLEMENT AND ADMINISTER ESOPs

The cost of implementation should generally be substantially less than the first year's tax savings. The primary costs are out of the way after the first year. The ongoing administration, although more complex to administer, costs about the same as other qualified plans. ESOPs should be implemented and administered by ESOP specialists who do this as a primary activity. ESOPs are not for all companies. With a few exceptions, they should not be implemented in companies that are not generally making a profit or that do not have the immediate realistic potential of doing so.

Although ESOPs have been used successfully to divest unprofitable divisions from public companies, such as in the well-known case of Weirton Steel, it is generally inadvisable to consider the ESOP a viable solution in companies that are not profitable. The author will take the liberty of quoting himself by saying: "An ESOP will not make a bad company good but will make a good company better."

ESOP = ESOT
Purpose → to broaden the base of capitalism.
A tax-qualified plan. A defined contribution plan.
ESOPs are employee trusts.

CHAPTER THREE

The Environment for ESOPs

More than 20 legislative acts have led to the present lofty status of ESOPs. The Tax Reform Act of 1986 created additional momentum that has further entrenched the ESOP as an instrument of corporate finance. The environment in Washington was one wherein the legislator's primary goal was to tackle the huge deficit and curtail tax shelters. Yet, on balance, the ESOP benefits were liberalized for corporations and the employees. The 1986 Act made ESOP financing more practical than ever before. It came on the heels of the Deficit Reduction Act of 1984, which was a hard act to follow.

ESOPs have become a movement unlike any this country has seen for many decades. A steamroller effect has become evident among an ever-increasing number of our legislators who hope to broaden the ownership of capital among the millions of employees who help create it.

The 1984 legislation, spearheaded by Senator Russell E. Long, was cosponsored by 47 other senators. A similar bill encouraging ESOPs had been cosponsored by 24 members of the House of Representatives. Interestingly enough, the sponsorship was bipartisan.

The 1984 and 1986 Acts are so broad in scope as to widen and resurface the path laid down by the Employee Retirement Income Security Act (ERISA) in 1974. ERISA stated congressional intent—to broaden the base of capitalism—when it formalized the interchangeable acronyms, ESOP and ESOT.

3.1 THE ESOP CONCEPT

The ESOP is quite simple in its concept. It merely involves a tax-qualified plan under which an employer may make tax-deductible contributions of cash or employer

[Handwritten margin note at top: ESOP → Employer makes tax deductible contributions of cash or employer stock to a trust. The trust assets are allocated among employee participants who receive distribution of cash or stock at their termination, death or retirement.]

stock to a trust. The trust assets are allocated among the employee participants, who will receive distributions of cash or stock upon their termination, death, or retirement. Hopefully, the trust assets will have risen in value prior to that time. Distributions of stock for which there is no public market are generally readily redeemable into cash.

[Handwritten margin note: ESOP Can borrow cash from any source, in order to buy stocks.]

Unlike other tax-qualified plans, the ESOP can borrow cash from any source, including the corporation or stockholders, in order to *buy* stock from the corporation or from stockholders for the benefit of the employee participants. Because the ESOP is a tax-qualified trust, cash contributed to it by the corporation to service the loan is tax deductible. Both principal and interest can be paid with deductible dollars, thereby permitting the loan to be discharged at a large discount.

Alternatively, the corporation can make tax deductible contributions of stock to an ESOP, thereby saving taxes with no disbursement of cash. Tax savings increase the size, value, and earning capacity of the company. The effect is to create new capital that employees can own without reducing the wealth of the business owners.

3.2 SLOW EARLY DAYS OF ESOPs

ESOPs got off to a slow start because relatively few employers were willing to put their companies on the line with a program that seemed too good to be true. A no-action, wait-and-see approach seemed appropriate.

For other entrepreneur-founders of private companies, putting stock in the hands of employees did not come naturally. From the employees' standpoints, cash in hand was better than idle paper that paid no dividends. From the IRS's viewpoint during that early period, there was suspicion that tax savings without a cash expenditure spelled S-C-A-M. The Department of Labor, very protective of its employee flock, also cast a wary eye on a plan whereby employees might possibly become the beneficiaries of overvalued employer securities in exchange for their expended labor.

In retrospect, all of these parties could have afforded to be much more optimistic. Indeed, the history of ESOPs in use has demonstrated that an overwhelming percentage of ESOPs have been highly successful in benefiting employee, employer, and the U.S. Treasury. In only an insignificant number of instances has there been a willful misuse of the ESOP concept to the detriment of employees. ESOPs have worked out so well for such a large variety of corporations and their employees that the government has enacted a stream of favorable legislation to encourage more widespread adoption of ESOPs.

Credibility is no longer a factor among companies who are considering the possibility of adopting an ESOP. It is estimated that ESOPs have saved hundreds of thousands of jobs since ERISA and have created thousands of new jobs because of the capital they have brought to ESOP companies.

By broadening capital ownership, ESOPs give more than mere lip service to the term *capitalism*. ESOPs can become the greatest boon to capitalism since the country adopted the philosophy as its mode of economic development.

ESOPs can borrow cash (from any source) in order to buy stock from stockholders or the corporation. Whatever the corporation contributes to the ESOP to service the loan (both principal & interest) is tax deductible

3.4 ESOPs AND MOTIVATION

3.3 REAL SOCIAL SECURITY THROUGH ESOPs

The Social Security solution for creating retirement security has always been easy, if unimaginative: Simply fund Social Security currently, and have employers and employees ante up more cash as needed. This is all well and good, but as businesses contribute ever-increasing amounts of their earnings into the Social Security fund, it reduces working capital and cash flow. This inhibits the company's ability to expand and create more jobs. Productivity is curtailed.

To the extent that employees own capital through stock ownership, they will become less dependent on Social Security. A reduction of the number of those on the Social Security rolls would decrease the amount of capital needed to fund the program. Corporate earnings that employers save by not contributing to the public system would be put to better use in their own companies. This would increase the value of the stock owned by the ESOP participants. Employees would have more disposable income to invest for their future security if their Social Security taxes were reduced or eliminated.

ESOPs have proven to be the most cost-efficient means of placing capital into the hands of employees. This is due to the fact that the capital they receive does not come from existing stockholders, but is derived from capital that would not have existed were it not for the ESOP. Millions of ESOP company employees are now capitalists who would not have been so characterized just a few years earlier. Many additional millions of employees will join their ranks as ESOPs proliferate.

3.4 ESOPs AND MOTIVATION

Numerous studies have shown that improved productivity is a by-product of stock ownership among employees. According to a study by the Survey Research Center at the University of Michigan, companies, the majority of whose stock is substantially owned by their employees, are one-and-one-half times more profitable than comparable companies that are owned conventionally. A National Employee Ownership Council study completed in 1986 demonstrated a correlation between the amount of equity owned by an employee in his or her employer firm and productivity improvement. The study found that ESOP companies outperformed their competitors to a greater extent in the post-ESOP period than they did in the pre-ESOP period. The more participative companies showed the greatest gain where stock ownership was also involved.

It has also been determined that the greater the amount of equity the employees owned, the greater the corporate profitability. MBA candidates at the UCLA Graduate School of Management have also correlated improved employee motivation with stock ownership by the employees.

A report by Michael Conte of the University of Baltimore and Joseph Blasi and Douglas Kruse of Rutgers determined that public corporations, 10 percent or more

Distributions to employees are taxed at termination of employment.

of whose stock is owned by employees, outperformed the various stock indexes. Other studies were quite consistent with these studies.

Equity ownership should be differentiated from management. Employees are more interested in equity accumulation in their ESOP account balances than they are in having a minority vote in the stock of the company. The greater their equity, the greater their motivation to achieve higher levels of productivity.

3.5 THE USE OF ESOPs TO SAVE JOBS

ESOPs have been used with increasing frequency to fund leveraged buyouts (LBOs) of companies by their employees. This occurs typically when the founder wishes to retire and becomes interested in looking for outside buyers. A number of leveraged ESOPs occur as a result of a corporation's decision to relocate to a better labor or economic environment. Employees in such situations would face mass localized unemployment. Management buyouts of corporate subsidiaries with the help of ESOPs have also become fairly commonplace.

State and local governmental agencies often encourage and help finance employee takeovers because of the potential harm a corporate relocation could create. Unions have joined the ESOP movement in order to maintain jobs among their membership. They have, upon occasion, encouraged employees to invest earnings into the business rather than into higher wages in order to assure the long-range well-being of their members.

In a number of employee buyouts, unions have gone along with wage reductions to help finance the corporate acquisition. The unions and the employees have an incentive to make the company succeed, since they will be getting a slice of the equity pie. Employees of ESOP companies will become capitalists in the truest sense.

ESOPs are being implemented overwhelmingly in healthy, growing corporations, companies with good management and a bright future. This is the most efficient means of putting stock into the hands of many employees. ESOPs require no contribution from the employee. Tax savings and increased productivity repay the company and its principal owners for contributing stock to the employee trust. ESOPs are proving their worth to corporations, major stockholders, employees, and the community at large. Their flexibility and value as instruments of corporate finance have given ESOPs a permanent status.

From the government's standpoint, tax revenue increases with corporate productivity. As ESOPs help companies become more profitable, the companies invest in capital equipment, expand, and hire more people. The corporations pay more taxes, as do their subcontractors and suppliers.

Employees must work in order to provide revenue for the government. Distributions of their account balances are taxed to the employees at termination of employment. These distributions provide a magnificent means of circulating cash throughout the economy with an eventual gain to the government.

CHAPTER FOUR

Exit Alternatives for Owners of Private Corporations

4.1 THE PREAMBLE TO OWNERSHIP TRANSITION

Founders of corporations go through various stages of growth—if they are fortunate. At the earliest stage, survival is the order of the day. In many instances, survival is at the forefront of the founders' thought processes throughout a major part of their business careers.

As founders increase their businesses' volume, profitability, and fair market value, they continue to build until such time as their inner clocks suggest that they slow down, which usually tends to trigger introspection and recurring thoughts of ways by which they can translate their achievements into a spendable form and smell the roses.

A large percentage of founders in their late 50s, 60s, and 70s have never prepared for retirement, either mentally or financially. Some at those ages who are prepared to retire financially have not prepared themselves psychologically to walk away from the business and into the realm of retirement.

What can they do in retirement that even comes close to the mental challenge and the variety of categories of events the chief executive officer (CEO) experiences that keeps the blood racing through his or her arteries? Most company owners who retire are less experienced at that new area of endeavor and ill-prepared for its challenges than they were when they dared to found their businesses.

Is one who is in his late 70s and in good health unable to cope with the hurly-burly of the daily business routine? Don't bet on it. When I was in my early 30s, I played a good game of four-wall handball. A frequent opponent of mine was an octogenarian who whipped the daylights out of me, using masterful strategy and conserving his energy by staying in one small area of the court while I was all over the place.

Like good wine, founders become seasoned with age. They are able to take problems in stride without missing a beat. Like my handball opponent, they learn how to expend less energy while accomplishing more through their vast storehouse of experience.

Many such owners do not dare contemplate total retirement and even become petrified at the possibility that they may have to play golf several times a week or function within one or two other categories of activities of which they might soon tire—then what? The chronology syndrome nonetheless prevails, and the founder realizes that the clock is ticking and it is timely to start becoming more liquid. Perhaps he or she knows of no way to sell the company stock and still continue to control and manage it. There are alternatives that the owner of the company should consider.

4.2 SELLING THE COMPANY TO AN OUTSIDE BUYER

Within a short time after selling the company to an outside buyer, or perhaps overnight, the former owner is often virtually banished from the business that had occupied his or her waking hours for a whole working career. This can be traumatic. Some sales are made on a workout formula, making a significant portion of the sale price dependent upon future profits. This type of sale can be particularly stressful to the selling shareholder, who is no longer in charge of the company's destiny.

Owners who sell to outside buyers often experience pangs of remorse due to their having placed the security of their loyal employees in the hands of strangers who owe no allegiance to those long-time employees. Those who were the most loyal are likely to be among the first to be discharged, because they tend to be among the most highly compensated. The founder often takes this route because it is often the only one with which he or she is familiar.

For companies that survive until their founders are ready to become *more* liquid, the destiny of the company is, most commonly, a sale to outside buyers. This is usually a path of least resistance.

Founders who have groomed children or other managers as their successors are to be commended for reducing the need to sell the company to outsiders. If the heirs are able to structure and finance the buyout in a manner that satisfies the founder's needs, such a succession plan might succeed.

If the buyer provides the total amount of financing and purchases 100 percent of the outstanding stock without requiring a four- or five-year workout nor the seller's taking back paper, the transaction, though quite rare, can be quick and relatively painless.

The disadvantages of selling to an outsider buyer include:

- The founder gives up his or her "toy" in life, the company, as well as the challenges and the brain stimulation—"if you don't use it, you lose it"

- Probable dislocations among the most valued and loyal employees

- Tax on the gain

- Loss of future salary and "perks"

- The trauma of losing power suddenly and facing a more sedentary lifestyle

- Possibly depriving a capable child or a manager of the opportunity to run the company.

4.3 THE INITIAL PUBLIC OFFERING ALTERNATIVE

Entrepreneurs typically relish the knowledge that whatever mistakes they make in the business are their own—as are the rewards. Is it any wonder then that they might be reluctant to make shares of their companies available for ownership by others who are not even remotely knowledgeable about the hands-on operation of their corporations?

If the business goes public, that is precisely what occurs. The financial results and operations are scrutinized by market makers who issue public reports, which include a prognosis of what the future holds for this once intensively private company. The company "comes out of the closet," financially speaking. In addition, the company must deal with "Big Brother," the Securities and Exchange Commission (SEC), whose presence looms large over the company's landscape. The SEC offers no accolades, only the potential for public criticism. Above and beyond that aspect are the costs of proper disclosure starting with the prospectus, the lawyers, the certified public accountants (CPAs), the investment bankers, and the most costly commodity of all, time away from profitable pursuits.

Entrepreneurs who go the route of an initial public offering (IPO) must be prepared to suffer the cost of diverting their attention, as well as that of other executives and staff members, from the companies' operations. The pressure to perform for others, the unnamed faces who invested in the companies' stock, can be excruciating and unceasing.

In the vast majority of IPOs, the number of new stockholders at the early stages is usually not great—unless we are talking about the Microsofts and Genetechs of the world, companies with unusual market appeal.

A *thin market* is one that has a small volume of stock sales in the public sector due to little demand, resulting from a dearth of interest in the company. A sale of a fairly sizable block of stock can depress the market, thereby reducing the per-share price at a time when the founder might want to diversify his or her holdings.

A sale by the founder is done through a secondary offering that requires a prospectus and becomes public information. The public, possibly skeptical about the fact that insiders want to sell, often beat the would-be seller to the punch by selling first, causing the price to decline.

As noted above, some IPOs are wildly successful. These are the ones that everyone knows about because of their tremendous visibility. Other IPOs might start out with a good public trading response, only to become flaccid shortly thereafter—or the market might remain strong permanently.

If the market starts out as a thin one, it tends to remain so for a few years—or indefinitely. In this instance, frustrated founders sometimes take the company private by tendering an offer for the public's shares so as to resume control again and build the company for long-term objectives the way they had done before the IPO, which had demanded short-term objectives.

4.4 THE MANAGEMENT BUYOUT ALTERNATIVE

Logical buyers of a private corporation are the managers, using management buyout (MBO) techniques whereby the MBO group of managers puts up some of their own equity capital, borrowing the balance of the amount needed to acquire the stock or assets of the company. The managers might attract equity capital from an investment group, who may or may not demand a control position.

The greater the equity, the smaller the debt that must be incurred. Without a source of outside equity, the company's future stream of earnings might be insufficient to service the debt, and banks might be resistant to providing the funds. Conversely, the greater the amount of debt that is available, the smaller the amount of equity that will be required. Equity is more expensive than debt.

Assuming that debt financing is available and the MBO succeeds, the burden of servicing principal with after-tax dollars through a leveraged buyout will retard growth, and it might take years for the company to regain its ability to resume its earlier growth trend.

In spite of this, MBOs can and often do succeed. It might take longer for the managers to reap the reward, because a corporation in the 41 percent tax bracket must earn $1.7 million to repay $1 million of principal, not considering interest payments.

4.5 THE ESOP ALTERNATIVE

The ESOP can be an alternative, or it can be used to facilitate a sale to an outside investor and can enhance an MBO's chance for success. By selling some of his or her stock to an ESOP, a founder can avoid the disadvantages that may be inherent in making an outright sale of the company to an outside investor.

The owner of the company can sell some of his or her stock to the firm's own ESOP, pay no capital gains tax, diversify personal assets—thereby receiving a supplementary income—and continue to effectively vote the stock sold to the ESOP.

After selling all of the stock that the founder needs for retirement, the balance of the shares can be transferred to one's offspring or other heir by means of a gift or purchase by the successor at such time as the founder wishes to relinquish control. Meanwhile, the selling shareholder can retain effective control as long as he or she wishes.

The employees not only will avoid displacement but will receive tax-free equity in the company and greater retirement security than any other program is likely to provide.

The ESOP and sale to an outsider are not mutually exclusive. The founder can sell a large percentage of his or her stock to the ESOP, deferring or possibly avoiding the tax on the appreciation. The remaining stock can then be sold to the outside buyer, transferring effective control over the ESOP shares as well to the buyers.

The ESOP does not preclude going public as well. Many public companies do have ESOPs. The IRC Section 1042 transaction (the ability of the selling shareholder to defer or possibly avoid taxes) is not available to public companies, but the other tax-advantaged benefits are.

The ESOP for the right company can serve as an exit for the founding generation on a stand-alone basis or in conjunction with other methodologies.

CHAPTER FIVE

Planning for Succession

Owners of private corporations do a great deal of planning as to the direction the business should take in order to capture market share. They put great thought into matters pertaining to personnel and into the purchase of equipment. They are loath to plan for business succession, however.

There are a number of possible reasons for owners being reluctant to plan:

- *Inertia*—Entrepreneurs, as a breed, are optimistic and often believe they will be able to work for many more years. There is therefore no sense of urgency in terms of thinking about eventually replacing oneself.

- *Confidentiality*—Owners of private companies often play things close to the belt and do not tend to share financial information about the company, something that would be necessary if one were to start grooming a successor.

- *Emotional blocks*—Making decisions relating to future involvement of family members in the business can involve dynamics that affect relationships among those other family members who are not to be involved in the company. It is no longer simply a business decision.

- *Fear of control erosion*—The entrepreneur does not want to create a situation that will undermine any element of control over his or her "baby," the company, whether real or imagined.

- *Lack of activity alternatives*—Owners of private companies all too often have devoted their entire energies to building the company, leaving little time for other interests. This can be a deterrent to replacing oneself in their primary area of interest.

- *Fixation on eventually selling the company*—Although the owner would prefer to have his or her child or a manager carry on the business, they have no cash which the owner will need in retirement and knows of no alternative.

- *Not good at training*—Entrepreneurs are often hands-on people and find it easier and more satisfying to make all decisions without taking time out to transfer this ability to possible successors.

Is there any wonder, then, why only one out of twenty family companies fail to reach the second generation?

Ownership transition should be anticipated five to ten years in advance. This requires foresight and the willingness to initiate a game plan. The owner should decide upon what his or her objectives are and work out a practical methodology and a timetable for achieving the objective.

Some of the more obvious approaches that will come to mind are:

1. Selling the company to an outside buyer.

Problems:

    (a) The seller must pay taxes on the gain.

    (b) The deal might be structured on a work-out arrangement and the seller might have to remain on a consulting basis for a few years to help gain the maximum value. The results will nonetheless be under the full control of the buyer.

    (c) The seller might have pangs of guilt for having abandoned some of the loyal managers whose future might be in jeopardy.

2. Selling the company internally.

Problems:

    (a) The managers seldom have adequate personal resources to buy the company.

    (b) If the owner bonuses the cash to the manager for the buyout, the owner is using his own money to buy himself out.

    (c) The owner will be taxed on the proceeds.

    (d) The manager will be subject to a phantom tax on the bonus.

    (e) If the company becomes leveraged, the owner will usually be a guarantor and must remain involved to assure the debt will be retired.

ESOPs create an internal market for the corporate stock with special tax advantages for both the corporate and the selling shareholders

Is there any wonder many company owners simply throw up their hands and do nothing?

The ESOP can be designed to create an internal market for the stock with special tax advantages to both the sponsoring corporation and the selling shareholder.

It can be used in various ways so as to blend in with the owner's timetable and its very presence will keep succession planning on the owner's mind. The owner might wish to sell a small part of his nonliquid stock portfolio to the ESOP at first and may decide to go into the planning more aggressively in a few years.

At any rate, the ESOP can help the owner keep focused to the idea of succession planning by its very presence. The ESOP will make it much more likely that the balance of the stock—which controls the ESOP—can be transferred to the managers or to the owner's child who is being groomed to run the business.

The ESOP can remove the feeling of helplessness that many owners face when contemplating transition of ownership planning because the ESOP is such a practical tool that has unusual tax advantages and can be very flexible in the way it is used.

CHAPTER SIX

ESOP versus Going Public versus Selling the Company

6.1 GOING PUBLIC

As noted in Chapter Four, a public offering is costly and the results are uncertain. It is in no way a panacea. An owner who wants to exchange stock for cash will consider the possibility of going public. In order for this to be a serious consideration, the company should have management strength, financial stability, good prospects for growth, and be in an economic environment that is conducive to a successful public offering.

If the objective is to get capital out of the corporation by creating a market for the stock, the entrepreneur may be disappointed. The offering price is determined at the due diligence meeting of the underwriters. The determining factor is the marketability of the issue. This, in turn, is related to the then current status of the stock market. The stock would quite possibly be offered through a regional exchange and there would be a thin market for the security. A sale of a significant portion of the owner's stock at the initial offering would be suspect. If the company is so good, why is the owner selling?

A thin market refers to the fact that the stock is held by relatively few stockholders and would not absorb large block sales of the securities. The price that the entrepreneur could hope to receive for his or her holdings might be well below the original offering price or even less than liquidation value.

Assuming the offering has been successful, it would still be impractical for the founder to plan on selling the bulk of his or her stock because of the rules prohibiting control persons from selling more than a fairly insignificant amount of stock at any point in time.

Underwriters do not come cheaply. They frequently demand a portion of the company in addition to their large fees. There are other significant expenses that detract from the attractiveness of a public offering, such as the burdensome costs for meeting the requirements of the securities laws. These are first noted with the filing of the 10K. Nonproductive expenses of such items as public relations–oriented annual and quarterly reports for the stockholders as well as the ongoing filings required by regulatory agencies divert additional working capital and management energies from the task of building the company.

One of the most dramatic aspects of going public from the entrepreneur's standpoint is the move from the picket fence home to the goldfish bowl. The owner will be under public scrutiny and will no longer be able to run the company on a shoot-from-the-hip basis.

This is not to say that private companies should never go public. Some corporations are made to order for having their stock widely held. Sadly, the ones that make it to the extent intended are few and far between. A private company has greater control over its true value than a public company because the latter is subject to the whims and vagaries of the public marketplace. Having said this, the valuation of private companies partially reflects the value of the public corporations in related industries.

It is important to remember that none of the companies on the New York or American Stock Exchange started there. There was a long road between the regional or over-the-counter exchanges and the big board. Those companies had the staying power to reach that austere status that made it big for their original stockholders.

On analysis, going public would probably be relegated to a distant second position when compared with the alternatives of selling to an outside investor, a group of investors, or the company's employees through an ESOP-assisted leveraged buyout (LBO) or partial buyout. The existence of an ESOP will not serve as a deterrent to going public. More and more public companies are implementing ESOPs for many of the same reasons that motivate private companies to do so in addition to reasons unique to public corporations.

6.2 LEVERAGED ESOP LOAN VERSUS PUBLIC EQUITY FINANCING

Private companies that require financing often consider going public as a means whereby the corporation can reach out to the public for equity financing. Where applicable, this can be a viable alternative to leveraged ESOP debt financing.

In the case of a public offering, the corporation would raise cash by selling a predetermined amount of stock on the open market, the value of which equals the cash requirement. It is always problematic as to whether a corporation will be able to realize the true worth of its stock in an initial public offering (IPO); if not, the offering would create equity dilution. Share and equity dilution to the shareholder's position is another possible cost factor created by a public offering. If the IPO succeeds in increasing the stock's value, the stockholder made the right choice.

A factor in the cost comparison with ESOP financing that is sometimes over-looked is the question as to whether the corporation has a qualified retirement plan for its employees that might be replaced by an ESOP. Contributions to such plans erode working capital and dilute equity. Had the equity raised in the offering gone to the employees instead of to the public, this would replace the benefits that the corporation would otherwise have had to purchase in order to maintain compara-ble employee benefits when compared with similar corporations.

The public offering, however, requires no debt service whereas the leveraged ESOP does. These are some of the tradeoffs. Interestingly enough, a number of companies that this author has assisted in going public have since gone private.

6.3 SELLING TO OUTSIDERS

This route is probably the most disruptive of all. It represents cashing in the chips both monetarily and activity-wise for the owner(s) as well as their loyal manage-ment team. A buyer will frequently tell the owner of the target company that he or she will not even consider buying the company unless the seller and top manager remain with the company for "X" years. The marriage generally lasts long enough for the new owners to learn the ropes and establish themselves with suppliers and customers. Then the relationship all too often falls apart. If the sale is stock for stock, it is tax-deferred but there is no diversification. Sale of the securities that are acquired in the merger triggers a tax on the gain down to the original investment in the founder's own company. A cash sale is taxed down to the basis.

6.4 SELLING TO AN ESOP

The stockholder wishing to sell stock in the private corporation can do so with tremendous advantages through an ESOP. The corporate owner can sell stock at a price that has been determined independently by scientific methodology. He or she can still operate the company with no new venture capital investors looking over his or her shoulders with bated breath wondering how quickly they can cash out and not concern themselves with the long-range welfare of the corporation and the people who devote their careers to making things happen. Through the ESOP, the selling shareholder creates no new direct stockholders or other bosses as one does in the public offering or in the selling to outsiders scenario.

The tax savings through an ESOP tends to help offset the dilutionary effect on the stockholders as does the fact that the ESOP can replace other forms of qualified plans which dilute equity. The owner can bring home a greater equity value by using an ESOP rather than the public or private sale. The deductibility of principal and the de-ferment of taxes through the ESOP route makes ESOP financing very compelling.

To qualify for the tax deferment for shareholders selling stock to an ESOP, the ESOP must own ≥ 30% of total value of company's stock. Code Section 1042 of Deficit Reduction Act of 1984

CHAPTER SEVEN

How You Can Defer or Avoid All Taxes by Selling Some or All Your Private Company to Employees

Prior to the 1984 Tax Act, the tax laws had been responsible for many private companies being sold to other corporations in stock for stock transactions rather than to their own employees. There is no tax on the exchange of stock by a corporate owner who sells 80 percent or less of the outstanding stock to another corporation for stock in that company. If one sells more than 80 percent, taxes are deferred until the shares acquired in the transaction are sold. The downside of this is that the seller is left holding the stock of just one company. If the stockholder sells the replacement stock, he or she will be taxed on the gain above the original basis of the securities in the acquired corporation. If the stock declines in value it will create a nerve-wracking experience due to the lack of diversification.

7.1 THE TAX-DEFERRED STOCK ROLLOVER

An improvement of windfall proportions brought about by the Deficit Reduction Act of 1984 affects stock sold by a shareholder to an ESOP after July 31, 1984. Code Section 1042 is the tax-deferred rollover provision, which, as the name implies, would, under proper circumstances, give the same tax break to an owner who sells shares to an ESOP that is enjoyed by the owner who sells shares to another corporation for stock in that company.

Actually, the sale to the ESOP is more advantageous in that an owner does not have to sell 80 percent of his or her stock holdings in order to receive favorable tax treatment. Moreover, the proceeds of the sale can be invested in a diversified portfolio. To qualify for the tax deferment (or, as we shall see, possibly tax avoidance), immediately after the sale, the ESOP must own 30 percent or more of the total value *[handwritten annotation at top: Stock of S-Corps does not qualify for the deferred rollover. If ESOP disposes of the shares acquired under a Section 1042 transaction, the corporation pays w/i 3 years a 10% excise tax (non-deductible). Employee distribution don't count in this.]*

of the company's stock or of each class of stock, including the stock in the sale being transacted. It does not matter how the ESOP accumulated the shares so long as the 30 percent mark has been obtained. Preferred stock is not included in determining the 30 percent. Sale of stock to the ESOP by two or more stockholders can be considered as though it is a single sale for purposes of the 30 percent rule so long as the sale is prearranged as a single integrated transaction. The 30 percent threshold rule can be complied with whether the ESOP acquires stock as a result of a contribution by the corporation or as a sale by stockholders.

7.2 STOCK THAT IS ELIGIBLE FOR THE NONRECOGNITION SALE

The stock sold by the stockholder under Code Section 1042 must have been held for at least three years and may not include stock acquired under an option or any other right that the employer may have granted the stockholder. It must not have been stock received as a result of a distribution from a qualified retirement plan nor may it be stock of a corporation that has had securities that have been readily tradeable on a securities market within a year preceding or following the sale. The selling stockholder must not be a C corporation if the nonrecognition of tax is to apply. Stock of S corporations does not qualify for the deferred rollover.

7.3 ESOP THREE-YEAR HOLDING REQUIREMENT

One of the government's objectives in providing the tax benefits to the selling shareholder under the Section 1042 transaction is to transfer stock to the employees' accounts. To ensure that this will be likely to occur, the Code stipulates that if the ESOP disposes of the shares of stock acquired under a Section 1042 transaction within a period of three years of the acquisition of those shares, the sponsoring corporation must pay a nondeductible excise tax of 10 percent of the amount of the stock disposed of by the ESOP during this period.

The tax, under Code Section 4978, is applicable if the value of the stock in the ESOP is less than 30 percent of the value of all employer stock held at the time of the transaction or if the total number of shares held in the ESOP within three years after the transaction date is less than the number of shares it held before the transaction date. Distribution of stock from the ESOP for statutory reasons including employee terminations, disability, death, or retirement is excluded from this provision.

The Section 1042 rollover provision has created an alternative to owners of private corporations that encourages them to sell their stock to the employee trust instead of to other corporations. The owner can still retain as much as perhaps 60 or 70 percent of the company stock and have the benefit of any future appreciation. The stockholder can sell incremental shares in the future, possibly at ever-increas-

Owner can retain up to 70% of stock y benefit y increased appreciation possible — selling incremental shares to ESOP on a tax-deferred (free?) basis. Corporation can make tax-deductible contributions to ESOP to fund this transfer

7.5 FLOATING RATE NOTE

ing values on a tax-deferred or possibly tax-free basis. The corporation could, of course, make tax-deductible contributions of cash to the ESOP, which would be transferred over to the selling stockholder and be tax-deferred.

7.4 QUALIFIED REPLACEMENT PROPERTY (QRP)

In order for the seller of the stock to defer the tax upon sale of his or her shares, the seller must invest in qualified replacement property (QRP), that is, securities of domestic operating corporations within 12 months from the date of sale, or, more precisely, within 15 months commencing three months prior to the transaction.

Qualified replacement property includes not only public or private corporate stock but corporate stock rights, bonds, debentures, notes, certificates, or other evidences of indebtedness in registered form or with coupons attached. These securities must be issued by domestic corporations, more than 50 percent of whose assets are involved in an active business or having no more than 25 percent passive income for the tax year preceding the year in which the replacement securities are purchased. Mutual funds, certificates of deposit, government securities, real estate, or securities of the sponsoring corporation or of a corporation that is a member of the same controlled group do not qualify as QRP under Section 1042. One can use the tax-deferred funds to bankroll a new operating corporation. If the replacement securities are sold, the gain above the basis of the original private company stock that had been sold will be taxed down to their original basis. Only those investments that are sold are taxed. The remaining replacement securities are not taxed.

The tax can therefore he spread over the seller's lifetime assuming all of the replacement securities are destined to be sold gradually over that time frame. If the securities are held until death, they would, prior to the 2001 tax change, receive a stepped-up basis and income tax would be avoided permanently. By investing directly in stocks, the selling shareholder acquires a fixed portfolio. The law may be amended to allow the basis to increase, once again, to 100 percent at death. It is possible, however, to create an actively tradeable portfolio without being taxed down to the original basis. That is by investing the 1042 proceeds in a floating rate note. This is described in the following section.

7.5 FLOATING RATE NOTE

Designer forms of securities, referred to as floating rate notes (FRNs), have been created by various highly rated corporations to qualify as QRP for this type of transaction. Some of these FRNs have a 40- to 80-year maturity callable in 30 years with 30-day floating rate and liquidity features. Because banks consider FRNs to be virtually perfect collateral, they will lend up to 90 percent against the floating note at close to a *wash* cost. This allows the selling shareholder to invest the amount borrowed in other investments without triggering capital gains tax down to the original basis as these investments are sold.

By using this strategy, one can create an actively traded portfolio with the borrowed funds and never have to repay the loan until death, at which time the basis is stepped up to the market value at that time, thereby avoiding any capital gains tax, as noted above.

7.6 HOW TO CREATE AN ACTIVELY TRADED PORTFOLIO WITH A FLOATING RATE NOTE

Floating rate notes are long-term bonds that qualify as QRP and they are generally issued by large U.S. corporations whose credit rating is AA or AAA. The FRNs pay a floating interest rate that is adjusted monthly or quarterly, the rate being based on LIBOR commercial paper minus some basis points, such as perhaps about 25 bps.

The interest rate charged by banks on loans using the FRN as collateral also floats and is based upon LIBOR plus some basis points, such as, say, approximately 50 bps, creating quite a narrow spread between the rate credited and the rate borrowed, the spread usually being in the range of zero to two percent. Because of their long maturity and call protection, they are not likely to mature during one's lifetime and are thereby unlikely to trigger capital gains recognition.

> **Example:** Let us assume that the selling shareholder is selling $10 million of stock to the ESOP. The sponsoring corporation borrows $10 million from a bank and lends the proceeds to the ESOP, which, in turn, pays it to the selling stockholder.
>
> The seller then purchases a $10 million floating rate note to the same or a different bank that will lend 90 percent, or $9 million or perhaps more against the note, the spread between the interest the note pays and the amount he pays on the borrowed sum being close to a "wash."
>
> The selling shareholder then invests the $9 million at will in virtually any kind of investment without triggering the tax on the capital gain down to the original basis. The seller, now the investor, can invest in mutual funds, real estate, gold coins, art, government securities or any other investment, even though they may not qualify as QRP. That is because the FRN is the QRP.

As noted above, by using this strategy, the selling shareholder is able to create an actively traded portfolio. It may be possible to borrow up to 100 percent of the $10 million sales proceeds by pledging some of the investments in addition to the FRN itself.

The investor can use some of his or her investment gains to pay down the loan during his or her lifetime or can wait until death for the estate to do so out of the investment portfolio.

7.7 HOW TO BOOTSTRAP A SELLER-FINANCED ESOP

Let's assume that the selling shareholder in the above example is Mr. Big who founded the company and wants to sell $10 million of his stock to Big, Inc.'s ESOP and be able to defer his taxes under Code Section 1042.

He would like to finance the transaction himself rather than having the corporation borrow from a bank. He feels that he would be a more lenient lender who would impose fewer covenants. Moreover, why not have the interest go to himself instead of to a bank?

There is, however, a problem in doing this because Section 1042 requires that he reinvest the proceeds in qualified replacement property within one year in order to defer his taxes on the sale. Unfortunately, the stock of Big, Inc. comprises the major part of his estate and he would be unable to come up with $10 million to invest in QRP within 12 months.

Here is where the FRN comes to the rescue and enables Mr. Big to "bootstrap" the $10 million sale of his stock to the ESOP and comply with Code Section 1042.

To simplify matters, Big, Inc. had $1 million of disposable cash in retained earnings. The steps involved in the seller-financed transactions are the following:

1. Mr. Big sold $10 million of his stock to the ESOP.

2. Big, Inc. loaned $1 million to the ESOP.

3. Mr. Big loaned $9 million to the ESOP and took back a 7 year, 10 percent note from the ESOP.

4. The ESOP paid Mr. Big $1 million cash.

5. Mr. Big obtained a $9 million bridge loan from a bank.

6. Mr. Big used the $10 million of cash to purchase a $10 million, 50-year floating rate note from a triple-A corporate issuer.

7. Mr. Big then used the $10 million FRN as collateral and a bank loaned him 90 percent, or $9 million.

8. He used the $9 million to repay the $9 million bridge loan.

9. Big, Inc. made tax-deductible contributions to the ESOP in an amount that was equal to principal and interest.

10. The ESOP used part of this contribution to repay its $1 million debt to the corporation and paid the balance to Mr. Big.

11. He paid no tax on the principal payments since this represents payment for his stock but did pay taxes on the interest payment.

Handwritten at top: Section 1042 stock sales may not be allocated to the shareholders ESOP account or to any family member's accounts for 10 years. (in-laws don't count). Up to 5% of stock sold by shareholder may go to ESOP account of family member owning < 25% of stock.

Result:

- The ESOP had two benign lenders: the corporation and the founding stockholder.

- Mr. Big complied with the requirements of Code Section 1042 and is able to avoid recognition of capital gains tax on the sale of his stock.

- He can reinvest the payments he receives in any investments.

- The interest payments he gets enhances his cash flow instead of that of some bank.

- The employees of Big, Inc. are given equity in their company and are incentivized to improve its value.

Handwritten: If I use Section 1042 to defer capital gains on sale, Gina can only receive up (to 5% of my stock sold to ESOP.) No restriction on liz.

Handwritten left margin: Prohibited persons

7.8 ALLOCATION ELIGIBILITY

In accordance with Code Section 402(n), the selling stockholder in a Section 1042 tax-deferred rollover transaction may not have any of the stock that is being sold allocated to his or her ESOP account or to that of certain family members during a nonallocation period as defined by statute. This period commences on the date the stockholder sells stock to the ESOP under Code Section 1042 and ends on the later of 10 years after the sale or the date the stock is allocated to the participants pursuant to the final amortization payment of indebtedness to acquire the stock. Stock owned by that individual's spouse, parents, brothers and sisters (both whole or half-blooded), ancestors or lineal descendents, including legally adopted children, will be considered to be owned by the individual for this purpose. Family members do not include aunts, uncles, nieces, nephews, stepchildren, stepparents, or in-laws.

This also applies to any other person who owns more than 25 percent (including stock owned by attribution under Section 318) of any class of the sponsoring corporation's outstanding stock or of the total outstanding stock or that of any other company that is in the same controlled group during a one-year period ending on the date the stock is sold to the ESOP or the date it is allocated to ESOP participants' accounts.

There is an exception to these restrictions. It is referred to as the *de minimis* rule. Under this rule, up to 5 percent of the aggregate amount of stock sold to the ESOP by the selling stockholder may be allocated to the accounts of the selling stockholder's lineal descendants during the nonallocation period provided that the lineal descendent is not a 25 percent stockholder.

These rules do not apply to stock sold by shareholders who do not elect to defer their taxes under Section 1042 unless, as noted above, they own 25 percent of the outstanding stock.

Stock that is owned by the ESOP or by any other qualified plan is counted as being outstanding when determining who owns more than 25 percent. Selling shareholders who are precluded from the allocation process cannot make up for this loss by participating in an equivalent qualified plan other than an ESOP.

ESOPs have always served to perpetuate companies and keep them in the hands of the founder's family, executives, and other employees. This trend has been accelerated by the tax-deferred rollover provision created by the 1984 Act, further broadening the base of capital ownership among the nation's employees. The law permits and encourages corporate owners to make partial sales of their companies, which has the positive effect of a gradual transition rather than a traumatic one that would come from a full sale. This will help assure corporate stability and continuity of the growth pattern that had existed prior to the sale. The owner will have an incentive to make the shares retained appreciate in value. This will have a positive effect on the ESOP equity holders as well.

7.9 PROCEDURES FOR NONTAX RECOGNITION ON STOCK SALE

In order to receive nontax recognition under Section 1042, the selling stockholder must elect such treatment in writing in the 1040 income tax return for the tax year in which the sale occurs. The shareholder must file on a timely basis, including extensions. Upon purchasing the qualified replacement property (QRP), the taxpayer must attach to his or her tax return the election "statements of purchase" which are to include the cost and description of the QRP and the date purchased. The statements must also denote the property that has been purchased as being qualified replacement property and be notarized not later than thirty days after the date on which the QRP was purchased.

7.10 THE CORPORATION'S CONSENT TO THE NONTAX RECOGNITION

The taxpayer must also attach to the IRS filings a written statement to the effect that the sponsoring corporation consents to the imposition of excise taxes in the event the ESOP does not adhere to the nonallocation provisions, to the three-year holding period under Sections 4979A and 4978(a) and to the requirement that the ESOP must not own less stock than it did immediately after the ESOP's stock purchase. This statement must be signed by the corporation.

It is therefore apparent that a selling shareholder cannot take advantage of the nontax recognition feature of Section 1042 without the sponsoring corporation's cooperation. There may be situations in which this fact might be used as a strategy for the majority stockholder to include a minority stockholder to tender his or her shares "while the offer is available."

7.11 HOW TO ACHIEVE TAX NONRECOGNITION WITH LESS BANK LEVERAGE

Stockholders who would like to sell their stock under IRC Section 1042 are often reluctant to do so because of the requirement that the transaction must result in the ESOP owning 30 percent or more of the company stock. This might require an excessive amount of leverage on the part of the company.

Let us assume that the corporation is valued at $20 million and Mr. Big, the stockholder would like to sell $6 million of his stock to the ESOP, the level needed to enable him to defer taxes. Unfortunately, the corporation, in its preliminary discussion with the bank, was informed that the bank was willing to lend only $4 million, $2 million less than the amount that was required for the Section 1042 transaction. Here are some strategies that might be considered.

(a) Prefund the Transaction

The corporation can make annual tax-deductible contributions to the ESOP of cash for one or two years. If, for example, the annual covered payroll is $3.5 million, the company can contribute 20 percent of payroll, or $700,000 in cash, to the ESOP for three years. Assuming the investment grows at 10 percent, it will be worth $2.5 million at the end of three years.

The $2.5 million can be used to supplement the bank financing to acquire stock from the owner.

This example disregards annual growth of the stock and annual payroll growth but it illustrates a concept.

(b) Selling Stockholder Takes Back a Note from the ESOP

Mr. Big can sell his stock to the ESOP and lend the purchase price to the ESOP by taking back a note from the ESOP trust. This note could be subordinated to the bank loan or could be done without the involvement of a bank loan.

The note is repaid by the corporation's tax-deductible contributions to the ESOP, which, in turn, are paid to Mr. Big. The principal payments come to him on a tax-deferred basis: He will pay taxes on the interest payments he receives.

(c) The Corporation Sells Newly Issued Stock to the ESOP

In the earlier example, the bank was willing to lend only $4 million of the $6 million that was required for a Section 1042 transaction. To solve this, the corporation could sell $2 million of authorized but unissued stock to the ESOP. This will accrue toward meeting the 30 percent threshold that is imposed by Section 1042.

ARC loans ESOP money to buy Treasury shares @ 30%. ARC donates the principal & interest amount to ESOP (tax deductible). ESOP pays it back to ARC. ARC gets full value + tax deduction.

This is accomplished by the corporation taking back a note from the ESOP. The corporation would make contributions to the ESOP in an amount that is equal to principal and interest. The ESOP promptly pays this to the corporation. The corporation recovers its outlay and saves taxes in the process.

The dilutionary effect is partially offset by the tax saving and by the interest the company will not have to pay to a bank for this part of the transaction.

(d) The Corporation Contributes Newly Issued Stock to the ESOP

The corporation can reduce the amount that it will eventually have to borrow by making tax-deductible contributions of newly issued stock to the ESOP. The stock that goes into the ESOP in this manner will count toward the 30 percent requirement for Section 1042. This strategy is similar to the one noted in subheading "A" above, except that this approach conserves cash for the company.

(e) Combination of All of the Above

The corporation can contribute both cash and stock to the ESOP.

7.12 TAX NONRECOGNITION ON AN INSTALLMENT SALE

Stockholders frequently sell their shares on an installment basis, whereby they are paid some cash up front and hold a note for the balance to be paid over a period of years. To comply with IRC Section 1042, the qualified replacement property must be purchased within twelve months after, or three months prior to, the sale of stock to the ESOP. Private Letter Ruling (PLR) 9102017, issued on October 12, 1990, stated that the selling shareholder who applied for the PLR could receive tax nonrecognition in connection with an installment sale. This could be accomplished by investing the cash received from the stock sale plus an amount of cash which equals the note's face amount in qualified replacement property within the time frame noted above. The cash could come from note installments received during the qualified period or from the selling shareholder's other liquid assets.

7.13 TAX REQUIREMENTS FOR THE TAX-DEFERRED ROLLOUT

An allocation to a prohibited person's account within 10 years after the sale or allocation of the proceeds of the sale, whichever is last, results in a tax to the employer.

This is a 50 percent excise tax on the value of the stock allocated to the prohibited individual.

If the selling stockholder sells any of the replacement securities, he or she will be taxed on the gain above the basis of the stock sold to the ESOP. The tax on the remainder of the replacement securities remains deferred. If held to death, stock receives a stepped-up basis and is never taxed under current law at the time of this book's publication.

Election of Code Section 1042 brings with it certain statutory rules that must be adhered to if the favorable results are to be achieved. These rules are:

1. Statement of election by the seller must be made in writing and filed on a timely basis, including filing extensions with the selling shareholder's personal tax return for the taxable year in which the sale took place.

2. Employer's consent to the 10 percent premature disposition excise tax must be made in writing by the employer and must accompany the seller's election statement when the latter is filed. The tax is imposed on the employer if the ESOP disposes of the stock within three years after the sale to the plan and the following occur:

   a. The ESOP holds less stock than it did immediately after it acquired it from the selling stockholder, or

   b. The stock purchased by the ESOP in the 1042 election falls in value below 30 percent of the total value of all the employer securities as of the date of disposition of the stock, but

   c. The excise tax does not apply if the disposition occurs as a result of an ESOP participant's death, disability, retirement after age 59½, or separation from service resulting in a one-year break in service.

3. The consent by the employer to the 50 percent prohibited allocation tax must also be filed in writing by the selling stockholder along with his or her election statement and the employer's statement consenting to the 10 percent premature disposition tax, all on a timely basis with the IRS. The statement attests to the fact that the employer consents to the imposition of an excise tax that is equal to 50 percent of the amount involved in the transaction if an allocation is made to any member of the prohibited group as defined in Code Section 409(n).

4. A notarized Statement of Purchase is required. The statement must be signed and notarized within 30 days of the date each item of qualified replaced property is purchased by the electing taxpayer. The notarized statement must be included with the selling shareholder's Form 1040 tax return for the year in which the sale occurred, notwithstanding the fact that the QRP may have

been purchased during the next year but before the tax return was filed. If the electing taxpayer buys the QRP within 12 months of sale of the employer securities to the ESOP but after the tax return was filed for that year, the notarized Statement of Purchase form must accompany his or her Form 1042 income tax return for the following year.

One should not count on the likelihood that they will be permitted to correct any but possibly the most minor deviation from these mandatory rules.

7.14 SELLING THE COMPANY TO OUTSIDERS

A point is reached when nearly every owner of a private corporation strongly ponders the advisability of selling the company. The owner is often asset rich and cash poor. Income from labor is a poor trade-off for capital that is tied up in the company.

So long as the owner does not sell the company, he or she cannot capitalize assets. Yet, the capital the owner would release to himself or herself upon sale can far exceed the salary he or she will continue to receive from the business, and it could be tax-deferred as opposed to being taxed as ordinary income. A partial sale, perhaps through a leveraged ESOP, can capitalize his or her wealth without turning off the faucet.

When companies are sold to outsiders, the first heads to roll are often those of the key executives who helped to build the company. Relocations of companies that are sold to outside corporate or individual buyers of companies is a frequent aftereffect that will call for family upheavals if the employee is to remain with the corporation. This scenario can be avoided if the owner sells his or her stock to an ESOP. The continued interrelationships with local suppliers, subcontractors, and banks make the ownership transition to an ESOP rollover far more preferable than the outright sale to corporations in other locations. Many communities recognize these attributes and have passed legislation that is beneficial to ESOPs. The tax-free rollover will help keep companies in the community (see Exhibits 7.1 and 7.2).

Exhibit 7.1

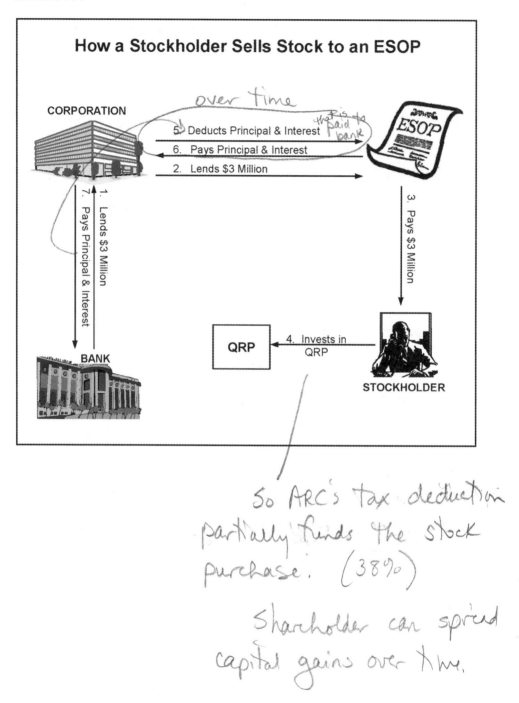

How a Stockholder Sells Stock to an ESOP

over time (handwritten)

CORPORATION

5. Deducts Principal & Interest _that is paid to bank_ (handwritten)

6. Pays Principal & Interest

2. Lends $3 Million

ESOP

1. Lends $3 Million

7. Pays Principal & Interest

3. Pays $3 Million

BANK

QRP

4. Invests in QRP

STOCKHOLDER

So ARC's tax deduction partially funds the stock purchase. (38%) (handwritten)

Shareholder can spread capital gains over time. (handwritten)

Exhibit 7.2

INCOME RESULT

TAX-DEFERRED ESOP SALE VS SALE TO OUTSIDER

ASSUMPTIONS:

Sale of $3,000,000 of securities (zero basis);
20% personal tax bracket;*
Taxable 10% yield on replacement securities;

	SALE TO OUTSIDER	SALE TO ESOP
Sale Proceeds	$3,000,000	$3,000,000
Less Tax	$ 600,000	$ 0
Available for Investment	$2,400,000	$3,000,000**

ANNUAL INCOME DIFFERENCE

ANNUAL INCOME VIA SALE TO ESOP   **$300,000**
LESS ANNUAL INCOME VIA SALE TO OUTSIDER   **$240,000**

ESOP'S ANNUAL INCOME ADVANTAGE***   **$ 60,000**

*IN THOSE STATES WHEREIN STATE LAW PARALLELS FEDERAL LAW, THE ESOP'S AD-VANTAGE WOULD BE EVEN GREATER.

**POSSIBLE FUTURE CAPITAL GAINS APPRECIATION ON THE REPLACEMENT SECURITIES IS NOT CONSIDERED IN THIS EXHIBIT.

*** COMPOUNDING IS NOT CONSIDERED HERE.

ESOP trustee selects an appraiser. Not the corporation's accountant or lawyer or anyone y financial relationship.

CHAPTER EIGHT

How to Value the Stock of a Closely Held Company

8.1 WHY HAVE A VALUATION?

An ESOP creates a market for the stock of private corporations. Stock will be contributed or sold to the ESOP. Employees will have stock in their ESOP accounts and a right price for measuring the value of the shares must be determined. It is the trustee's responsibility to determine fair market value by engaging an independent appraiser.

8.2 INDEPENDENCE OF THE APPRAISER

The 1986 Tax Act requires that an independent appraiser or appraisal firm be used to perform the valuation of stock which is not readily tradable on an established market and is either contributed to an ESOP or purchased by it. This requirement became effective for transactions occurring after December 31, 1986. The valuation must be done in writing and must reflect the value of the stock as of the date of the transaction. The Act further provides that the name of the valuation appraisal firm be reported to the IRS. Stock for which there is a readily tradable market on an established exchange requires no appraisal. In order to be considered independent, the appraiser must be selected by the plan's trustee. This does not preclude the corporation's paying the appraiser's fee, however, so long as the ESOP's trustee has the right to terminate the appraiser's appointment, thereby establishing the fact that the plan is the client of the appraiser.

Independence also suggests that the valuation should not be performed by anyone who has financial dealings with the company or in a paid advisory position

[Handwritten note at top: ESOP must pay fair market value for stocks. It must be done for "adequate consideration" as determined by trustee or named fiduciary.]

with the firm, such as its attorney or accountant. If the accounting firm is large enough to have a "Chinese wall" separating its various pertinent departments, the valuation section might very well qualify as being independent under the law although some would feel that the independence of this is questionable.

8.3 ADEQUATE CONSIDERATION

Corporations that have ESOPs are parties to various types of transactions involving the sale or purchase of employer securities.

All of the following ESOP transactions have one thing in common—they must be done for adequate consideration. *Adequate* has been defined by ERISA as the fair market value of the assets as determined in good faith by the trustee or named fiduciary pursuant to the terms of the plan and in accordance with the regulations proposed by the Secretary of Labor. The ESOP cannot pay more than fair market value for the stock it purchases.

- A contribution of employer stock to an ESOP

- A contribution of cash, which is used by the ESOP to purchase stock from the corporation or from stockholders

- Purchase of stock held by the ESOP trustee

- Distribution of cash by the trustee to ESOP participants in lieu of employer stock

- Purchase by the trustee of stock from ESOP distributees

The Department of Labor (DOL) proposed adequate consideration regulations that will serve as a guide to appraisers as to fair market value and will enable them to establish appropriate discounts for lack of marketability, control premium, repurchase liability, and so on. Two criteria for determining adequate consideration are:

1. *Fair market value*—requiring that the value placed on an asset reflect its fair market value as defined in the proposed regulations

2. *Good faith*—requiring that the fair market value assigned to the stock must be determined by the plan trustee or named fiduciary in good faith as defined by the proposed regulation

The DOL regulations define fair market value and require that the value be determined at the time of the ESOP transaction and that it be documented in writing for the purpose of the specific transactions and performed by parties with demonstrable expertise. The regulations require that there be good faith on the fiduciary's part, with no conflict of interest between the valuing fiduciary, the ESOP, and the plan sponsor.

Corporation = plan sponsor

The DOL's definition of fair market value is: ". . . the price at which an asset would change hands between a willing buyer and a willing seller when the former is not under any compulsion to buy and the latter is not under any compulsion to sell, and both parties are able as well as willing to trade and are well informed about the asset and the market for such asset."

The fiduciary has the responsibility of assuring that the ESOP not pay more than adequate consideration for plan assets notwithstanding the independent appraisal.

8.4 THE VALUATION REPORT CONTENTS

The valuation report must be in writing and is required to contain the following information at the very minimum in order to determine fair market value:

- Qualifications of the individual(s) making the valuation

- The value of the asset, the method or methods used, and the reason for the valuation in light of the methodology that is being employed

- A thorough description of the asset being valued

- The purpose of the valuation

- The valuation's effective date

- All factors that were considered in the course of performing the valuation (must include any agreements, restrictions, and understandings, as well as obligations that would limit the use or disposition of the property)

- A dated signature of the person making the valuation report

- The valuation's significance or relevance, taking into account the methods being used for the valuation

Appraisal reports for securities that do not have a generally recognized market must contain an assessment of all other factors including the following eight basic items of information noted in Revenue Ruling 59-60:

1. The nature of the business and the history of the enterprise from its inception

2. The economic outlook in general and the condition and outlook of the specific industry in particular

3. The book value of the stock and the financial condition of the business

4. The earnings capacity of the company

5. The dividend-paying capacity of the company

6. Whether or not the enterprise has goodwill or other intangible value

7. Sale of the stock and the size of the block to be valued

8. The market price of stocks of corporations engaged in the same or similar lines of business having their stocks actively traded in a free and open market, either on an exchange or in the over-the-counter market

Different weight is assigned to the various elements enumerated above, depending upon the nature of the company being valued. Net asset value is given far less weight in a service company than is discounted cash flow. The converse is true for asset-rich companies such as those that own heavy equipment or land and buildings that are integral to the operations of the business. Cash flow discounts vary with the degree of risk in achieving the projected cash flow. It is often said that today's value is the present value of future benefits.

The very existence of an ESOP and the manner in which it will be used can affect the value of the stock. If, for example, the leveraged ESOP's funds are to be used to infuse working capital into the company for growth and profit enhancement, the value can be greater than it would were the funds to go off balance sheet to purchase shares from stockholders.

The proposed termination of an existing pension or profit-sharing plan can affect the valuation because of the discontinuance of future contributions.

In making a comparison with comparable public corporations, the market price relative to cash flow, earnings, book value, and debt-free cash flow is considered in the valuation process.

8.5 METHODS FOR VALUING STOCK

The primary methodologies that are generally used in valuing stock of privately held corporations include the following.

(a) Asset Method

The going-concern asset method reflects the company's value as being based on net assets or its adjusted book value, actually the liquidation value, and is employed in valuing companies that have a significant amount of equipment or other tangible assets and their earnings are not indicative of their real value. The actual market value of the assets rather than the depreciated value is used.

This method, though simple, is seldom used in valuations for ESOP since it does not reflect a realistic going concern value. Buyers are more concerned with other factors than assets in arriving at a figure they will pay for a company. They are more concerned with earnings a company will provide. Inventories as carried on the balance sheet do not reflect their true value and accounts receivable or payables are

The trustee cannot pay more than fair market value for stock, but can pay less. It is a negotiated price.

not shown on the balance sheet, yet these are of great importance in determining the return the buyer can expect on his or her investment.

(b) Discounted Cash Flow Method

company value → present value of the projected future income stream.

This method is given great importance in cash flow-intensive companies and is based upon the notion that the present value of the projected future income stream for a specific number of years reflects the going concern value of the company. The projection must be realistically based upon the company's most recent financial results and a proper discount rate must be applied. Add-backs such as payouts to present owners for fringe benefits and excessive compensation that could be reduced by a replacement in that position will affect the discounted cash flow positively.

The buyer will have predetermined the rate of return that he or she needs in order to justify the risk of investment. After all, running a business carries with it greater risk than purchasing a bond from a triple A–rated corporation.

The presence of an ESOP will bring tax advantages to the table that will have a positive impact upon cash flow which, in turn, can improve earnings. The tax savings should therefore be taken into consideration in calculating the present value of the future income stream in arriving at the capitalization or price the buyer should be willing to pay.

(c) Comparable Sales Method

This methodology considers prices that have been paid for purchasing other companies in the same industry similar to the company being appraised. In using this approach, it is important to determine whether a portion of the purchase price was for employment agreement, covenant not to compete, or other such factors.

(d) Comparability with Public Companies Method

This method involves a comparison using the price/earnings (P/E) ratio of public companies in the same industry. One can determine the multiple of earnings factor by dividing the published price of the stock by the company's earnings, and those that are most similar to the company that is being valued are considered as relevant.

If there had been recent sales of the company's stock, the price at which the stock was sold can be considered in arriving at the valuation. The larger the block of stock that is traded, the more relevant it would be.

The price the trustee pays is a negotiated price and can differ from the fair market value determined by the independent valuation. Nonetheless, the trustee cannot pay more than fair market value. In some instances, the selling shareholders may wish to give the ESOP a break to better assure the likelihood that the company will be able to service the loan.

If the selling price is substantially below the fair market value determined by appraisal, the IRS could contend that the difference should be treated as a gift and be taxed as such. We have never seen this occur since the appraiser has great latitude in the assumptions that may be used in determining fair market value.

8.6 FAIRNESS OPINION

Fairness opinions have become essential ingredients in multi-investor ESOP transactions. They are usually rendered by an independent financial advisor who is retained by the board of directors, the ESOP committee, the trustee, or by one of the other parties to the proposed transaction to assure that the various interests are protected.

The financial advisor will opine, usually in the form of a one-page letter, as to the fairness of the transaction, taking into consideration the viability of the valuation that had been performed. The fairness opinion is updated to the time of the shareholder vote as to any substantive changes which may affect the earlier opinion as to the fairness of the stockholders.

Valuation experts delve deeply into numerous other factors, such as the firm's share of the market and its potential for maintaining that share. They look at the first-line and second-line management team and consider the various aspects of management succession and perpetuation of the company. The corporation's technological capabilities, research and development status, lines of credit, adequacy of physical plant, and potential for expansion are some of the other considerations in arriving at fair market value of the company. The valuation will, in the end, reflect the fact that today's value is the present value of future benefits.

The use of a formula in valuing a company does not relate to many of the tangible and intangible factors of the immediate and distant economic and political environments that can influence the company's future. Appraisal by formula, even if permitted, would, over a period of time, produce unrealistic valuation results, fall apart, and lack the credibility inherent in independent appraisals. As noted, appraisals must be performed by independent appraisers in any event.

8.7 CONTROL PREMIUM, MINORITY DISCOUNTS, AND MARKETABILITY DISCOUNTS

(a) Control Premium

The shareholder who has the controlling interest of a corporation can call the shots as to how the company is to be run, whether to pay dividends, decisions on making acquisitions or divestitures, or selling the company. For this reason, valuation firms generally agree that the control block of stock deserves a control premium,

Control stock deserves a premium between 20-40% Minority stocks are similarly discounted.

ranging from about 20 percent to as much as 40 percent, depending to some extent on the perception of the valuation firm.

Once the ESOP has paid a control premium for the stock, it will continue to value shares that it acquires in the future on a control premium basis and the accounts of ESOP participants will also be valued on that basis.

(b) Minority Discounts

Transactions in which the ESOP trustee frequently engages can involve minority interests that have no control over important decisions such as compensation, dividends, or determination of corporate policy. As a consequence, the valuation specialists will most likely assign a minority discount to the value of the stock. A minority discount is the inverse of a control premium (i.e., a control premium in reverse).

Some appraisers contend that a minority discount is not called for if the private company stock valuation takes into strong consideration the value of comparable public company stocks. They point out that stocks listed on major exchanges reflect a minority discount; consequently, an additional discount would be redundant.

If there is little or no market for the shares, one might impute a marketability discount of 10 percent to 35 percent in relation to public company stock that is actively traded. This discount for lack of marketability could be reduced or eliminated by other factors.

(c) How to Sell a Minority Share but Get a Control Price

Sometime a major stockholder might not be ready to sell more than a minor block of stock to the ESOP currently, but fully intends to sell a controlling interest some time in the future. This may be due to the corporation's inability to obtain financing or perhaps the firm's unwillingness to become too highly leveraged.

It may be due to the fact that the company is expected to grow substantially over the next several years and the shareholder would like to sell more stock later on when the shares will have a higher fair market value. The problem with this is that the shareholder, upon selling less than half of his or her stock to the ESOP, will be hit with a minority discount on the sales proceeds. There may be a way whereby the selling shareholder can sell a minority block of stock to the ESOP and still receive a control premium price.

If the initial sale to the ESOP is less than 50 percent, authorities feel that the trustee may be able to pay a control premium if, according to the DOL-proposed regulations [DOL Prop. Reg. Sec. 2510.3-18(b)(4)(ii)(l)(l)], the ESOP obtains a binding option at the time of the sale to acquire a controlling interest within a reasonable period of time and not subject to early dissipation. Many practitioners consider this to be approximately four or five years or perhaps until the end of the loan term for the stock transaction. There seems to be little doubt that the selling stockholder should receive enterprise or control value. It should be noted, however, that there have been no rulings on this.

(d) Marketability Discount

A put option for the distributee can justify a significant reduction or possibly elimination of a marketability discount if the financial condition of the company warrants a realistic expectation of its ability to repurchase the stock. A good funding program will help assure that the company will have the capability to ultimately purchase the stock in the ESOP account. This can have a positive effect on the value of the stock in that it may substantially offset the discount for lack of marketability.

8.8 INFORMATION THE APPRAISER NEEDS

The information that the valuation firm requires is extensive. The more thorough and well organized the data is, the easier it will be for the appraiser to come up with an accurate and reliable appraisal. The appraiser will do on-site walkthroughs with meeting with key managers. Here are some of the items that will be requested by the appraiser:

- Description of the company and its products

- History of the firm

- Audited or reviewed financial statements for five or more years (includes balance sheets, income statements, capital statements, and cash flow statements)

- Pro forma projections

- Budget

- List and descriptions of subsidiaries

- Stockholder list

- Compensation of the highly compensated employees

- Patents or royalties

- Leases

- Contracts

- Copy of qualified plan

- History of dividends, if any

- Previous bona fide sales offers for the company

- Copy of the ESOP plan and trust

- List of board members

8.9 SUMMARY

If anything goes wrong with respect to an ESOP transaction, it is almost invariably because of the perceived inadequacy of the valuation. The consequences might be that when a company takes a tax deduction for its contribution of stock to the ESOP, it had better be certain that fair market value is the criterion on which the amount of the deduction is based. If the stock has been valued at too high a price, a disallowance of the deduction may be the unpleasant result. If a major stockholder sells stock to the ESOP at a price that is greater than fair market value, the stockholder may be asked to pay an excise tax.

Conversely, if the ESOP trustee purchases stock from a terminating employee-participant at a price below fair market value, the former participant may litigate for a more favorable price. Use of an annual valuation will generally be adequate for transactions that do not involve a party-in-interest (the corporation or an officer, director, or 10 percent or more stockholder). For one that does involve a party-in-interest, the value should be updated as of the date of the transaction.

If the valuation is done by those professionals who are experienced in performing valuations for ESOP purposes, it will undoubtedly be well documented and provide comfort for the fiduciaries.

Companies whose stock is listed on a national exchange and which are readily tradable pose no problem in valuation. For ESOP purposes, fair market value of stock that has a readily tradable market will be considered to be the average of the closing prices of the stock in question for 20 consecutive trading days immediately preceding the date of the ESOP transaction.

$$\begin{array}{r} 20.5 \text{ weeks (5 mos)} \\ 40\overline{)1000} \end{array}$$

Must include all employees > 21 yrs of age who have completed 1 yr (and 1000 hours) of service, unless the company grants complete vesting immediately upon participation. Part-time employees may be allowed to participate.

CHAPTER NINE

Eligibility for ESOP Participation

9.1 ELIGIBILITY

As is true with all other qualified plans, an ESOP must include all employees of the sponsoring corporation who have reached the age of 21 and completed one year of service during which they worked at least 1,000 hours. There are certain exceptions. Employees in a plan that grants complete vesting immediately upon participation may be excluded until they have completed three years of service. Seasonal industries are an exception to the 1,000-hour rule. These rules are covered under Code Section 410(a).

Although there is a minimum age (21), there is no maximum age above which an employee meeting the other requirements can be excluded from the plan. They become eligible on the earlier of: (a) the first day of the plan year after completion of the service requirement, or (b) six months after completion of the service requirement. Nonresident alien employees whose earned income is derived entirely from sources outside of the United States border are to be excluded from participation in an ESOP. Although part-time employees (less than 1,000 hours of service in a year) can be excluded from the plan, they may be included if the plan is so designed to permit this. The minimum employee participation standards must be met on at least one day of each quarter.

A plan may specify that employees who are members of a collective bargaining unit may be excluded from the ESOP so long as retirement benefits had been the subject of good faith bargaining between the union and the employer.

An alternative to the foregoing qualification items is the percentage test, which assures satisfaction of the coverage requirement if the plan meets the following criteria:

- 70 percent or more of all employees are covered;

- The percentage of non–highly compensated participants is 70 percent or more of the percentage of those that are highly compensated ($85,000 or more under Code Section 410(a)).

- There is no discrimination in the way employees are classified for eligibility that favors highly compensated employees, and the amount of benefits contributed to the ESOP qualified plan for the non–highly compensated employees comprises 70 percent or more of that contributed for the benefit of the highly compensated employee segment.

The separate line of business rules, often referred to as the "SLOB rules," provide that only employees who work for a subsidiary or a division that is in a separate line of business from the parent corporation may be excluded from the ESOP Code Section 401(a). For this exemption to apply, the subsidiary or division must have a minimum of 50 employees. This must be applied in a nondiscriminatory manner and not with the intent to circumvent the coverage rules such as by not making eligibility available to rank and file employees in one division while including employees of another division that consists only of managerial staff.

(a) Employees Who Are Excluded if Stock Is Sold Under Code Section 1042

If a selling shareholder elects to defer taxes under Code Section 1042 he or she, certain family members, and shareholders who own 25 percent of the stock will be excluded from participation in the ESOP. This will be discussed more thoroughly in Chapter 11.

ESOPs may provide that participants who have incurred a break in service (failure to complete more than 500 hours in a specified 12-month period) will no longer be considered plan participants. In order to become eligible again, the former participant may be required to complete a year of service following the break.

(b) Controlled Group

Employee eligibility extends to employees of a controlled group.

A corporation is part of a controlled group if a parent corporation has 80 percent or more of the voting power or 80 percent of the value of all classes of stock of another corporation, or if at least 80 percent of all classes of voting stock is owned by five or fewer persons and more than 50 percent of the value or voting power of the stock of each of the corporations. However, the ownership in each corporation must be identical to be considered as part of the controlled group.

The rules for testing for eligibility must be applied to all of the corporations in the controlled group.

CHAPTER TEN

How to Fund an ESOP at Zero Net Outlay

An ESOP's purpose is to provide ownership of company stock to the employees. Pension plans and traditional profit sharing plans are precluded from having more than 10 percent of their assets in the form of employer stock. Assets of those plans are thereby invested away from the company while the ESOP invests its assets back into the company or can be used to purchase the owner's stock.

The regulations say that the assets of the ESOP must be invested primarily in employer stock but do not define what *primarily* really means. Practitioners generally perceive this to mean that 51 percent of the assets in company stock is a good, safe number for meeting this specification. If there is a good rationale for cash even in excess of this percentage, it can probably be justified on audit.

The ESOP's fiduciaries are not insulated from the diversification rule as it applies to assets other than employer stock. Another area of departure between ESOPs and other qualified plans is the fair-return-on-investment rule. Accumulation of equity in the corporation for the benefit of employees is the rationale for ESOPs. It is understood that relatively few privately owned corporations pay dividends. It is hoped that the ESOP will assist companies increase the per-share value of their stock. The employees or their families will benefit from any capital appreciation that might occur in their ESOP accounts when they terminate, die, or retire.

Suppose a corporation in the 40 percent combined tax bracket wishes to contribute a total of $250,000 to its ESOP but will do so with zero net cash outlay. If the company contributes $150,000 of authorized but unissued stock to the ESOP, it will save $60,000 in taxes with no out-of-pocket cash leaving the corporation. The company also contributes $100,000 of cash to the ESOP at an after-tax cost of $60,000.

Exhibit 10.1

HOW TO FUND AN ESOP AT ZERO NET CASH OUTLAY

EXAMPLE:

CONTRIBUTION TO ESOP	CASH FLOW
$150,000 STOCK:	$60,000 INCREASE ($150,000 × 40% Tax Bracket)
$100,000 CASH	<$60,000> DECREASE ($100,000 less $40,000 tax savings)
$250,000 TOTAL CONTRIBUTION OUTLAY	$-0- NET AFTER-TAX CASH

The $60,000 annual increase in cash flow brought about by the tax savings created by the $150,000 of stock to the ESOP offsets the $60,000 after-tax cost of contributing $100,000 of cash to the other plan. Result: zero net after-tax cost for funding both qualified plans.

The employees get a stake in the company's future along with building a diversified portfolio (see Exhibit 10.1).

CHAPTER ELEVEN

Contribution and Allocation Parameters of the ESOP

11.1 EMPLOYER CONTRIBUTION LIMITS

ESOPs, as instruments of corporate finance, can be used for a wide variety of corporate and stockholder objectives. The uses are limited only by the user's creativity and knowledge of the legal limitations imposed by applicable law.

Administrators of qualified ESOPs must have a thorough knowledge of the various categories of rules that are unique to ESOPs. These practitioners must also be familiar with the statutory limitations of all other qualified plans. Some of the more critical ones are addressed in this chapter. The amount of deductible contribution a corporation can make and the extent to which allocations can be made to the accounts of ESOP participants are interdependent on the contributions to, and allocations in, other qualified defined contribution plans and *defined* benefit plans that a sponsoring corporation makes available to its employees.

ESOP transactions involve not only the ERISA regulations but encompass corporate and estate planning laws as well. These transactions can range from those that are very elementary to some that are exceedingly complex.

To structure an ESOP transaction, one must be particularly familiar with the Code sections that govern the tax-deductible amount the sponsoring corporation can contribute to the plan (Section 404) as well as the amount that can be allocated to the accounts of participants (Section 415). In applying the limits imposed by these sections, all qualified plans must be considered.

1099 consultants are not ESOP participants.

401K deductions are not added back for purposes of determining total payroll.

Bonuses & Commissions can't count if they result in lower paid employees facially discrimination.

Jane & Gha's salaries don't count if Jane take deferment.

CONTRIBUTION AND ALLOCATION PARAMETERS OF THE ESOP

11.2 ELIGIBLE COMPENSATION

The eligible compensation on which corporate contributions to an ESOP are based must be W-2 wages of the eligible participants. Independent contractors, those who receive 1099 income, are not included as ESOP participants. (A sample Employee Stock Ownership Plan Participation Statement is shown in Exhibit 11.2 at the end of this chapter. This statement shows the total amount of a company's stock that a participant owns and the value of the participant's ESOP account balance.)

The ESOP documents can define eligible compensation to include or to exclude bonuses or commissions so long as this is not discriminatory against those employees on the low end of the compensation scale.

The maximum amount of eligible compensation that can be considered for determining allocations to a participant's account is $170,000 as of 2001, however, the amount of allocation cannot exceed $35,000. This is increased after December 31, 2001 to $200,000 indexed in annual $5,000 increments after that and raises the $35,000 to $40,000 with annual increases of $1,000. Husbands and wives can each have these amounts contributed and allocated as of January 1, 1997. Prior to that date, the compensation of each was attributed to the other.

Calculation of the amount of deductible contribution a corporation can make to an ESOP (Code Section 404) is based upon taxable wages. Employee deferrals to a 401(k) plan as well as deferrals to a Section 125 cafeteria plan are not added back to these eligible wages or considered. In no event, however, can the corporation's deductible contribution exceed the amount that can be allocated to the participants' accounts under Code Section 415.

When a stockholder of a C corporation sells stock to an ESOP and elects tax deferment under Code Section 1042, that person's compensation as well as that of certain family members is excluded from participating in the ESOP, and their compensation is not included when determining the amount that can be contributed or allocated to the ESOP. This is also true of those other employees and certain family members who own 25 percent of the outstanding shares outside of the ESOP and as a participant of the ESOP. This will be discussed in greater detail later in this chapter.

11.3 EMPLOYER CONTRIBUTION LIMITS TO A NONLEVERAGED ESOP

After December 31, 2001 the sponsoring C corporation or S corporation will no longer be limited in the amount of deductible contribution that it can make to a nonleveraged ESOP to 15 percent of the eligible payroll of all plan participants, as it had been (Code Section 404(a)(3)), or 25 percent if leveraged or with a money purchase plan component, namely, a combination plan.

11.5 LEVERAGED ESOP

The 2001 Tax Act permits the corporation to make tax-deductible contributions of up to 25% of a participant's qualified pay: a combination ESOP is therefore not required after 12/31/01.

If tax deferral is taken that persons compensation & certain family members doesn't count towards totals.

11.4 COMBINATION ESOP

An ESOP is defined under Code Section 4975(e)(7) as a qualified defined contribution employee benefit plan that is a stock bonus plan or a combination of a *stock bonus plan* and a *money purchase plan* that is required to invest primarily in qualified employer securities. The Code section permitted the employer to increase the deductible contribution it can make from 15 percent to 25 percent of covered payroll through the addition of a money purchase plan. The money purchase plan segment is less flexible than the stock bonus plan. A stock bonus plan permits flexible contributions while the money purchase plan defines the percentage of compensation that must be contributed annually. This is known as a combination ESOP.

25% of payroll

A typical C corporation or S corporation combination ESOP plan might have been a mandatory employer contribution of 10 percent of covered payroll with the balance subject to the stock bonus plan limit. This has meant that an additional amount ranging from 1 percent to 15 percent could be contributed under the framework of the stock bonus plan at the discretion of the company. The corporation could make tax-deductible cash or stock contributions ranging from 11 percent to 25 percent through the combination ESOP described above. A company cannot establish a money-purchase pension plan ESOP unless it is accompanied by a stock bonus plan ESOP; however, the terms of the plans can differ from each other. Combination plans are seldom used since contributions to ESOPs can amount to as much as 25 percent of covered payroll as of 2001.

11.5 LEVERAGED ESOP

If the ESOP in a C corporation is leveraged, Code Section 404(a)(9) has permitted the company to make a tax-deductible contribution of up to 25 percent of covered payroll for the payment of principal, even if no money purchase plan is involved, if the amount in excess of 15 percent is for the payment of principal in connection with an acquisition loan. The corporation may contribute unlimited amounts of interest over and beyond the 25 percent limit. However, for contributions occurring after 2001, the 25 percent limit applies to both leveraged and non-leveraged ESOPs. The corporation may contribute unlimited amounts of interest over and beyond the 25 percent limit.

An S corporation ESOP can borrow to acquire employer stock. However, the maximum amount that can be contributed is 15 percent of payroll but, unlike a C corporation ESOP, interest is included in this limit. The 25 percent contribution limit is available to an S corporation ESOP only if it is a combination plan.

Is this still true?

ARC can pay (tax-deductible) dividends on ESOP stock used to repay the ESOP loan to purchase that stock. This can be over & above the 25% payroll contribution.

CONTRIBUTION AND ALLOCATION PARAMETERS OF THE ESOP

Corporate contributions in excess of the limits for deductibility may result in an *from shareholders, who took a note* excise penalty tax on the amount of the excess contribution (Code Section 4972).

11.6 DIVIDENDS

Some transactions are so large as to require a greater amount of leveraging than can be serviced by 25 percent of covered payroll. Code Section 404(k), enacted under the 1984 Tax Act, permits a sponsoring employer to deduct dividends on stock that is an ESOP if the dividends are paid on the stock acquired by the ESOP loan and used to repay that loan. The dividend is deductible in addition to the annual 25 percent contribution. Since a corporation cannot deduct dividends other than through a C corporation ESOP, the company would create a different class of stock to sell to the ESOP. In this way dividends, if paid to the ESOP stock, would not have been paid on stock held outside of the ESOP. S corporations, unlike C corporations, cannot have a different class of stock and cannot deduct dividends.

If no more than one-third of the contributions to the ESOP are allocated to highly compensated employees, interest, forfeitures, and dividends can be allocated to the ESOP participants' accounts over and beyond the 25 percent Code Section 415 limits. The corporation can deduct these as well.

Dividends may also be deductible if they are paid in a C corporation and passed through within 90 days to the employees on the shares allocated to their ESOP accounts. If the IRS deems the dividends to be unreasonable, the service may determine that they are contributions and, as such, would constitute annual additions. Dividends used to service a loan for the acquisition of stock can be deducted only if they are paid on the shares acquired subsequent to August 8, 1989, with the proceeds of the loan. See Chapter 18 for more complete details about dividends.

The manner in which dividends may be used should be spelled out in the ESOP document. If it is not, the plan can authorize the board of directors to make this decision.

The administrator must allocate to the accounts of the participants an amount of stock having a value equal to or greater than the value of the dividend allocated to the accounts.

The use of dividends to service ESOP debt to purchase stock is particularly useful in situations in which the covered payroll is small and the company would be unable otherwise to make adequate deductible contributions to service the needed level of debt. Dividends should also be considered if the corporation has other qualified plans that effectively eat into the Section 415 limits.

In a leveraged ESOP, shares are released from allocation to participants' accounts as debt is amortized. The price the ESOP paid for the shares when it acquired them is the cost basis and continues as such when the shares are allocated to the participants' accounts. The cost basis of the shares does not change so long as the stock remains in the ESOP trust. Forfeitures retain their original cost basis when they are reallocated, as they do not leave the trust. The plan administrator must track the cost basis of the ESOP shares to determine the average cost for a participant's tax reporting in the event shares are ever distributed to that individual.

In summary, the Code sections that apply to the deductibility of employer contributions for all qualified plans must be considered when designing a transaction. Because ESOPs are treated as instruments of corporate finance, the contribution perimeters are substantially more liberal than for other qualified plans.

11.7 CONTRIBUTION LIMITS ON ESOPS IN CONJUNCTION WITH OTHER QUALIFIED PLANS

The contribution limit is aggregated among all defined contribution plans under Code Section 404(a)(3). A corporation that has both a defined benefit plan and an ESOP covering the same group of employees can make tax-deductible contributions of up to 25 percent of covered payroll or the amount calculated to be needed to meet the pension plan's minimum funding requirement. However, if none of the employees are covered by both the ESOP and the defined benefit pension, the plans do not have to be aggregated for purposes of determining the contribution limit. Thus, if the defined benefit plan's minimum funding requirement was found to be, say, 35 percent and the leveraged ESOP contribution was 25 percent, the company could deduct 65 percent of the compensation in addition to dividends and unlimited interest. The contribution the company makes to its qualified profit-sharing plan must also be aggregated with that of the ESOP.

11.8 ALLOCATING THE BENEFITS

Corporate contributions to the ESOP are customarily allocated to participants' accounts in accordance with their compensation, service with the company, or a combination of both. Most generally, compensation is the only criterion that is used. The allocation formula must be nondiscriminatory. Typically, the total covered payroll is divided into units equaling $100 of annual compensation. The amount of corporate contribution allocated to a participant's account will be determined by the ratio that his or her unit count bears to the total. The more highly compensated individuals will receive the greatest allocation.

It is possible to allocate the contributions on a per capita basis so that each participant receives the same allocation irrespective of compensation. Thus, the janitor would have the same amount allocated to his or her account as the vice president. This technique is uncommon, however, since it would not give the more highly compensated employees proportionate weight, a form of reverse discrimination. It would also reduce the eligible payroll for leverage and tax shelter purposes.

Forfeitures from those employees who terminate prior to becoming fully vested are treated in different ways, depending on the type of qualified plan. In a defined-contribution plan (e.g., stock bonus plan or ESOP), forfeitures are real-located to the accounts of the remaining participants unless the contributions are limited by formula in the plan's design, in which case forfeitures are used to re-duce the employer's contribution for the plan year. This same reduction of em-ployer contribution treatment is true of money-purchase plans (e.g., money-pur-chase ESOPs).

Allocation of forfeitures is computed in the same manner as corporate contribu-tions. This rewards tenure and loyalty. Employers should place emphasis on this desirable end result in selecting the types of benefit programs they wish to adopt.

In a leveraged ESOP, shares that are used to collateralize a loan are allocated to participants' accounts as the shares of stock are released from pledge as the loan is repaid. This is done on a pro rata basis and in accordance with the same allocation method used for employer contributions and forfeitures (see Exhibit 11.1).

Exhibit 11.1

MODEL: Allocation of Shares to Corp, Inc.
Employee Stock Ownership Trust Participants

Payroll of ESOP Participants: $1,000,000
Corporation Contribution to ESOT: 15 percent of payroll, or $150,000

EMPLOYEE	SALARY	PERCENTAGE OF PAYROLL	AMOUNT CREDITED TO ACCOUNT
Vice President	$90,000	9.0%	$13,000 (9% × $150,000)
Department Head	$45,000	4.5%	$6,750 (4.5% × $150,000)
Clerk	$20,000	2.0%	$3,000 (2.0% × $150,000)
Other (in aggregate)	$845,000	84.5%	$126,750 (84.5% × $150,000)
TOTAL:	$1,000,000	100.0%	

11.9 ALLOCATION EXCLUSIONS

When a shareholder of a privately held corporation sells stock to an ESOP and elects to defer taxes under Code Section 1042, the provision that permits nonrecognition of tax on the sale, a whole series of rules governing prohibited allocation becomes applicable.

The complexity of the IRS Code sections that dictate which employees may or may not have stock allocated to an ESOP account for their benefit warrant discussion in greater depth. Assuming that a selling stockholder has adhered to the requirements of Code Section 1042, one must consider the consequences to the fiduciaries of the ESOP. It is of critical importance that stock not be allocated to certain parties that are identified categorically in the Code.

Administrators must be aware of parties who are not permitted to share in the allocation of stock in the ESOP. If a shareholder sells stock to an ESOP and elects to defer taxes under IRC Section 1042, he or she and certain family members will be excluded as participants in the plan until the later of the following events: (a) 10 years after the date those shares are sold to the ESOP or (b) the date the stock sold in the 1042 transaction has been fully allocated to the participants' accounts.

11.10 FAMILY MEMBERS WHO ARE PROHIBITED FROM PARTICIPATION

Family members who are prohibited from having stock allocated to their ESOP accounts are those pursuant to Code Section 267(b), namely, the seller's spouse, lineal descendants, ancestors, and brothers and sisters, whether they are half- or whole-blood siblings. They are prohibited from receiving allocations of the stock that was purchased by the ESOP pursuant to Code Section 1042 until such time as the nonallocation period ends.

If the selling shareholder's child has been adopted legally, the child is eligible to have stock sold by the selling shareholder allocated to his or her ESOP account.

11.11 FAMILY MEMBERS WHO CAN PARTICIPATE IN THE ALLOCATION

Confusion often occurs as to which family members of the selling shareholder are excluded from having stock sold by their relative in accordance with a Section 1042 election. Those who are not in the prohibited allocation category are aunts, uncles, nephews, nieces, stepparents, and stepchildren. They can have stock sold by their relative allocated to their ESOP accounts without running afoul of this provision.

If any shareholder elects 1042 deferral all shareholders w/ ≥25% stocks are precluded from participating in ESOP permanently. *Their families

CONTRIBUTION AND ALLOCATION PARAMETERS OF THE ESOP

11.12 STOCKHOLDERS WHO OWN MORE THAN 25 PERCENT OF THE SPONSOR'S STOCK DIRECTLY OR BY ATTRIBUTION

If any shareholder elects tax deferral under Code Section 1042, other stockholders are prohibited from having that stock allocated to their ESOP accounts if they own stock above a prescribed threshold. Specifically, a stockholder who owns pursuant to Code Section 318(a) more than 25 percent of any class of the outstanding shares of the sponsoring corporation, or of a controlled group in which the sponsor is a member, is precluded permanently from having stock allocated to his or her ESOP account. Outstanding shares include all of the shares in the ESOP that are allocated to the accounts of the participants for purposes of the more-than-25-percent reallocation.

Stock allocated to the stockholder's ESOP account also counts for purposes of this rule. Stock options that the individual has also count toward the more-than-25-percent calculation. Stock owned by the stockholder's spouse, parents, children, and grandchildren are deemed to be owned by the shareholder in determining whether a stockholder's stock ownership exceeds the 25 percent threshold. Stock owned by other relatives is not attributed to the shareholder in determining whether he or she has more than the 25 percent threshold ownership.

11.13 HOW TO DETERMINE IF ONE OWNS MORE THAN 25 PERCENT

The evaluation of the foregoing factors, and certain additional qualification factors in determining whether one has reached the threshold of being a more-than-25-percent owner, must be done within a period of time that begins 12 months prior to the date of the Section 1042 sale to the ESOP and ends on the date of that sale. The rules relating to prohibited transactions are very complex and the Code sections are not clear on a number of related issues. It is always advisable to seek competent advisors in dealing with this aspect of ESOPs, as with all other facets of ESOP planning.

One who meets the definition of a more-than-25-percent owner is precluded from having stock allocated to his or her account so long as the stock sold to the ESOP in a Section 1042 transaction remains in the ESOP. Neither the selling shareholder who elects Section 1042 nor the family members as defined by Code Section 318(a) whose stock is attributed to the seller will be permitted to have shares allocated to their ESOP accounts from the date of the Section 1042 sale to either the date of the tenth-year anniversary of the sale or the date the stock sold in the Section 1042 transaction has been fully allocated to the participants' accounts, whichever is later.

Notwithstanding the foregoing, which relates to the family member-prohibited allocation group, there is a de minimis rule that applies to children as well as grandchildren of the shareholder who sells under a Section 1042 election. They, in the ag-

Neither Jane nor Gita would be eligible to participate in ESOP if Jane's takes advantage of Section 1042 tax deferment for 10 years. Gita could have 5% of those 1042 shares.

gregate, can have a portion of the shares sold by their parent or grandparent allocated to their accounts so long as the amount allocated does not exceed 5 percent of those Section 1042 shares.

Violations can trigger an excise tax of up to 50 percent of the amount of the stock that was wrongly allocated with respect to the prohibited transaction rules. The tax is levied against the sponsoring corporation.

The excise tax will be imposed pursuant to stock that was allocated to the accounts of the selling shareholder or family members described above during the nonallocation period. The tax will be imposed if at any time stock is allocated to those shareholders and family members who own more than 25 percent of the outstanding stock of the corporation or of any class of outstanding stock.

With these rules in mind, it would seem appropriate to see how they can affect the strategies that should be used to accomplish various corporate and personal stockholder objectives. It is evident that the amounts that employers can contribute to an ESOP will be affected by the limits on amounts that can be allocated to employee participants.

It might be advisable to provide those who are excluded from participating in the ESOP with a nonqualified benefit plan, such as one of those described in Chapter 45. Nonqualified plans will not trigger the excise tax described above.

Exhibit 11.2

```
                    YOUR FAVORITE CORPORATION
                  EMPLOYEE STOCK OWNERSHIP PLAN
                     PARTICIPATION STATEMENT

FOR  ROBERT ALLEN                          FOR THE YEAR ENDING DECEMBER 31, 2000
```

	OTHER INVESTMENTS ACCOUNT	COMPANY STOCK ACCOUNT
THE BALANCES IN YOUR ACCOUNTS AS OF 12-31-99	$ 0.00	258.9500 SHARES
COMPANY STOCK PURCHASES ALLOCATED TO YOUR ACCOUNTS	-10,357.42	1,035.7421
PRINCIPAL NOTE PAYMENTS ALLOCATED TO YOUR ACCOUNTS	-6,797.06	906.2743
VESTED INTEREST DISTRIBUTIONS PAID TO YOU	0.00	0.0000
FORFEITURES ALLOCATED TO YOUR ACCOUNTS	0.00	0.0000
THE COMPANY'S CONTRIBUTIONS FOR THE YEAR	17,446.80	0.0000
THE BALANCES IN YOUR ACCOUNTS AS OF 12-31-00	$ 292.32	2,200.9664 SHARES

EACH SHARE OF THE COMPANY'S STOCK ALLOCATED TO YOUR ACCOUNT HAD AN APPRAISED VALUE OF $10.00 AS OF 12-31-00, AS COMPARED TO $7.50 AS OF 12-31-99.

THE TOTAL VALUE OF YOUR EMPLOYEE STOCK OWNERSHIP PLAN ACCOUNTS WAS	$22,301.98
YOUR VESTED PERCENTAGE AS OF 12-31-00 WAS	100.00%
THE VESTED VALUE OF YOUR PLAN ACCOUNTS AS OF 12-31-00 WAS	$22,301.98

THE COMMITTEE MAY DIRECT THE TRUSTEE TO USE ANY AMOUNTS IN YOUR OTHER INVESTMENTS ACCOUNT TO PURCHASE COMPANY STOCK. ANY STOCK PURCHASED WILL BE REFLECTED IN YOUR COMPANY STOCK ACCOUNT.

PLAN COMMITTEE

BY_____

1998: S-Corps can have ESOPs.

CHAPTER TWELVE

ESOPs for Subchapter S Corporations

12.1 INTRODUCTION

The Taxpayer Relief Act of 1997, generally referred to as TRA '97, signed into law on August 5,1997, made it possible for Subchapter S corporations to have ESOPs, effective as of January 1, 1998. Until that date, ESOPs were available only to C corporations. The ESOPs applicable to Subchapter S corporations can best be described as being of a modified form, in that certain major ESOP incentives that are available to C corporations are not available to Subchapter S corporations. Nonetheless, it may be possible to achieve the best attributes that both have to offer.

12.2 TAX FLOWTHROUGH ATTRIBUTES OF S CORPORATIONS

Most of the corporations that have elected to be taxed under Subchapter S have done so to avoid double taxation; that is, taxes are not paid at the corporate level as they are in a C corporation, but are passed through to the stockholders pro rata to their ownership.

It is common practice for earnings to be distributed to the shareholders in an amount that is roughly equal to their tax obligation. The undistributed earnings are retained in the corporation although the shareholders will have already paid taxes on those retained earnings, referred to as the triple-A account. The retained earnings boost the shareholders' basis.

S-corps. Retained earnings have already been taxed as personal income. They boost shareholders basis.

S-Corps shareholders are not eligible for tax deferred re-investment. However, they & their families are eligible for participation in the ESOP.

12.3 UNAVAILABILITY OF THE 1042 TAX-DEFERRED ROLLOVER

The benefits of tax-deferred sale of stock under Code Section 1042 are not available to shareholders of a Subchapter S corporation who sell their stock to the company's ESOP. Only C corporation–sponsored ESOPs can provide this tax advantage to selling shareholders. Some stockholders of Subchapter S companies may not need a tax deferral on the sale of their shares because, in many cases, they have already paid their taxes on the corporate earnings at the time they were distributed but left in the company, thereby increasing the stockholder's basis in the stock. The fact that the Section 1042 benefit is not available to S corporation shareholders may not be a deal killer to companies in which this practice has occurred.

C corporation shareholders who sell their stock to an ESOP under Section 1042 will be excluded from participation in the plan as will certain family members and other 25 percent shareholders and their families. Such is not the case when stock is sold to an S corporation ESOP. This can also narrow the gap between S and C corporation ESOP transactions when considering the loss of the ability to defer capital gains tax.

12.4 DIVIDEND DEDUCTIBILITY

Unlike C corporations, Subchapter S corporations cannot have a different class of stock. Moreover, even if they could, the S corporation would not be able to deduct dividends. C corporations can deduct dividends payable to stock in the ESOP if used for debt service or passed through to the participants. The use of tax-free distributions on unallocated shares in a Sub S corporation ESOP can usually compensate for this inasmuch as they can be used to service ESOP debt over and beyond the deductible contribution limit of the ESOP.

12.5 LEVERAGED S CORPORATION ESOPs

C corporation ESOPs permit the corporation to make deductible contributions of up to 25 percent of covered payroll to repay principal of the loan, plus an unlimited amount for interest plus dividends, but ESOPs for Subchapter S corporations are limited to 15 percent of covered payroll, or 25 percent after 12/31/01, whether or not the ESOP is leveraged. The 15 percent or 25 percent after 12/31/01 includes both principal and interest. This limitation, as noted above, is mitigated by the fact that distributions to the ESOPs unallocated shares can be used to repay debt that the ESOP incurred to acquire the stock to which the distribution is made.

It may be possible to use the distributions that are made on the allocated shares by having the ESOP use those distributions to buy newly issued stock from the corporation. The S corporation would then use the proceeds of the sale of stock to re-

ARC makes distributions on unallocated shares to repay ESOP debt.

S-corps — may require employees to accept cash instead of stock when they leave.

pay the lender. This will possibly eliminate the difference in the amount of principal that can be serviced on a deductible basis between a C corporation ESOP and an S corporation ESOP.

12.6 DISTRIBUTIONS TO TERMINATED PARTICIPANTS

TRA '97 made it possible for ESOPs in Subchapter S corporations to require that the employee participants receive cash distributions when they terminate, retire, or die, rather than receiving stock. This was made part of the law because of the intrinsic nature of Subchapter S corporations. If, for example, a terminating employee rolled the distributed stock into another qualified plan, such as an individual retirement account (IRA), this could upset the sponsoring corporation's Subchapter S election—certain entities are precluded from owning Subchapter S stock, and an IRA falls into this category. However, at the time this is being written, the IRS is considering ruling favorably on a request that if an IRA does hold stock of an S corporation for no longer than a single day, the Sub S corporation election is not upset.

Another reason for requiring that ESOP participants receive cash rather than stock when they terminate, retire, or die is because a Subchapter S corporation is limited as to the number of stockholders it can have. If stock were distributed to employees who left, it is possible that the 75-stockholder limit might eventually be exceeded, causing the sponsoring corporation to experience an involuntary forfeiture of its Subchapter S election. For purposes of the 75-shareholder rule, the ESOP trust is considered to be only one stockholder, regardless of the number of participants in the ESOP.

12.7 PROHIBITED TRANSACTION RULES

ESOPs for C corporations are exempt from certain prohibited transaction rules in ERISA. TRA '97 made these same exemptions equally applicable to Subchapter S corporations that sponsor ESOPs. They are exempt from the rules that govern pension and profit-sharing plans such as those rules requiring that the assets of those plans must be diversified and must generate a reasonable investment return.

12.8 SUBCHAPTER S CORPORATION ESOPs AS AN EMPLOYEE BENEFIT

Stockholders of Subchapter S corporations have the advantage of having corporate earnings passed through to them without undergoing taxation at the corporate level. The ESOP, as a stockholder, will also benefit from the earnings pass-through in the form of pro rata distributions.

These distributions to the ESOP will be credited to the accounts of the employee participants on the shares that are allocated to their ESOP accounts. The fact that these distributed profits will go into their accounts in cash will help the employee participants relate the effect of productivity improvement to profitability enhancement. Alternatively, as noted above, distributions on unallocated shares could use the cash to pay down ESOP debt.

If the non-ESOP stockholder is in, say, the 33 percent federal and state tax bracket, the corporation will most likely distribute 33 percent of its net earnings to the stockholders for that year. The ESOP can possibly use part of its pro rata share of the distributions to purchase stock from the company or from a stockholder.

All of the net earnings are subject to tax by the stockholders, but only the non-ESOP stockholder will have to pay the tax on its pro rata share since the ESOP is a tax-exempt entity. Under present law, if the ESOP owns 100 percent of the stock of the company, it will pay no tax at all since the ESOP is a non-tax paying entity.

The corporation can make tax-deductible contributions of stock to the ESOP in lieu of cash if it wishes to have a cashless benefit program. Alternatively, the earnings can be retained in the corporation after having been taxed at the stockholder level. Distributions that are made to the ESOP are not subject to the Code Sections 404 and 415 contribution and allocation constraints. In this respect the ESOP for a Subchapter S company can possibly be a richer benefit for the employees than for a C corporation ESOP, because in the latter, the profits are typically retained in the corporation and are not passed through to the stockholders.

By the same token, if the corporation retains the stockholder-taxed earnings or uses these earnings to acquire inventory and equipment or for marketing purposes, the stock of the company will be more apt to increase in value. Stock valuation updates will reflect the increased stock value in the participants' accounts. Because of the tax-exempt status enjoyed by the ESOP, it will be able to keep all of the distributed earnings it receives.

12.9 CONVERSION—S TO C/C TO S CORPORATION

An S corporation that converts to a C corporation can maintain its same fiscal year end by converting within 75 days of its year end. By doing so, the company can avoid having an interim short fiscal year which would require an interim financial statement.

In converting from a C corporation to an S corporation, the built-in gains will remain taxable at C corporation rates for a period of ten years after the date of the conversion. This can be offset by any built-in losses that had been incurred while a C corporation. The bank loan to the ESOP that was incurred and guaranteed by the corporation during the C corporation period can constitute a built-in loss that could help mitigate the tax on the built-in gain. This should be examined thoroughly by one's tax advisors in deciding whether or not to make the conversion.

Such a conversion to a Subchapter S status might be considered in the year following the sale of stock to the ESOP under Section 1042 by the shareholder. The company must generally wait for five years to switch back to Subchapter S after relinquishing its sub S election unless approval is given by the IRS for an earlier election.

If the inventory method used by the C corporation is last in–first out (LIFO), electing to be taxed as an S corporation will cause the corporation to include their LIFO reserve for the last year as a C corporation and for the three subsequent years, a total of four years.

In a Subchapter S corporation, the earnings are not taxed at the corporate level, but are passed through to the stockholders. Let us assume that the 100 percent stockholder is in the 39.6 percent federal income tax bracket and that with the state tax the effective rate is 45 percent. If the corporation with a $2 million annual includable payroll has a simple ESOP to which it contributes stock valued at 15 percent of the payroll, or $300,000, the corporation will pass through to the stockholder the earnings for the year reduced by $300,000. The stockholder in the effective 45 percent tax bracket would save $135,000 in personal taxes with no cash expenditure on the part of the corporation.

An ESOP can enable the stockholders of a Subchapter S corporation to exercise considerable control over the amount of income tax the stockholders will pay in any given year. It is also worth noting that stockholders who are employed by the company will be included in the ESOP and have stock allocated to their ESOP accounts. After 12/31/01, the $2 million payroll would allow the corporation to contribute stock valued at 25 percent ($500,000), saving $225,000 in taxes with no cash outlay.

It should also be noted that any distribution that is made to the outside shareholder must be made to the ESOP pro rata to the percentage of stock that the ESOP owns.

12.10 SUBCHAPTER S CORPORATION ESOP STRATEGIES

(a) Strategy 1: Increasing the Deductible Contribution with a Combination ESOP

A strategy is available for increasing the S corporation's deductible contributions to its ESOP. S corporation ESOPs have been limited to 15 percent of covered payroll contributions whether the plan is leveraged or not until 12/31/01, after which date the contribution limit is 25 percent of payroll. As noted earlier in this chapter, it is possible to increase the deductible contribution of cash or stock to 25 percent of covered payroll by designing a combination plan, which is a basic stock bonus plan ESOP and a money purchase plan. This is referred to as a *combination ESOP*. The stock bonus plan will allow the corporation to contribute from 1 percent to 15 percent of payroll (25 percent after 12/31/01), and the money purchase plan allows

No set amount of stock (30% in C-Corps) must be sold to S-Corps ESOP.

the company to make a fixed contribution of from 1 percent to 10 percent as determined at the plan's inception.

The percent of payroll contribution selected for the money purchase plan ESOP cannot generally be changed easily once it has been chosen. If maximum contributions are made to both plans, the corporation would be contributing cash and/or stock valued at 25 percent of covered payroll. Thus, a corporation whose covered annual payroll is $2 million can contribute and deduct $500,000 of cash and/or authorized but unissued stock to a combination ESOP.

Strategy 2: Selling to a Subchapter S ESOP as an Alternative to Stock Redemption

If the S corporation redeems the stock of a stockholder, the company cannot treat the transactions as an expense; the stockholders do not receive any tax relief because the taxable income is passed through to them.

If the stockholder sells to the ESOP, the corporation can deduct the cash contribution from the earnings that are passed through to the stockholders of the Subchapter S corporation. Moreover, if the selling stockholder remains an employee, a proportionate amount of the stock sold will be allocated to his or her account.

There is no statutory requirement as to the amount of stock that must be sold to the ESOP, because the rules pertaining to Section 1042 tax-deferred sales are not pertinent to Subchapter S ESOP transactions.

The stock redemption route does not benefit the employees, but selling to the ESOP keeps the employees in the loop. Whether the sponsor is a C or an S corporation, the ESOP can be a very effective employee benefit. It is cost effective for the sponsoring company, and it is an alternative means of getting equity to the employees without actually making them stockholders. The ESOP trustee becomes the sole stockholder for the ESOP. The employee participants are beneficiaries of the ESOP trust.

The employees benefit by seeing the stock that is allocated to their accounts appreciate. This should be conducive to their developing an ownership culture and increasing their productivity, a further advantage over a stock redemption by the corporation.

Strategy 3: The Subchapter S ESOP as an Exit Vehicle

From the selling stockholder's standpoint, there is some virtue in not electing to defer the tax on the sale of his or her stock under Code Section 1042, even if it were available. A prerequisite of Section 1042 is that the transaction result in the ESOP's owning 30 percent of the outstanding shares. Another is that the selling stockholder must reinvest the proceeds of the sale in qualified domestic securities within 12 months after the sale. This usually means that the corporation must borrow to

Can begin as S-corps, then when stock in ESOP approaches 30%, switch to C-corps & begin selling the rest of the stock under Section 1042.

12.10 SUBCHAPTER S CORPORATION ESOP STRATEGIES

meet the requirement that the transaction result in 30 percent ownership. This might cause the company to run afoul of covenants imposed by its present lenders. At the very least, heavy leverage might retard growth.

It might be advantageous from the corporation's viewpoint to purchase stock from a selling shareholder piecemeal, as cash flow permits contributions even though the seller will pay capital gains tax on the sale. In this way, the company need not leverage itself for the stock purchase. Moreover, the stockholder will be under no restrictions as to how the proceeds of the sales to the S corporation ESOP must be invested. When the stock in the ESOP approaches the 30 percent threshold for a tax deferred sale to the ESOP, the S corporation can change to a C corporation and start selling stock piecemeal under Section 1042 deferring taxes on the sale without leveraging the company. The owner can even take back a note from the ESOP.

While the shareholder is selling stock to the ESOP as an S corporation, a pro rata share of the stock being sold will be allocated to his or her ESOP account. This allocation will help in some measure to offset the capital gains tax that the shareholder must pay on the gain of sale. When he or she sells under Section 1042 to the C corporation ESOP, shares will no longer be allocated to his or her account. The cash allocated to the seller's account cannot be used under Section 1042 to buy stock from him or her.

Stockholders who foresee the need to cash out at some future date might want to start the process a number of years in advance of their retirement date. By selling their company stock gradually, they can start their diversification program and use a modified dollar cost-averaging system.

A pro rata share of the tax savings the S corporation gets for making cash contributions to the ESOP to purchase a portion the stockholder's stock through the ESOP is passed through to the selling stockholder. The effect of this is that the seller gets a partial personal tax deduction for selling his or her own stock. Upon termination, retirement, or death, the stockholder will also be entitled to receive distributions of his or her ESOP account balance in the form of cash from the ESOP or from the corporation. This will supplement the cash proceeds of the sale of his or her stock.

Per the 2001 law, a 50 percent penalty is imposed on allocations to those participants who own 10 percent or, with their families, own 20 percent of the ESOP's assets, as if all shares are allocated and as if synthetic equity were ESOP shares.

Strategy 4: Neither Owner Nor Corporation Pay Taxes

Mr. Big, the sole stockholder of a corporation, can sell all of his stock to the ESOP, recognizing no tax under Code Section 1042. In the following fiscal year the corporation elects to be taxed as a Subchapter S corporation. The company would pay no tax since the taxable income would be passed through to the stockholder, the ESOP, a tax-exempt entity.

CHAPTER THIRTEEN

How ESOPs Can Increase Working Capital and Cash Flow

Perhaps the most elementary ESOP transaction is one that can be used to increase working capital and cash flow while making equity available to ESOP participants. To accomplish these results, the corporation simply contributes authorized but unissued stock or treasury stock to the ESOP. The deductible, though cashless, transaction will save taxes, thereby increasing operating capital and cash flow.

The amount the corporation can contribute to the ESOP on a deductible basis is limited to 15 percent of covered payroll in a given year (25 percent as of 12/31/01).

If the sponsoring company's covered annual payroll is, say, $1 million, the corporation can contribute up to $250,000 in the form of cash and/or stock after 12/31/01 and, assuming a 40 percent combined tax bracket, the corporation would save $100,000 in taxes. If the corporation's contribution is all in the form of stock, the tax savings increases working capital by that amount.

Another way of looking at this transaction is to relate the tax savings to the net after-tax profit the corporation would have to earn on sales to achieve the same result. If the company nets 5 percent after taxes on sales, $100,000 of tax savings is equal to the net after-tax profit on $2 million of sales without need to hire additional personnel or incur short- or long-term overhead.

At first glance this method might appear to be dilutionary—but is it really? Possibly not. Here is why. The dilutionary effect is, in great measure, offset by the company's use of the tax savings to grow the company's value. Another offset to dilution occurs by adding back the after-tax cost of the contribution to the profit-sharing plan that was discontinued, thus adding cash flow and working capital, thereby increasing the value of the corporation.

The owner of the company will also be a participant of the ESOP and will have a pro rata amount of the shares that the company contributed to the plan allocated to his or her ESOP account. This is an offset to dilution.

Another offset to dilution is the fact that productivity will most likely occur, increasing profitability and adding further value to the corporation. The effect is that the corporation gives a slice of a larger pie to the employees, and the original stockholders keep the rest of the larger pie.

CHAPTER FOURTEEN

How to Increase Working Capital and Cash Flow by Converting a Profit-Sharing Plan or Pension Plan to an ESOP

14.1 PARTIAL CONVERSION

Contributions of cash to a qualified profit-sharing plan result in a tax deduction for the corporation but nonetheless reduce working capital and cash flow. If the corporation is in the combined 40 percent state and federal tax bracket and contributes $200,000 of cash to a qualified profit-sharing plan, it will save $80,000 in taxes but will decrease working capital and cash flow by $120,000.

If the profit-sharing plan were converted to an ESOP, the company could contribute newly issued company stock to the ESOP instead of cash. A corresponding contribution of employer stock to an ESOP in the same amount will be tax deductible, saving $80,000 in taxes, thereby increasing its working capital and cash flow by $80,000 since neither the cash nor the tax payment leaves the pockets of the corporation. The difference between the two plans from a working capital and cash flow standpoint is a reduction of $120,000 by contributing cash to the profit-sharing plan versus an increase of $80,000 by contributing stock to the ESOP, or $200,000 in favor of the ESOP. This amounts to $2 million of increased working capital in the course of a decade, assuming no change in payroll or annual contributions.

If covered payroll increases at a 10 percent compounded rate and proportionately greater annual contributions are made, working capital would be improved by $5.2 million over the decade. If the corporation is able to earn 10 percent net on the capital that it gained as a result of choosing an ESOP over another form of qualified plan, this will add an additional $5.18 million of working capital, for a total of $10.3 million over the 10-year span.

This is referred to as a partial conversion since existing assets of the profit-sharing plan would continue to be invested in a diversified portfolio as before. All new contributions would be invested in employer stock.

Studies have demonstrated dramatic productivity improvements among ESOP companies. If this is factored into the subject company's working capital improvement, the $10.3 million gain noted above would be further enhanced. Although this is a compelling feature of the ESOP, it should not be treated in isolation of other characteristics of the various forms of qualified plans.

14.2 CONVERTING THE PROFIT-SHARING PLAN

The act of converting a profit-sharing plan to an ESOP can be done by the fiduciaries without seeking approval of the employee participants. A full conversion refers to using the existing assets in the profit-sharing plan to purchase stock of the sponsoring corporation.

When considering whether to use some or all of a profit-sharing plan's assets to buy employer stock in a full conversion to an ESOP, the question will arise as to whether the employees should participate in the decision. An election on the part of the employees to convert their existing profit-sharing plan account assets into employer stock in an ESOP may be considered an offering of stock that would require the company to make full disclosures concerning the corporation and the securities being offered. This is done in the form of an offering memorandum.

Alternatively, if the fiduciaries use the assets of the existing plan to purchase employer securities without seeking the participants' approval and the account balances are subsequently decreased as a result of the conversion, there could possibly be a cause of action against the fiduciaries under the prudent person rule or because the conversion was not for the exclusive benefit of the employees.

The corporation can consider guaranteeing that the employee will not suffer a loss if he or she leaves the company during the term of the ESOP loan. Certainly, this would tend to build an argument for prudency, though it would not eliminate the fiduciary risk. If a profit-sharing plan is converted partially or fully to an ESOP, the participants maintain their vesting status that existed in the profit-sharing plan.

It is generally felt that using up to 10 percent of a profit-sharing plan's assets to buy employer stock falls within the realm of diversification and the decision to do this could be made by the plan trustee.

A *partial* conversion is one whereby the assets of the profit-sharing plan are maintained in a separate cash account in the newly created ESOP, and the new contributions are made to the ESOP in the form of stock or cash, which is used to purchase stock. The assets in the cash account can continue to be invested in money instruments or diversified securities other than stock of the sponsoring company. The fiduciary responsibility must be maintained to assure diversification and a fair return on investment in connection with the nonemployer security assets.

A technique that might be considered to make the participants more receptive to the idea of allowing their profit-sharing plan assets to be used to buy company stock would be to allow the employees to compare the investment gain in the other investment account and the stock account for one or two years after the partial conversion. The switching of assets might be less traumatic to the employees if the annual valuation attests to the fact that the employer stock had appreciated to an amount at least equivalent to the investments in the cash or other investment account. Thereafter, the use of the cash account to purchase employer stock might reduce the exposure to fiduciary liability.

Employers tend to make more generous contributions to ESOPs than they had been making to profit-sharing plans due to the fact that ESOPs permit the cash to remain in the corporation while profit-sharing plans are a drain against the cash flow and working capital of the corporation. If, for example, a corporation had been contributing 5 percent of covered payroll to its profit-sharing plan and subsequently contributes 15 percent to an ESOP, the plan participants would be essentially just as well off if the stock value declined by approximately 66⅔ percent. The contribution to a leveraged ESOP is likely to be even higher.

Of course, this is a theoretical example and the employees would undoubtedly feel very uncomfortable about the decline in the value of the stock. It is quite likely that if the company were doing that poorly, many of the employees would have already been discharged. By the same token, since contributions to a profit-sharing plan can only be made out of profits, it is obvious that the employer would not be in a position to make further contributions to the profit-sharing plan until such a time as the company turned around. A contribution of employer stock to an ESOP would tend to increase working capital and cash flow and should offer further security to the employees as a result of the corporation's improved capital position.

As a general rule, it can be risky and therefore inadvisable to convert all of the diversified assets of a profit-sharing plan to employer stock.

In such a conversion, the assets of the profit-sharing plan could be used to purchase stock from the corporation or from stockholders who are willing to sell. Purchase of stock from the corporation will infuse working capital and cash flow into the company. The improved working capital position could possibly benefit the participants significantly by increasing the value of the stock in their accounts more rapidly. This strategy is more likely to be used in those situations where the alternative would be a sale of the corporation to outside buyers. Assuming this to be the reality of the situation, the argument for the transition of the assets would be fortified.

If the profit-sharing plan's investments have historically outperformed the employer stock, it might be unwise to reinvest the existing investments into common stock of the sponsoring corporation. Such action might invite litigation by an employee participant.

There are those corporations whose stock has not performed as well in the past as it is expected to perform in the future. It may be untimely to convert the profit-sharing plan and use the assets to buy common stock of the employer. It might be more appropriate, though, for the assets of the converted plan to purchase preferred stock whose dividend outperforms the yield experienced in the converted plan. Preferred stock gives the employees a good measure of downside protection as well, since it is not so volatile as common stock. The dividends are deductible by the company and are paid in cash directly to the employees. This is described in Chapter 18.

Assuming the assets of the converted plan are not used to buy employer stock, those assets could be frozen in a separate account with separate records being maintained. At some future date it might be considered more timely to use some or all of the assets of the former plan to purchase stock from the company or from stockholders. Distributions to terminating employees would be made from the stock account and from the other asset account.

While profit-sharing plans can be converted, the Pension Benefit Guaranty Corporation will deem the conversion of a pension plan to an ESOP a termination, and all of the account balances of participants will become fully vested and subject to distribution (see Exhibit 14.1).

Exhibit 14.1

MODEL:

Conversion of a Profit-Sharing Trust to an ESOP Using Part of the
Assets to Increase Company Working Capital

$3 MILLION DIVERSIFIED STOCK ASSETS

CORPORATION

(2) $1 MILLION CASH

(3) $1 MILLION STOCK

(1) $3 MILLION CASH INVESTMENTS

—Corporation has a profit-sharing trust with assets of $3 million.
—It forms an Employee Stock Ownership Plan.
—Assets are converted from the profit-sharing trust to the ESOP.
—$1 million of the assets are liquidated and used to purchase stock of sponsoring
    corporation.
—Employer-participants retain vesting standing they had prior to the
    conversion.

Summary:

The corporation's cash flow, working capital, and net worth are increased by $1
million.
The employees participate in the growth of their company.
Future contributions are used to purchase employer stock.
NOTE: Fiduciary and prudency aspects must be considered.

CHAPTER FIFTEEN

How to Convert or Terminate an ESOP

A question frequently arises as to how one might convert or terminate an ESOP in the event it does not work as well as the employer had hoped or perhaps the company becomes bankrupt, merges with another corporation, outlives its original purpose, or perceives that its repurchase liability is going to be too large to contend with out of cash flow.

ESOPs can be terminated either completely or partially. In the former instance, the ESOP's assets must either be rolled into another qualified plan or distributed to the employees, who, in turn, can roll their account assets into an IRA. The employees become 100 percent vested in the event of a complete termination of the ESOP. In a termination, distributions are made as soon as practical.

Alternatively, the ESOP can be converted into a profit-sharing plan or into a 401(k) plan. The assets of the ESOP can be frozen and new cash contributions can go into the profit-sharing plan to which the ESOP as been converted. The cash would be invested in diversified investments.

If a participant rolls his or her ESOP account balance into an IRA within 60 days of the distribution, there will be no tax exposure.

If an ESOP is to be terminated, it may be a good idea to request that the IRS issue a letter of determination in order to dispel any issue concerning whether the plan was ever intended to be a permanent plan. However, the law does not require IRS approval of a plan termination.

3-20 vesting: After 3 years — 20% vested w/ 20% added each year after that. 7 yrs = fully vested.

5 year cliff vesting: 0 vesting until 5 years, then 100% vested.

CHAPTER SIXTEEN

Vesting Benefits

Qualified plans, whether they be pension plans, profit-sharing plans, or ESOPs, are seldom designed so as to be fully vested in the first year. This would create undue costs due to early employee terminations, but, possibly more important, it would not meet with most employers' desire to use benefit plans as "golden handcuffs" to help dissuade employees from terminating. They would have too much to forfeit if they left the firm prior to being fully vested.

The 1986 Tax Act provides a safe harbor guideline in the form of two minimum vesting schedules. An ESOP's vesting provision must be no more stringent than either of these in order to be considered nondiscriminatory. One of the safe harbor vesting schedules, the so-called 3-20 vesting, provides that those participants with fewer than three years of participation in the ESOP will have zero vesting. They will become 20 percent vested after three years of participation, and vested in increments of 20 percent thereafter, with full vesting after seven years of participation.

The other safe harbor schedule is the five-year cliff vesting schedule under which employees with fewer than five years of participation will have zero vesting. Five years of participation triggers 100 percent vesting. If a plan is top heavy, that is, too heavily weighted in favor of officers or highly compensated employees, the plan can be required to vest more rapidly—possibly immediately. Employers can have the plan designed to give the employees credit for the prior years of service, that is, service that commenced prior to the ESOP's effective date. This is not mandatory, however. Plans can be designed to have the vesting schedule start as of the date the ESOP is installed.

The 3-20 vesting schedule appears to be the most popular among the corporations structuring new plans. In the case of an ESOP that has been converted from a profit-sharing plan, the participant in the ESOP will retain the vesting status that is at least as favorable as that which he or she had in the profit-sharing plan.

Complete vesting for all participants will be triggered by the act of terminating the ESOP. This is true of all other tax-qualified plans as well.

The vesting guidelines are useful in helping plan designers avoid the pitfalls that might lead to discriminating in favor of officers, shareholders, or highly compensated employees. The vesting schedule and all other provisions of the ESOP must fit fundamental requirements benefitting employee participants and their beneficiaries.

CHAPTER SEVENTEEN

Distributing the ESOP Benefits

Employees or their families almost invariably want cash when they retire, become permanently disabled, die, or terminate for any other reason. Private corporations, as a general rule, prefer that the ESOP participants have cash rather than stock upon leaving the company's employment. If there are too many shareholders, registration of the stock under securities laws might be required. As an ESOP participant, the employee has a beneficial interest in the ESOP but is not a stockholder. The plan's single stockholder entity is the trustee.

Public companies have a different mentality. They usually like to see their stock owners proliferate. Since there is a market for public stock, shares distributed from ESOPs of public companies are simply sold in the marketplace. The greater the number of stockholders, the greater the marketability.

In order that ESOPs of private companies maintain credibility among the employees, precise rules governing distribution of benefits have been promulgated. The Tax Reform Act of 1986 went the full nine yards in tightening up the rules for the benefit of the participants. Plan account distribution rules apply to stock acquired by the ESOP after 1986 and pertain to stock bonus plans as well as to ESOPs. The plans can be amended to apply to pre-1987 stock as well as post-1986 stock so as to eliminate the administrative burden of tracking the two categories of plan assets.

ESOP participants who terminate from the company and its ESOP because of death, disability, retirement or other reasons are subject to distribution rules. The corporation can make the distributions in cash or in company stock subject to their right under Code Section 409(k)(1) to demand stock, one exception to this being a bank. Another exception lies in the corporate charter or bylaws which can override this Code Section by requiring that substantially all of the stock must be owned by the employees or by the ESOP. The word *substantially* is commonly construed to mean 80 percent or more.

ESOPs have regulations that differ from other qualified plans in significant ways. Noteworthy among these are the rules that govern distribution of the ESOP participants' balances. ESOP rules require that the plan must begin to distribute a participant's vested account balance no later than one year following the end of the plan year in which the participant terminates due to death or disability, or reaches normal retirement age, or the fifth plan year following the plan year in which the participant terminates from service for other reasons. This means that distributions must begin by the end of the sixth plan year after the plan year in which the participant terminates. There is an exception where the ESOP is leveraged.

17.1 LEVERAGED DISTRIBUTION RULES

If the ESOP has borrowed funds to acquire stock, the ESOP is not required to make distributions of a participant's account balance that includes stock acquired with an exempt loan until the end of the plan year in which the final loan payment has been made.

In the case of a leveraged ESOP, distributions must be completed by the end of the plan year in which the loan has been repaid in full, or by the date the distributions would otherwise have to be completed according to the general rule if this exception did not exist.

17.2 DISTRIBUTION METHODS

The distribution may be made in a lump sum, based upon the value of the stock at that time. Alternatively, it can be made in installments, in which case each installment will be measured by the fair market value of the stock at the time the installment is made.

If the participant puts the stock to the company, the corporation can either redeem the stock in a lump sum or give the terminating participant a promissory five-year note which pays interest and is backed up by adequate security. Stock of the company cannot be used as adequate security but segregated corporate assets can be used. Special bonds have been designed to meet the requirements of adequate security.

17.3 NONLEVERAGED DISTRIBUTION RULES

In a nonleveraged ESOP, if the participant quits or is fired, distribution must begin in the fifth year following the year of termination of employment. Benefits are *not* distributed if the employee resumes employment prior to the end of the fifth year.

If the payout is in installments, the payments must commence within 30 days from the date the participant exercises the put option. The installment payments must be made at least annually in substantially equal periodic payments over no more than a five-year period (six annual installments including the first one) unless the participant elects a longer period. The installment period may be extended an additional year for each $155,000 (or fraction thereof) by which the balance in the participant's account exceeds $780,000, the respective limits in 2000. They are adjusted periodically according to cost-of-living changes. The payout period must be set forth in the plan document. It must not be subject to the plan administrator's discretion.

The sponsoring company must provide adequate security and credit the participant with reasonable interest on the unpaid balance. The sponsoring employer stock is not considered to be adequate security.

17.4 LIBERAL DISTRIBUTION PRACTICE

A policy of account balance distribution can be more liberal but not less liberal than these rules so long as the treatment is administered uniformly. For example, the general practice might be to have the ESOP pay out balances up to, say, $5,000 at the time of termination but to defer distributions if the account balance is higher than this amount. This would preclude further administration of relatively smaller accounts while discouraging employees from terminating in order to receive more substantial distributions.

17.5 DIVERSIFICATION RULES

The Tax Reform Act of 1986 imposed a requirement that the ESOP permit participants to begin to diversify their account balances gradually so that the liquidity will be available when they approach the age of retirement. Diversification rules are set forth under IRC Section 401(a)(28). These rules apply to ESOPs of both private and public corporations. The regulations also apply to accounts of terminated participants whose account distribution is being deferred. The diversification rules apply to stock acquired by the ESOP after December 31, 1986. Persons who have participated in the ESOP for 10 years and who have reached age 55 must be permitted to diversify 25 percent of the stock balance acquired after 1986. They have 90 days after the close of the plan year to elect to diversify. The eligible participants of private companies must be given three investment choices other than employer stock in order to avoid it being considered a security by the Securities and Exchange Commission.

The diversification period must continue for five years so that when the participant reaches age 60, he or she has 90 days after the end of the plan year to elect to diversify or not. Fifty percent of the stock allocated to his or her account after 1986 must be subject to diversification if the participant so elects. By the end of the plan year in which the participant reaches age 65, 100 percent of the post-1986 stock must be subject to the participant's right to diversify. The trustee must satisfy the participant's election for diversification within 90 days from the end of the election period.

17.6 HOW TO DIVERSIFY THE ACCOUNTS

The ESOP can make cash payments to participants who have elected diversification of their account balance of the plan or can offer three alternative investment funds, and participants can elect to have the account assets transferred to investment funds. If the plan satisfies the diversification requirement by distributing cash, the 10 percent early withdrawal tax does not apply.

Although stock of the private sponsoring company can be made available as an investment choice, it might be considered a securities sale, from the Securities and Exchange Commission's viewpoint, requiring a form of registration and complete disclosure.

The participants must be given a complete description of other alternative investment funds, including a history of fund performance.

Although the diversification requirement pertains only to employer stock acquired by the plan after the end of 1986, it is advisable to apply the diversification rules to all of the assets in the participants' accounts. This measure would eliminate the need to track which stock was pre-1987 and which stock was post-1986, thereby simplifying the administration process.

IRS Advance Notice 88-56 provides a $500 de minimis rule when the amount is less than $500. Diversification is permissible but is not required.

17.7 DIVIDEND DISTRIBUTION

Dividends payable on stock allocated to participants' accounts in a C corporation ESOP may be distributed to the participants at any time; however, if the dividend is distributed more than two years after the ESOP received the dividend, the distribution of the dividend may be made in cash or in stock, subject to the right of the participant to demand stock. Again, this can be superseded by the charter or bylaw provision.

In order for the corporation to be able to deduct the dividend, the corporation must pay it directly to the ESOP participants or to the ESOP, in which case the ESOP must distribute it within 90 days of receiving it.

Upon termination of employment, employee participants seldom wish to have distributions in the form of stock that is not publicly traded. They want liquidity. Aside from this, unless they roll the distribution over into another qualified plan, they will be taxed on the distribution and will need cash for that purpose.

17.8 WITHHOLDING

Withholding rules affecting qualified plans were promulgated by the Unemployment Compensation Amendments Act of 1992, affecting all post-1992 distributions. The employer must withhold 20 percent of the taxable distributions not paid out as an annuity over a minimum period, often years, unless the distribution is transferred trustee-to-trustee to an IRA or successor plan of a different employer.

The ESOP is given an important exemption from this requirement in that the rule only applies to cash distributions. Dividends are also exempt from withholding.

The lesser of 20 percent of the amount of the distribution or the total cash amount must be withheld. Therefore, if a participant's account consists of $8,000 of stock and $2,000 of cash, then 20 percent of $2,000 ($400) must be withheld, but if the mix were $9,000 and $1,000, respectively, only $100 is to be withheld.

If the account were all in stock and the stock was distributed, there would be no withholding, but if the value of the stock were all paid out in cash, withholding would apply.

17.9 PUT OPTION

ESOP companies whose stock is not readily tradeable on a public market must give the participants a put option that would require the employer to purchase their ESOP account shares within 60 days after they are distributed to the employee. If the option is not exercised within that time frame, the terminated employee must receive another put option for an additional 60-day period following the next stock valuation. If the participant does not exercise the second put option, the company is no longer required to redeem the stock. Banks are an exception to the put option requirement inasmuch as they are precluded by law from redeeming their stock.

The options can provide for a lump sum or an installment payout, the latter beginning within 30 days after exercise and in substantially equal payments over not more than five years from that time, or if the ESOP has any indebtedness it can be extended for the full term of the loan but not to exceed 10 years. The installments must not be less frequent than annual. The corporation must provide a reasonable rate of interest as well as adequate security.

Some states require that corporations redeem stock essentially only out of retained earnings. If a corporation's retained earnings are inadequate in this context, the company may defer the put options until it can meet the retained earnings requirements. This applies to nontradeable shares that the ESOP acquired after December 31, 1979.

Subchapter S corporations are not required to distribute stock because of the possibility that a terminated employee might roll the stock into an IRA or another qualified employee benefit trust, thereby causing the sponsoring company to lose its S election since its stock cannot be owned by an employee trust other than an

ESOP. Another reason for not distributing S stock is that S corporations are limited to 75 stockholders and the distributions could possibly violate this requirement.

17.10 BUY–SELL AGREEMENTS

ESOPs cannot be required to purchase stock at some future unknown date at an undeterminable price. For this reason, a put option cannot be imposed upon an ESOP. The ESOP may have the right to purchase stock from the terminated participant if the corporation is unable to do so. In this same context, an ESOP cannot enter into a mandatory buy–sell agreement that would require it to buy the stock upon a stockholder's retirement or death. The corporation can enter into such an agreement and the ESOP can be given an option to buy the stock.

In the event an employee exercises the right to demand stock at the time of distribution, he or she still must be given a put option. Private company employers seldom wish to have stock in the hands of terminated employees. As a result, the ESOP regulations provide them with a safeguard under which the employer or the ESOP may be given a right of first refusal to reacquire the stock from the distributee or from his or her ESOP account at fair market value. If the distributee receives a bona fide offer from a third party, the company or the ESOP may meet the higher price within 14 days of receiving written notice from the distributee concerning the offer.

ESOPs of public companies do not require put options since their stock is readily tradeable in the public marketplace. If the stock is subject to certain trading limitations, the plan must provide a put option covering those shares. ESOPs of banks are not required to contain a put option where such banks are precluded by law from redeeming their own shares.

The ESOP trustee will look to the corporation for liquidity in order to make cash distributions or repurchase stock from those participants who are disabled, die, or retire. The corporation can oblige by making tax-deductible cash contributions to the ESOP to the extent needed within the limitations set forth by the regulations. Some firms choose to establish sinking funds comprised of liquidity instruments ranging from certificates of deposit (CDs) to annuities to life insurance held within the corporation or by the ESOP. There are pros and cons to the various approaches. The liability will not generally be significant in the early stages of the ESOP due to the younger average ages of the ESOP population and the shallow vesting at that stage. Nevertheless, the problem should be anticipated and provision made to accommodate the future cash out needs.

17.11 DISTRIBUTION OF ACCOUNT BALANCES

Unless the distributee elects otherwise in writing, distribution of account balances must commence within one year after the end of the plan year in which employment terminates due to death, disability, or retirement or within one year after the end of the plan year which is the fifth plan year after termination for any other reason. This is, in effect, the sixth year. The distributions may be made at a rate of 20 percent annually over the next five years.

If any stock in the participant's accounts was acquired by leverage and any debt still exists, the distribution may be delayed until the plan year following the plan year in which the debt is paid in full, but the delay cannot exceed ten years. The payout must then be made over a period that does not exceed five years in substantially equal periodic payments that are not less frequent than annually. As previously noted, in 2001, the payout period is extended one year for each $100,000 of account balance in excess of $780,000 up to five additional years. These amounts are indexed for inflation. In 2000, they were $145,000 and $735,000, respectively.

Benefit distributions must begin on April 1 following the year in which the participant reaches age 70½ whether or not he or she is still employed. Prior to the 1986 Tax Reform Act, this applied only to participants who owned more than 5 percent of employer stock. The Act makes this provision applicable to all participants as of 1989.

17.12 TAX ON DISTRIBUTIONS AND ROLLOVERS

ESOP participants who are age 59½ or older and who have participated in the plan five years or more can elect to have a once-per-lifetime five-year averaging distribution election on lump sum distributions. This permits them to be taxed on 20 percent of the distribution and disregard any other taxable income for the purpose of computing the tax. This figure is multiplied by five in arriving at the taxable income on the distribution. Five-year averaging is available to the participants' beneficiaries. All plans sponsored by the employer that permit five-year averaging must be grouped by the distributee in order to receive this form of tax treatment.

Taxes can be deferred by participants or their beneficiaries on distributions of stock or cash that are rolled into other qualified plans within 60 days after distribution. This is applicable if the spouse is the beneficiary. Any remaining distribution is ineligible for five-year averaging. An ESOP participant's rollover to an IRA whose sole asset is employer stock can be rolled over to a qualified plan again. A participant might consider creating a separate individual retirement account (IRA) to allow for this possibility.

In the event of a lump-sum stock distribution that is not rolled over into another qualified plan, and assuming that the distributee does not elect five-year averaging, the cost basis of the stock or the current value, whichever is lower, is taxed as ordinary income. This cost basis is the value of the stock at the time it was contributed to or purchased by the ESOP.

Long-term capital gains treatment is afforded to the stock's unrealized appreciation upon subsequent sale of the distributed shares. The stock's full market value is subject to tax in non–lump-sum distributions.

A 10 percent excise tax is applicable on pre–age 59½ distributions from qualified plans subject to a number of exceptions. The Tax Reform Act of 1986 granted an exclusion to distributions from ESOPs made prior to January 1, 1990, so long as the majority of assets were invested in employer stock for the preceding five years.

Other exceptions to the penalty tax on distributions are death, permanent disability, dividends, distribution of excess 401(k) deferrals or contributions, life annuity payments, transfers or rollovers to other qualified plans, divorce settlements, allowable medical expenses, and early retirement after age 55. The last two do not apply to individual retirement plans.

ESOP participants are not taxed on the unrealized appreciation of such stock or of stock qualifying for a lump-sum distribution. However, a participant may elect to be taxed on the gain currently if it is advantageous to do so. The distributee is taxed as ordinary income on the appreciation above the basis when he or she ultimately sells the stock.

The final regulations relating to distributions from statutory ESOPs permit flexibility in using either lump sum or installment payments, or they may limit their use to only one of these methods of distribution. The distribution can be in the form of cash rather than stock if the company is *substantially* owned by the employees.

In the matter of distributions that occur prior to the participant's attaining age 59½, the excise penalty tax is waived for statutory ESOPs or stock bonus plans where the benefits have been invested in stock of the sponsor for at least five years or for the life of the ESOP. Stock that was transferred from other qualified plans can be aggregated for purposes of this regulation.

The rules permit the substitution of an acquiring company's stock for that of the acquired company insofar as distribution rules are concerned. The final regulations apply to transactions made after December 31, 1989.

Employers must withhold 20 percent of terminated ESOP participant's taxable distributions, namely cash distributions as opposed to distributions of stock, the latter being exempt from immediate taxation. The employee is taxed only when he or she sells the stock.

17.13 THE DISTRIBUTION POLICY

The ESOP plan document should contain distribution rules that must be adhered to throughout the ESOP's existence by the board of directors, the ESOP committee, the ESOP trustee, and the administrator of the plan. The way these rules should be carried out operationally must be applied uniformly by those persons or bodies. They should therefore be put in writing in the form of a distribution policy to serve as a guide for everyone who is involved with the operation of the ESOP. This would assure that the plan provisions will be interpreted in a consistent manner. The policy should not be in conflict with the plan document and must not be discriminatory.

The distribution policy is needed because the law has only minimum requirements that must be contained in the ESOP plan document. Both the ESOP plan document and the distribution policy should be designed so as to reflect the objectives of the corporation and its shareholders. It should not conflict with the company bylaws, Articles of Incorporation, shareholder or buy–sell agreements, existing loan covenants, whether the company operates as a C or an S corporation, or other pertinent factors.

The distribution policy should instruct the fiduciaries as to how the company should finance its obligation to cash out terminating employees. Should it rely upon future cash flow or should a sinking fund be created so as to prepare against the impact of fiscal surprises?

A clearly constructed distribution policy will enhance the company's ability to cope with its ability to meet its repurchase obligations and better enable the company to communicate the ESOP policy to the employees.

Qualified plans are generally precluded from amending the plan to eliminate benefits that are optional, such as when benefits will be distributed. It is possible to make distribution procedural changes once the benefit has been allocated to the participant's account on options that pertain to allocations to occur in the future.

17.14 THE ASSET DIVERSIFICATION EXEMPTION

The 1986 Tax Reform Act required that participants with 10 years of participation and who reach age 55, 60, and 65 be given the right to diversify 25 percent, 50 percent, and 100 percent, respectively, of their account balance. This applies to post-1986 contributions. They must have three investment choices other than company stock.

One of the most important ways in which ESOPs differ from other forms of corporate qualified plans is the fact that they have been granted an exemption from the diversification rules except for the specific limited diversification rule previously noted. The ESOP assets can be composed totally of employer stock with the exception just described.

17.15 WITHHOLDING

Since 1983 ESOPs have been permitted to make voluntary withholding from distributions and certain other qualified plans. Now in 2001 the ESOP must withhold 20 percent of the value of the distribution for federal income tax for those employee participants who do not elect to roll over their distribution to another qualified plan. Excepted are distributions that are as an annuity, installments for one's lifetime expectancy or for a 10-year period or longer. Withheld amounts need not exceed the amount of cash in the distribution so that no stock needs to be sold in order to meet the required withholding. Minimum distributions for those who are age 70½ or above are also excepted from the withholding requirement.

17.16 TAX TO THE PARTICIPANT

A lump sum stock distribution from the ESOP of one who is 59½ or more the amount of taxation as ordinary income is the fair market of the stock or the ESOP's cost basis, whichever is less in addition to the amount of cash distributed. The net unrealized appreciation is taxed as long- or short-term capital gains depending upon how long the distributed stock had been held prior to its being sold or rolled over to an IRA is not taxable, unless the distributee elects to be taxed currently.

CHAPTER EIGHTEEN

Deductible Dividends—Only Through ESOPs

Dividends paid in a non-ESOP environment create a double taxation event because they are nondeductible by the corporation and taxable to the recipient. The corporation receives no tax deduction and the recipient is taxed. The ESOP rules changed this. The Deficit Reduction Act of 1984 permits a corporation to pay dividends to an ESOP and deduct them from the sponsoring C corporation's taxable income, provided that they are used to pay ESOP debt to acquire stock or are passed through to the employee participants.

18.1 HOW YOUR CORPORATION CAN DEDUCT DIVIDENDS TO SERVICE DEBT

The Tax Reform Act of 1986 extended the opportunity for a C corporation to deduct dividends paid on the stock in the ESOP that is purchased with the proceeds of an exempt loan. This applies to both allocated and unallocated shares and they are deductible by the company in the year they are actually applied to debt service.

This provision came about in order to enable corporations to add to their ability to service ESOP loans in those instances where the covered payroll is small relative to the amount of debt the ESOP incurs for the purchase of stock, keeping in mind the limitations imposed by Code Sections 404(a)(9)(A) and 415(c), which govern the amount of principal the corporation can deduct and the amount that can be allocated to the participants' accounts.

Dividends, in order to be deductible, must be considered to be reasonable. This determines whether or not it is a dividend. Among the factors to be considered are whether it represents a reasonable return on investment and reasonable compensation.

Technical Advice Memorandum 9304003 dated 9/30/92 stated that dividends used to repay debt of an ESOP are not deductible under Internal Revenue Code (IRC) Section 404(k) if the amount of the dividend is deemed not to be reasonable. The IRS held that the dividend, to be deductible under this section, should be continuing and reoccurring and at a rate normally used in the regular course of the business on comparable securities. The IRS addressed a case involving a dividend of more than 63 percent of the ESOP's stock value. The ESOP loan was incurred to acquire stock from a selling shareholder and the transaction was not recurring. The IRS disallowed the dividend, stating that it exceeded the rate that might be paid on a continuous basis by the company.

The use of dividends in servicing ESOP debt is sometimes the deciding factor in determining whether a leveraged ESOP transaction is workable. This is true when the covered payroll is inadequate to accommodate the amount of debt servicing that is needed for the transaction. The dividend deduction is over and above the 25 percent of covered payroll deduction for servicing principal in leveraged ESOPs.

The Financial Accounting Standards Board (FASB) issued its FAS No. 96 on December 31,1987 pertaining to the accounting treatment of ESOP dividends. It provided that they should be recorded as a credit to income tax expense. They should not be credited to stockholder equity which would bypass the income statement.

Payment of dividends to be used to service ESOP debt is deductible if the appropriate shares of stock are released from the suspense account to the participants' account balances.

18.2 PASSING THE DIVIDEND THROUGH TO EMPLOYEES

Code Section 404(k)(2)(A)(i) prescribes that dividends that are paid on the shares that are allocated to the employee participants' accounts and which are purchased with the proceeds of an exempt loan and which are used to repay that loan may be deductible if paid directly to the participants or their beneficiaries by the corporation. Alternatively, they can be paid to the ESOP, which, in turn, would distribute them to the participants or to beneficiaries. To be deductible, they must be passed through to the employees within 90 days of being contributed to the trust. The dividends are taxable to the participants but they are exempt from the 10 percent early distribution tax. The plan document must state whether the fiduciary or the board of directors will decide to pass the dividends through to the employees from time to time or whether it is done automatically.

ESOPs help employees build capital without their contributing any cash since the employer is usually the sole contributor to the ESOP. This results in the participants receiving tax-deferred compensation over and beyond the wages they receive for their labor. If the ESOP helps to increase productivity, the dividends that are paid on the stock allocated to participants' ESOP accounts will further enhance their current feeling of well being while the underlying stock adds to their retirement security.

An additional element of compensation can now be expected as a result of the 1984 Tax Act in the form of tax-deductible dividends—an immediate or nondeferred return on equity. This is the element that had been missing in ESOPs. It is difficult for employees with limited patience to rely solely on the value that can be realized sometime in the future.

What is often needed in order for one to appreciate one's wealth is tangible evidence of its existence. This comes most effectively in the form of current spendability. The deductibility of dividends had been talked about for years, but when the first realization of this tax break came, it was for the benefit of ESOP companies.

The payment of tax-deductible dividends is an ideal way to help avoid a penalty tax for excess accumulations of retained earnings in the company. If a corporation has no profit and no current or accumulated retained earnings, the payment of *dividends* may be treated as a return of capital and therefore ineligible for deductibility. Laws of the various states might also restrict the declaration of dividends if such payments would impair capital. The dividend is deductible in the company's tax year in which the dividend is paid or distributed directly to the participant. The dividend pass-through provision provides the corporation with another distinct advantage. Employees will come to a better understanding as to the meaning of equity ownership. They will quickly learn that dividends will be paid on their shares in a manner commensurate with corporate profits. The fact that dividends are related to additional productivity will not be lost on them.

The deductibility of dividends applies to any form of stock in the ESOP that meets the definition of qualifying employer securities. It may be advantageous to pay no dividends to non-ESOP shares because of their double taxation while paying deductible dividends to ESOP shares. This can be accomplished by providing a class of stock for the ESOP that differs from that held by other stockholders. Dividends paid on ESOP shares are not deductible in a Subchapter S corporation. Moreover, Subchapter S corporations cannot have a different class of stock.

Tax-deductible dividends paid to ESOP participants have an advantage over bonuses since there is no Federal Insurance Contribution Act (FICA) tax on dividends while FICA is payable on bonuses. Withholding is not required on such dividends, whether they are applied to stock purchased with employer contributions or employee contributions. Some firms have a practice of paying bonuses to all employees. The amount that would otherwise be paid in FICA taxes can be used to increase an ESOP company's dividend so long as the dividend is reasonable.

Public corporations that pay dividends and have an ESOP can obtain greater tax savings by passing dividends through to the ESOP participants. As the ESOP shares allocated to ESOP participants increase, so can the dividends and the tax savings. If desired, the distribution could be applicable only to vested shares. State law should also be reviewed in this regard.

The Economic Growth and Tax Relief Reconciliation Act of 2001 would let the employees deduct the amount of the dividends they receive if they reinvest them into the ESOP in employer stock. The allowable deduction is 25 percent for 2002 through 2004, 50 percent for 2005 through 2007, 75 percent for 2008 through 2010 and 100 percent for 2011 and thereafter.

The deduction can be denied if the dividends are unreasonable or if they constitute avoidance or evasion as determined by the Secretary of the Treasury.

CHAPTER NINETEEN

ESOP Account Diversification Rules

19.1 INTRODUCTION

ESOPs must give plan participants the opportunity to diversify the assets of their ESOP accounts upon attaining their ages and tenure in the plan. This requirement came about as a provision of the Tax Reform Act of 1986 and applies to stock that either was contributed to or was acquired by the ESOP after December 31, 1986.

The diversification requirement applies to those who have been plan participants for 10 years or more and who have attained age 55. Therefore, it is timely to revisit and update this subject matter; a significant number of ESOPs have reached the maturity stage at which many employees are eligible to choose diversification.

Internal Revenue Code (IRC) Section 401 (a)(28) is the code section that governs the requirement for diversification; however, there are many confusing aspects that require the clarification this chapter endeavors to provide.

The diversification rules pertain only to post-1986 stock that has been allocated to the account of a "qualified participant": one, as noted earlier, who is age 55 or older with 10 or more years of plan participation.

The ESOP must permit such a qualified participant to invest 25 percent of his or her account balances in other forms of investments except employer stock. They can do this within a "qualified election period," which commences with the initial year the participant becomes eligible or qualified. The qualified participant has six plan years to elect to diversify the post-1986 stock accounts, starting with the first year he or she becomes eligible. The qualified participant can elect to increase the amount of his or her post-1986 stock account up to 50 percent in the sixth year after becoming eligible.

The election to diversify the account must be made by the participant within 90 days after the end of the plan year in which he or she becomes qualified (eligible) for diversification and within 90 days after the close of each plan year during the six annual election periods. The plan trustee must implement the election within 90 days from the end of each election period. The election to diversify is applicable to all stock that is allocated to the account as of the last day of the prior plan year.

The shares of post-1986 stock in an eligible participant's account that are subject to the election for diversification in any election year other than the sixth year are 25 percent of those shares that were ever allocated to the account before the most recent allocation date. This number is reduced by any shares that had been diversified or otherwise distributed or transferred from the account previously. It is permissible to round out fractional shares to the nearest whole share.

19.2 THE *DE MINIMIS* RULE

If the amount of post-1986 stock in the participant's account has a fair market value of $500 or less, the shares will not be subject to diversification. For this *de minimis* rule to be available, the plan document must provide for it.

19.3 IMPLEMENTING THE DIVERSIFICATION ELECTIONS

The eligible participants must be given a preliminary form within the aforementioned 90-day period following the plan year, directing them to make a diversification election, and a final election form within 180 days following the plan year. This procedure must be used for each of the election years. There are three methods an ESOP can use to meet the diversification election requirements. They are:

1. The ESOP can make a distribution of the segment of the participant's account that is subject to the diversification election. It can be made in the form of either cash or stock. This must be done within 90 days after the last day of the annual election period.

   a. If the distribution is in the form of cash, the withholding rules apply and the distributed cash is taxable to the participant unless he or she rolls the amount distributed over into another tax-qualified plan such as an IRA or a profit-sharing plan.

   b. If the cash or stock is not rolled over into an IRA and the participant has not attained the age of 59½, he or she will be subject to the premature penalty tax of 10 percent of the amount distributed. No such tax applies to distributees who have attained age 59½.

Distributions of stock from nonpublic-company ESOPs are subject to the put option requirements applicable to other nondiversification distributions.

2. The ESOP can offer the participant a minimum of three specific investment selections other than securities of the sponsoring corporation. Each investment choice must be fully subscribed and the participant must be provided with their historical performance.

A number of authorities feel that employer stock of a nonpublic company should not be offered to the participant as an investment choice because this might be construed as a securities sale, subjecting the company to compliance with the Securities and Exchange Commission. Notwithstanding this, it is customary practice to allow the eligible participant to elect not to diversify—an option that some say could be construed as a sales offering of employer stock.

Before the eligible participants are notified of their investment choices, the contributions for the prior plan year must have been made, the stock allocations to the participants' accounts must have been prepared, and the appraisal of the stock must have been done.

When the participant notifies the ESOP designee of his or her investment selection, the trustee will have the corporation liquidate the applicable employer shares in the participant's account and purchase the investment choice for the account. Because no distribution is made to the participant, he or she is not charged with taxable income.

3. The participant can direct the ESOP designee to transfer the amount designated for diversification to another qualified defined contribution plan that offers three or more investment choices other than employer securities. There is no taxable event for the participant so long as the transferred account remains under the shelter of a qualified plan. The plan to which the assets are transferred must provide complete disclosure about the investment choices, including their track records. The ESOP document must dictate which of the various options will be made available to the participant, in compliance with the diversification rules.

4. The trustee can make a distribution of cash in an amount that is equal to the value of the employer stock in the participant's account.

5. The plan can distribute the stock that is in the account subject to the put options and, if applicable, the articles and bylaws provisions.

As noted earlier, ESOP participants must be given the right to make their diversification within 90 days of each of the plan eligibility years. It is good practice to provide them with written information some time in advance of that point, so that they know the investment choices that will be available to them when they become eligible for diversification, notwithstanding the fact that there is no requirement to do so.

By the time the ESOP participant reaches retirement age 65, the diversification that will have occurred will make it far easier for the corporation to exercise the put for the remaining employer securities.

The diversification rules provide an answer to those who might question the wisdom of putting all of one's eggs into a single basket. Diversification requirements are designed for ESOP participants who are arriving at an age at which it might be too late to weather a decline in the value of the sponsoring company's stock. The diversification of assets is likely to provide one with considerable peace of mind.

CHAPTER TWENTY

Leveraged Buyouts and the ESOP

Founders of privately held corporations who are interested in succession planning should have a working understanding of how they can transfer the equity of their business to an ESOP and effective control to the management group even though the managers may have very little cash available to invest in the company.

20.1 LEVERAGED BUYOUTS

A leveraged buyout (LBO) involves the acquisition of a company, the assets and cash flow of which are used by an investor to obtain and service the financing required to make the acquisition. This technique has been on the financial scene for many years, but, until the 1980s, was referred to simply as "getting a loan to buy a business." A great deal of sophistication has been added over the years to facilitate the leveraged transfer of the stock or assets of companies from one party to another.

Leverage can be accomplished through the use of third-party equity investments or loans. Businesses are seldom bought without the use of outside funds, since buyers generally do not have adequate cash on hand. Even if they did, it is almost invariably more advantageous to use other people's money (OPM), since this expands one's capability to make larger acquisitions than would otherwise be possible.

Quite frequently, acquisitions can be made on a shoestring or in some cases on no string at all. The price must be right. The financing must be well tailored and the new owners must be capable of churning out a profit sufficient to make the transaction worthwhile for all parties. Indeed, an LBO can permit an individual with limited resources to acquire an extraordinarily large firm. Many LBOs are the unsung smaller deals that never even hit the last page of the financial section. The prerequisites for newsworthiness are much more stringent than they were in the 1980s. The fees for putting an LBO together today are often larger then the whole financing package was in those days. A multibillion dollar acquisition price is in the ho-hum category and the investment banking fees can be many millions of dollars.

Larger-sized LBOs are usually structured by an outside coordinator or quarterback who brings the other advisors and players together. Smaller LBOs can sometimes be put together essentially in-house. However, it is still important to consult with outside advisers. The large LBOs involve venture capitalists, banks, and insurance companies that provide the capital source. Venture capitalists are rewarded by interest income, equity kickers such as convertible debentures, common stock, preferred stock, or by getting their investment return through a public offering or eventual sale of the company.

An ESOP would provide an alternative that could be more advantageous. In an LBO transaction, outside investment groups, corporations, management teams, or the employees are the buyers. Management and employee buyouts are becoming a more frequent occurrence as the viability of using LBOs in conjunction with ESOPs emerge.

The tax leverage afforded by an ESOP/LBO involved in LBOs can be awesome. A one-to-one or two-to-one debt to asset ratio is textbook for an established, well-run corporation. Nine or ten to one is not an uncommon leverage ratio for some of the large LBO transactions. Somewhere about midway offers a comfort zone for the less adventuresome players. The debt loan must be supportable if the deal is to succeed. The underlying assets and the restructured cash flow are the determinants of this. The corporation's ability to deduct principal payments in an ESOP transaction increases the cash flow available for debt coverage.

Cash flow rides on the backs of management as does the security and profitability for the lenders and investors. Their management and operating talents are often a mandatory ingredient. The top executives are therefore frequently given the opportunity to cash in on the big capital gains stakes. The financial participation sometimes comes out of their pockets to make them try harder. For the most part, their net outlay, if any, can be zeroed out by incentive bonuses.

The act of public companies going private has become commonplace. The stock of some public companies is underpriced, selling far below liquidation value. The company's assets may provide sufficient collateral for financiers. The enhancement of the deal could come from a strategic performance study involving a paring down of expenses coupled with a good marketing plan to increase cash flow. This could portend a return trip from being private to going public or selling out to a larger corporation as a means of cashing out the lenders and entrepreneurs.

The smaller LBO transactions have the same basic prerequisites for success as those of behemoth proportions. The degree of sophistication and the number of players grow exponentially with the size, however. A large financing might involve venture capitalists, pension funds, and insurance companies that take a subordinated position to the commercial banks, with each represented by separate counsel. A relatively small LBO might involve only an individual buyer (who may or may not take back some of the paper), a seller, the bank, and their respective counsel.

20.2 LEVERAGING THE LEVERAGED BUYOUT WITH AN ESOP

A buyout coupled with a leveraged ESOP can improve the ability of a management group to buy out private or public companies. The ESOP improves the doability of the deal and has many social attributes that are lacking in other forms of LBOs by outsiders. From a broad perspective, the management group, the corporation, the economy, and the social fabric of the country is far better off when an ESOP is involved in a corporate takeover. The economy is weakened by a traditional LBO simply because the ownership is reduced to perhaps one individual or at best a handful of investors. The ESOP broadens the ownership and places equity in the hands of employees, where it will do the most good.

The leveraged ESOP allows a management group to invest a minimal amount of equity capital into a new corporation (NEWCO). NEWCO forms an ESOP which borrows money from a lender. Principal and interest are repaid from ongoing corporate earnings being contributed to the ESOP which, in turn, discharges the debt. The contributions for principal and interest are tax deductible. The tax savings go into marketing, production, and equity appreciation, swelling the pie size. Management's slice may become more valuable than its 100 percent share of the traditional LBO would have become.

There are other elements to the leveraged ESOP that can further enhance management's equity position, including the use of other classes of stock, dividend deductibility, offsets to other qualified plans, and lower interest rates. These were enlarged upon in Chapter 18.

20.3 PUBLIC COMPANY DIVISION DIVESTITURE

An LBO opportunity often exists when a large public company makes a decision to divest itself of one or more divisions or subsidiaries. The reasons are varied. These units may not be profitable or they may be very profitable but require too much of the parent company's attention, capital, or both. The parent may wish to concentrate its energies in another direction. It may want to raise capital to make acquisitions that are better suited to the company's blueprint for the future. Obsolescence of products occurs almost as soon as a technical product is introduced to the public. This occasions management's thinking in the direction of a spin-off unless some alternative use can be found for equipment and personnel that has greater bottom-line gratification.

An ideal target is a division that is at the receiving end of an economic downswing, once having been a good performer and possessing the potential of becoming one again. The parent wants to massage its annual report and rid itself of the subsidiary, often at a bargain basement price. A talented operator who has a knack for rekindling situations of this kind can build up the bottom line to make a killing on resale several years hence.

Public companies can range in size from a $1 million market value to one in the megabillions. Those on the lower rung can be closely controlled by a small number of shareholders, yet they may have a relatively large number of outside stockholders to whom the major stockholder must report. These companies can be essentially private in effect. In some instances, the major stockholder, often the founder, has no practical means of selling his or her stock because of the Securities and Exchange Commission (SEC) restrictions and the thin market. A secondary offering of his or her stock can become a sell signal to other stockholders who then stampede the market and depress the stock price before the founder has a chance to sell any securities. This could thwart the founder's ability to achieve a viable succession plan.

This is sufficient motivation for the board of directors either to seek an outside buyer for the whole company or take the company private through an LBO by the management group. Such a scenario for small or medium sized public companies is not uncommon.

The proposed leveraged buyout must be penciled out vis-à-vis a feasibility study to determine whether the transaction will work. If the deal is too highly leveraged, the cash flow going forward may not support the debt service requirement. Even if the loan obligation can be paid by future corporate earnings, the margin may be so thin as to leave an insufficient cushion for marketing and production expansion so that the company may not be able to cope competitively. The firm might be forced into bankruptcy or liquidation.

Although the management group would own one hundred percent of the corporate stock, how much equity would this translate into? Might the management group not fare better with a smaller piece of a larger pie? If there were a vehicle through which after-tax earnings could service the debt load more easily, leaving more for equity appreciation, the owners could look forward to a more lucrative and secure future. The leveraged ESOP may be the route to explore.

20.4 USE OF ESOPs IN CORPORATE DIVESTITURES

Large public corporations generate hundreds of profitable subsidiaries and divisions each year. These spin-offs occur due to the parent companies' desires to (1) concentrate their energies and resources on their primary area of endeavor and (2) maximize their efforts to gain market share over their competitors.

These new entities are sometimes put up for auction with a bidding process determining who the lucky new owner will be. The parent company uses this auction process to assure its stockholders that it has attained the maximum value for the entities.

Management buyouts (MBOs) are often successful in the bidding due to the managers' inside track. They often know of the board's plan to sell the subsidiary or division long before others learn about it. Management knows more about the real potential that may not be reflected in the financial news and other documents available to outside corporate or individual buyers. All other things being equal, the board's sympathy would tend to lie with the managers. This is particularly true if the managers' proposal involves an ESOP, as this will benefit all employees, not just a few at the top. The ESOP also brings to the table extraordinary tax savings that increase the likelihood of a successful buyout. This concept will be more apparent with an understanding of how the ESOP is used in conjunction with a divestiture.

20.5 THE MBO/ESOP MECHANICS

One of the numerous ways that divestitures occur might involve a management group that creates a new corporation, "NEWCO," the purpose of which is to acquire the assets of the division being spun off by the public parent corporation. The managers invest funds to purchase some of NEWCO's stock.

NEWCO's board establishes an ESOP, which obtains senior debt and possibly mezzanine, or subordinated, debt to acquire the balance of NEWCO's stock.

If the amount of debt financing that can be obtained is insufficient, an outside equity investor may have to be found, in addition to the management group.

Senior debt is the least expensive debt, because the lender is first in line to be paid out of corporate earnings. The senior lender is collateralized by the assets of the corporation and stands before all others in the event of liquidation. Banks are the most common source of senior debt financing. The cost might range from prime to prime plus 3 percent.

Subordinated debt is more costly, because the lender stands in line behind the senior debt provider regarding the availability of the corporation's cash flow to repay principal and interest. Insurance companies and pension funds are the major sources of subordinated debt. By assuming greater risk, these lenders will probably tack on an equity "kicker," such as warrants. The parent company might, in some cases, provide some of the subordinated debt by carrying some of the paper.

Some state and local governments, desiring to preserve their tax bases by discouraging businesses from leaving the area, will make subordinated loans with favorable terms.

Equity is the most expensive form of financing, with the investor requiring a 30 to 40 percent return on investment. It is used in situations in which debt financing is not available.

NEWCO services debt by making annual contributions to the ESOP that are equal to principal and interest payments. The contributions are tax deductible and, accordingly, the corporation can deduct both principal and interest within liberally prescribed limits. The ESOP might acquire a different class of dividend stock, such as convertible preferred or a super common that is convertible to the highest form of voting common at the end of the term period.

The dividends paid on the ESOP stock are tax deductible, and the stock is typically designed to convert into fewer shares of voting common. The result of this arrangement is to transfer more of the equity to the equity investors who hold the common stock, which effectively partially offsets dilution that might otherwise be experienced by the equity investors, possibly increasing their equity by as much as 15 percent to 30 percent.

It is a certainty that an ESOP will reduce the risk to the lenders and to the equity investors because of the advantages noted above. Risk reduction is of great importance to those who provide the capital. An ESOP should be considered as a viable instrument in corporate divestitures.

20.6 DILUTIONARY OFFSETS

By deducting principal payments, the corporation saves 40 cents on the dollar. Thus, for each $100,000 of annual principal payments made, the ESOP allows the corporation to save $40,000 annually for the period of the loan. If the loan is for seven years, the tax savings are $280,000, adding that amount to the value of the company.

Overall interest costs are reduced further by the company's ability to use tax savings on principal payments to accelerate the paydown of the debt, which can be added to the list of equity dilution offsets that the ESOP brings to the transaction.

Quite likely, if the ESOP were not available as an employee benefit, the company might feel obliged to restore a costly retirement benefit similar to that which the predecessor company provided. This, too, is a dilution offset.

Another offset to dilution is the increased productivity that a well-run ESOP brings to the company, increasing the company's value.

CHAPTER TWENTY-ONE

The Leveraged ESOP for Business Succession

21.1 THE DILEMMA OF NONLIQUID STOCK OWNERSHIP

Private companies tend to take on the founder's characteristics and the corporate personality is as distinguishable as his or her own. The owner's goals are mirrored in the philosophy that governs the direction of the company. Ralph Waldo Emerson said "A company is the lengthened shadow of a man."

A private business, aside from legal definitions, has a finite existence. Unless it is endowed with a strong second-line management team, it is as fragile as the thin life thread of its founder.

An entrepreneur's major asset is often his or her corporate stock. While the owner is alive and productive, the corporation is a virtual "goose that laid the golden egg." It continues to spin off income within the limits of reasonable compensation set forth by the Internal Revenue Service (IRS). The owner is currently paid for his or her labor—not ownership. Unlike public corporations, private companies seldom pay dividends.

The owner's ownership of the company stock is a paradox. It is an asset, but it is nonspendable so long as he or she controls the company. It is in another sense a liability. The stock will be taxed in one's estate, notwithstanding the fact that the owner could not use the capital during life without relinquishing the company to others. The bottom line is that the owner is compensated for labor and not for capital while he or she remains the major stockholder. Founders often become sorely tempted by the equity they are sitting on but cannot use or even touch.

The most common method used by owners of private corporations to transform their nonliquid capital into cash is to sell the company. Ideally, most would prefer to sell only a portion of their stock; however, one seldom wishes to acquire less than 51 percent of a private company. If the owner sells the controlling interest, he or she is generally out of a job. An entrepreneur would find it difficult to work for others in any event. Individuals can sell all other forms of property such as real estate, automobiles, coin collections, or sailboats without forfeiting their vocation or their potential for earned income. Not so with the entrepreneur's private company. The sale of their life's blood, their avocation in life, is the biggest decision that many entrepreneurs face. Selling the company usually means giving up something in which they have invested substantial emotional capital.

Aside from the emotional attachment to the company, the owner must weigh the financial price he or she is willing to pay for keeping the capital in a nonspendable form. If the owner's stock in the company is worth $5 million, it is costing that individual approximately $5 million of otherwise spendable pretax funds.

Many business owners are experiencing the frustration of being wealthy but nonliquid. They face the specter of estate taxes, essentially a nine-month call on about half their assets by the government at an indeterminate time. The Treasury Department will not accept stock certificates. It relates only to cash. An owner's failing health may become the catalyst for considering the subject of mortality and perpetuation of the company.

The need for liquidity to pay estate taxes is a most compelling reason for selling a private corporation. Sometimes companies are sold by the executors at a distressed price. More often, a business is sold by the founder while he or she is still very much alive and able to negotiate a better price. The owner may not be actively pursuing an opportunity to sell the company, but will be receptive if a prospective buyer broaches the subject in a serious vein. A new owner might require the founder's talents for a period of time in order to assure a smooth transition. The founder's availability could enable him or her to command a more attractive price for the company.

If the founder has one or more potential heirs to the chief executive officer's (CEO's) suite, whether offspring or other executives, who have demonstrated an ability to take over as chief executive officer, the founder will in all likelihood be motivated to retain the company for their benefit. The question is how to accomplish this transition if the owner cannot afford to give them the company and the heirs do not have the cash to buy the stock.

Private firms that were built with the help of capable, loyal, long-time executives often try to explore every possible technique to permit the executives to buy the owner out. Some of these transfer arrangements are so generous that the owner all but gives the company away, thereby depriving his or her family of the true worth of the accumulated wealth.

Since there are many more private companies than public ones, and because a private company is an extension of an individual, an entrepreneur whose working career is finite, it follows that there are more private companies that are overtly for sale. There are also more compelling reasons for private company owners to consider selling companies or finding alternatives.

A leveraged ESOP might be a viable alternative. It will let the owner sell the company stock tax free, still keep the company, and remain in the driver's seat for as long as he or she wishes, eventually transferring effective control to managers or heirs on a practical basis.

21.2 HOW A PRIVATE COMPANY OWNER CAN PROVIDE FOR SUCCESSORSHIP THROUGH A LEVERAGED BUYOUT

Mr. Big, the founder of Alpha Widgets, Inc., owns 100 percent of the company stock. He would like to step down in the near term, diversify his assets, but still perpetuate the company. Independent appraisal places an enterprise (control) value on the company at $16 million. The stock has a history of increasing in value 10 percent annually and this trend is expected to continue. The company has a covered annual payroll of $3 million and the payroll is also expected to grow at an annual compounded 10 percent rate.

Pretax earnings before the $400,000 annual contribution to its profit-sharing plan amounts to $2 million for the current year and are projected to increase at a 10 percent annual compounded rate. The profit-sharing plan has $3 million of assets, the investment performance of which is mediocre.

Bill Big, Jr., vice president and son of Mr. Big, has demonstrated an ability to succeed his dad as CEO. He also aspires to that position.

(a) The Problem

Mr. Big's wealth is locked into the stock of his privately owned corporation. It comprises the bulk of his estate. He cannot afford to give the company to his son even if the gift tax laws permitted this to occur. Bill Jr. has no funds with which to buy Dad's stock. How can Mr. Big pass effective control of the company to his son and still get his capital out of the company? He learns what can be accomplished through the use of an ESOP and formulates his objectives.

(b) Mr. Big's Objectives

- Perpetuate the company that he founded, sell 70 percent of his company to an ESOP under Internal Revenue Code (IRC) Section 1042, transfer the balance to his son, Bill Big, Jr.

- Reward those loyal employees who helped build the company by providing them with equity in the corporation.

- Do all of the above tax efficiently.

(c) Solutions

- The corporation converted its profit-sharing plan to an ESOP, thereby saving $400,000 of annual contributions that would henceforth be used by the company for ESOP debt service.

- Alpha Widget's bank extended a seven-year term loan of $11.2 million to the corporation which, in turn, loaned it to its ESOP.

- The corporation created a second class of stock, a super common stock that pays dividends.

- Mr. Big sold the dividend stock to the ESOP under IRC Section 1042. He would invest the proceeds in qualified replacement property (QRP) within 12 months and defer the federal capital gains tax on the transaction and his state of residence permitted tax deferral as well.

(d) Mechanics

The corporation is permitted to deduct 25 percent of covered payroll for principal debt reduction. Twenty-five percent of the $3.5 million of annual payroll is $875,000. Scheduled annual principal payments on the $11.2 million seven-year loan are $1.6 million, a shortfall of $725,000.

To solve this problem, the corporation declared a 6.5 percent noncumulative annual dividend on the $11.2 million of stock that was sold to the ESOP, resulting in a dividend of $728,000.

The deductible $875,000 contribution plus the tax-deductible $728,000 dividend add up to $1.6 million, the annual principal payment. No dividends are paid on the common shares that Mr. Big retained since they would not be deductible by the corporation.

The company can deduct an unrestricted amount on its interest payments.

The stock is held in a suspense account and is released and allocated to the ESOP participants' accounts as principal is amortized. The allocation is prorated to their compensation.

(e) Gift of Stock to His Son

Because the ESOP debt was reflected on the balance sheet of the corporation, the value of the outstanding stock was reduced by 70 percent. Therefore, the value of the 30 percent traunch of stock that Mr. Big retained was reduced.

The fair market value of 100 percent of the stock was valued at $16 million before the debt. After incurring the $11.2 million debt, the corporation's value fell to $4.8 million.

(f) Minority and Marketability Discounts

Mr. Big's sale of 70 percent of the outstanding stock to the ESOP left him with a 30 percent minority interest in the company. The appraiser subjected the value of the 30 percent block of stock to a 25 percent minority discount.

Mr. Big's intention was to make a gift and/or sale of this stock to his son. Bill Big, Jr., would have no guaranteed market for the stock, thereby increasing the discount to 45 percent. The value of the 30 percent traunch of stock was reduced from $4.8 million ($16 million $\times$ .30 = $4.8 million) to $2.64 million.

Mr. Big, with the consent of his wife, made a gift of stock to their son of $1,370,000 of stock. This fell within their combined lifetime exclusion in 2001 of $1.24 million plus the $20,000 annual gift exemption. Mr. Big sold the remaining $1.29 million of stock to his son, Bill, taking back a long-term note. The corporation would bonus Bill the required payments.

(g) Summary

- Mr. Big receives roughly the after-tax equivalent of what he would have had left to invest after a taxable sale to an outside purchaser.

- Mr. Big invests the proceeds he received from the sale of his stock to the ESOP into a diversified portfolio of stocks and bonds of domestic corporations, thereby deferring his taxes. If he retains those investments until death, they receive a stepped-up basis and income taxes on the gain will be deferred forever.

- Bill Big, Jr., acquired 30 percent of the outstanding stock of the company at a large discount. His stock was 100 percent of all of the stock outside of the ESOP trust, giving him effective control of the board that effectively controlled the ESOP.

- As ESOP participants terminate, the corporation can redeem the shares from the ESOP, thereby shrinking the number of shares outstanding and increasing Bill's percentage ownership.

- Mr. Big was able to perpetuate the company.

- The cash flow that was diverted from future contributions to the profit-sharing plan would be used to help service ESOP debt.

- The corporation was able to deduct the ESOP's purchase of the stock.

If the company in the 40 percent combined tax bracket had no ESOP, it would have to earn $20.95 million to repay principal, ignoring interest. With an ESOP it must earn only $11.2 million, saving $9.75 million of future earnings, making the company stronger in the years ahead.

CHAPTER TWENTY-TWO

How an ESOP Can Make a Leveraged Management Buyout Company Healthier

ESOPs are ideally suited to enhance the value and ongoing financial health of corporations that had originally been acquired by means of a leveraged management buyout.

This is so because of the unique ability of ESOPs to fulfill dual corporate needs as follows: (1) ESOPs are tax sheltered instruments of corporate finance; and (2) they are tax-qualified employee benefit plans. In the first role, ESOPs provide capital for an acquisition transaction by making the sponsoring corporation eligible to receive tax incentives. They infuse capital into the corporation in the form of tax savings by allowing the company to deduct principal as well as interest.

A corporation with no ESOP in the 40 percent combined tax bracket must earn $1.67 million to repay $1.0 million of principal, ignoring interest. By letting the company deduct principal payments, it saves $670,000 of future before tax earnings. This is a substantial reduction in the amount of pretax profit that a company must earn in order to discharge its acquisition debt. An ESOP will therefore help the company get this phase behind it on an accelerated basis and get on with the business of growth.

By lowering the threshold of earnings that will be diverted to debt service, the company will be able to produce earnings in excess of this level, all of which will go into growth. The ESOP will make the company stronger and will bring greater equity to the stockholders in the years ahead.

Alternatively, ESOPs will permit lenders to justify higher levels of financing because of the increased debt coverage ratio the tax savings create. This might be in the form of working capital lines and will allow the managers to take on larger projects, increase market share, and expand more rapidly and effectively. A dollar diverted from taxes is a dollar more that is available for expansion.

By maximizing a corporation's cash flow available for debt service, an ESOP can increase the amount of leverage the company can service by about one third. Financing that would otherwise have been delayed because of high interest rates can perhaps proceed since the tax savings on principal payments might be considered an offset to higher interest.

An ESOP's second role as a qualified employee benefit plan eliminates the company's need for alternative costly pension plans, profit-sharing plans, or matching contributions to a 401(k). Corporate contributions that would otherwise go into those off-balance-sheet employee trusts can be used to secure acquisition debt through ESOPs.

Because shares of stock are allocated to the accounts of employees, well-run ESOPs are likely to improve productivity and profitability.

22.1 HOW ESOPs INCREASE CORPORATE VALUE

Exhibit 22.1 shows how an ESOP can increase the post-transaction value of a corporation that had been acquired in a leveraged buyout (LBO) by a management group. The example assumes that a pension or a profit-sharing plan to which the company had been committed to make future contributions was replaced by an ESOP. Exhibit 22.1 reflects the present value of the savings of future contributions to those plans.

Exhibit 22.1

How the ESOP Brings Added Equity to LBOs	
Pre-LBO value	$10,000,000
Present after-tax value of savings on future pension or profit sharing contributions	455,000
Present value of tax savings	1,710,000
Post-LBO value	$12,165,000

CHAPTER TWENTY-THREE

ESOPs And Total Succession Planning™

Why Total Succession Planning™ Is a Must for Private Company Owners

23.1 HURDLES OF TRANSFERRING OWNERSHIP

Owners of privately held companies that have survived the "barracudas" and have achieved the lofty status of steady growth in profitability and market share should be applauded. They have outlasted many that have fallen by the wayside.

Yet, the odds that a successful, mature privately held corporation will transcend the founder's generation are approximately only one out of twenty. The hurdles that founders of such companies must overcome are staggering.

Generally, tax laws have been designed to discourage perpetuation of private companies, notwithstanding the fact that a successful company brings many benefits to federal, state, and local governments.

One successful tax-paying enterprise supports a whole ecosystem of tax-paying entities, including employees, suppliers of inventory and equipment, professional advisors, the merchants and service providers that employees patronize, and the businesses that those merchants and service providers support.

If a successful privately held company is sold to a larger company, it is often relocated and absorbed into the acquirer; the unneeded departments are discarded, and any trace of the founder's creation no longer exists. The suppliers and service providers of the acquiring company replace those that had served the acquired company. This signals loss of a significant tax base for the local community.

Confiscatory gift taxes make it impractical for the founder to simply give the company stock to an heir who might be groomed to succeed his or her parent as CEO. Bonusing stock to a key manager subjects the recipient to a phantom tax. Managers, after having paid taxes, can seldom save sufficient cash to purchase stock from the owner. If the bulk of the founder's assets are locked up in the company, he or she cannot afford to retire without finding a way to liquefy the company stock. For this reason, the amorous advances of "tire-kickers" become ever more compelling.

Many founders of private corporations, upon reaching the age when they would like to retire, realize that their primary assets are nonliquid. Aside from their homes, the stock of their companies often comprise the major portion of their worth. At some point in time, they develop a burning desire to become liquid. Selling the company becomes a recurring thought, but to whom should they sell? Their children, the managers, or outsiders?

23.2 THE LOYALTY FACTOR

A business owner's success is usually due to an ability to cultivate good managers and other employees, dependable and loyal suppliers, and customers of long standing. It is only natural that owners of successful companies have a strong sense of pride in their accomplishments and wish to perpetuate their companies, not only to repay the loyalty of their managers and employees by protecting their interests but, in many cases, as a monument to themselves. The subject of disposition of businesses is an active one. KMPG Peat Marwick surveyed 6,000 owners of corporations that had sales ranging from $10 million to $200 million and determined the following:

1. Forty-five percent have considered selling their companies.

2. Another 35 percent plan to sell within 3 years.

3. Forty percent of those considering a sale are thinking about retirement.

4. Thirty-two percent have considered offers for their businesses.

It has been determined also that more than $7 trillion of private company stock will be ready to be transferred to a new generation over the next decade.

23.3 THE NEED FOR A SUCCESSOR

Another hurdle that must be overcome if the company ownership is to pass from the founder's generation to a successor is the founder's reluctance to relinquish control and his or her uncertainty as to when this transfer should occur. Founders are often fiercely independent, which is what compelled them to go into business for themselves initially. For the entrepreneur to train others to someday sit in the "catbird seat" means giving up some of that independence—an often traumatic experience. To prepare for successorship, an owner must start grooming a likely candidate— possibly a son, a daughter, or someone outside the family—well in advance of the time he or she decides to retire.

The owner must have a far-reaching perspective of what he or she wants to do with the business some years into the future. By preparing for successorship early on, the founder will have a wider range of options when the time comes for an ownership transition and will thus be able to wait out, and possibly ignore, the myriad of tempting offers that will inevitably materialize. Effective strategic planning for perpetuating a company demands that the founder address a number of key issues and develop a knowledge of several disciplines. The business is often the major part of an owner's wealth, the founder having perhaps devoted most of his or her working career to creating this asset.

23.4 PREPARING A SUCCESSION PLAN

It is common practice for CEOs of successful companies to prepare a business plan and update it regularly. The plan covers, among other things, sales, earnings, and expense projections for the next year or several years, new product development, and expansion programs. Preparation of a business plan requires a great deal of time and thought but relatively little emotional expenditure.

A succession plan and exit strategy involve much more preparation and introspection than preparing a business plan. The chief executive officer (CEO) must examine his or her own psyche and contemplate how he or she might hold up under the unfamiliar terrain of retirement or adjusting to a lesser role in a beloved business involvement. One must examine one's own mortality. This may be difficult for an energetic founder to do, so the business succession plan is all too often put on the back burner.

It is certainly worth the founder's time and effort to prepare a business succession strategy for maximizing the value of the business, while simultaneously designing an exit strategy.

23.5 SUCCESSION AND EXIT PLAN COMPONENTS

The exit strategy should:

- Allow the owner total flexibility as to when to exit, whether gradually or on a certain date

- Have the right successor CEO and other managers in place to let the founder walk away, mentally as well as physically

- Minimize or eliminate tax erosion of the fruits of the owner's labor in the transfer process

- Ensure the selling shareholder the maximum postsale income

- Provide loyal managers and employees with a sense of security and the incentive to continue to increase the growth effort

- Give the owner a clear road path of rewarding retirement activity

- Maximize the value of the estate that the family will be able to keep through proper estate liquidity planning

- Create a workable course of action for the CEO's other dependents who are not involved in the company

To accomplish this strategy, the owner of a privately held midsized company must commit to having a Total Succession Plan™ or TSP™.

23.6 WHAT IS A TOTAL SUCCESSION PLAN?

TSP is a term the author has coined that incorporates the components of a workable plan to perpetuate the founder's corporation. TSP incorporates not only succession planning but also investment strategy planning, estate liquidity planning, estate transfer and tax planning, and retirement activity planning. A small number of firms provide a one-stop service for overseeing TSP, which is a holistic rather than a piecemeal approach to business perpetuation. These sections will set forth some of the strategies for TSP, the disciplines that must be evaluated, and steps that should be followed.

The earlier the owner starts the planning process, the greater the number of options that will be available. Founders or second-generation owners typically spend two-thirds of their adult life building their company, which might amount to as much as 80 to 90 percent of their estates. They devote little or no time to strategizing as to how they might position the company for maximizing the value of this primary asset for their family's benefit when it is time to consider retiring.

In consulting with hundreds of companies throughout the country, the author has found that all too often the reason for lack of planning is that the owner does not know what questions to ask of advisors. Moreover, the advisors seldom offer advice when they are not asked specific questions—a stalemate.

23.7 THE ESOP AS A CORNERSTONE FOR TOTAL SUCCESSION PLANNING

ESOPs, because of their flexibility, lend themselves as an ideal component of total succession planning for owners of profitable, growing, midsize, closely held corporations. Objectives of all company founders differ from one to another, yet there seems to be a commonality of threads of these objectives among a large percentage of such corporate owners that surfaces when they reach their late 50s or older.

A typical owner wants to continue working for awhile and to remain in control, but is apprehensive about the fact that most of his or her assets are nonliquid, and he or she would like to start diversifying. The owner recognizes that it is virtually impossible to sell a minority share of the company at a worthwhile price. Accordingly, he or she looks to other means of getting cash out, such as perhaps doing an initial public offering (IPO). Sadly, relatively few companies have the qualifications for a successful IPO, nor is the timing always just right in the public marketplace.

One of the strategies that keeps coming to the forefront of an owner's thinking is whether or not to sell to a strategic buyer. But a founder whose child works for the company would often rather pass the reins of control to flesh and blood than to a stranger. Such an owner wonders how he or she can do this and still have the financial means to retire. If there are more than one offspring, only one of whom is actively involved in the business, how does one treat them all fairly? Does *fair* mean *equal?*

Some owners consider a management buyout, but the managers seldom have sufficient financial means to purchase the company. Here is where the ESOP proves itself to have the flexibility to help solve many of the succession planning issues. By implementing an ESOP, a founder can create a private marketplace for the company's stock while maintaining effective control and deferring, or possibly avoiding, tax on the sale of the shares.

For example, the founder can sell up to 99 percent of the shares to the ESOP, while retaining 1 percent. That share is 100 percent of the shares outside of the ESOP trust, allowing board control, which, in turn, appoints the ESOP committee that directs the trustee as to the vote. The six grave issues on which the vote must be passed through to the ESOP participants can, except for liquidation, be pretty much circumvented if that is the founder's intent.

The founder, having sold down to a modest percentage of stock and invested the sale proceeds in other qualified replacement property, will be highly diversified and can someday easily give, bonus, or sell the remaining shares to the offspring, manager, or imported executive, which would then pass effective control to those select individuals. Perhaps life insurance or other assets can be the great equalizer for the children who have no interest in the business.

It is generally advisable that the cashing-out process start perhaps five or ten years prior to the time the founder anticipates retiring, although the process can, under proper circumstances, take place closer to retirement.

23.8 PREFUNDING THE ESOP

In order for the owner of a private company to defer taxes on the sale of stock to an ESOP under Code Section 1042, the transaction must result in the ESOP owning at least 30 percent of the outstanding stock of the company. (See Chapter 7 for further details.) The ESOP, backed by the corporation, can borrow 30 percent of the value of the company from a lender, and the company can service the debt with pre-tax dollars.

If the owner would like to have his or her corporation become less leveraged while still qualifying for tax deferral, there are some strategies that can accomplish this. The company can contribute cash or authorized but unissued stock to the ESOP for one or two years, deducting the contribution from taxable earnings. The cash would reduce the amount that would have to be borrowed and so would the stock, which accrues toward the 30 percent threshold. When tax savings, productivity gains, and other qualified plan offsets are considered, there may be little or no net dilution where newly issued stock is contributed to the ESOP.

23.9 MOVING CLOSER TO SUCCESSION

After the ESOP owns 30 percent of the outstanding shares of the corporation, the founder can releverage the company and sell additional traunches of stock with no recognition of capital gains tax. Alternatively, he or she can sell one share at a time without further leverage by having the company simply make tax-deductible cash contributions to the ESOP that will be used to purchase additional shares from the stockholder—almost like having a tax-free pension.

When the founder feels that he or she has cashed out through the ESOP to a sufficient extent on a tax-deferred or possibly tax-free basis, he or she can transfer the remaining stock to the chosen successor. This transfer can be done by gift (keeping in mind the gift tax constraints) or by selling the stock to the family heir, manager, or other designated person who will then, and *only* then, assume effective control of the company's destiny, as he or she would then assume effective control of the stock held by the ESOP.

By deferring or avoiding the taxes, the selling shareholder recognizes that he or she can sell substantially less than 100 percent of the stock to the ESOP and still have as much to invest as compared with selling to an outside buyer. Alternatively, the shareholder could transfer the stock to a family limited partnership (FLP) and the heavily discounted limited partnership units can be given to the child or children. The partnership could sell the stock to the ESOP under code section 1042, so that it would not be subject to any tax. The proceeds invested in qualified replacement property, allow the offspring to become more liquid and diversified.

CHAPTER TWENTY-FOUR

ESOP—A Practical Means to Succession Planning

Owners of privately held corporations have a liquidity problem when the bulk of their estates are in the form of the stock of their companies. Their problem is exacerbated if an owner wishes to transfer control to a child immediately or sometime in the future.

An owner who will need cash at retirement cannot afford to give the company to the heir apparent, and the son or daughter typically has little or no funds to pay Dad for his stock. Even if the owner is willing to give the stock to the child, gift taxes will cost Dad about 50 cents on the dollar after the lifetime exemption and annual exclusions are used up.

24.1 CASE STUDY

Assume that Johnson Equipment Co., Inc., would fetch $10 million on the open market. Upon selling, the founder, Mr. Johnson, would be left with about $7 million after taxes, assuming the 30 percent federal and state tax bracket. Selling the company to an outside buyer would solve Mr. Johnson's liquidity problem, but it would deprive his son, Paul, of the opportunity to succeed his father as company commander. Paul might even be fortunate to have a job under the new regime.

Instead of selling 100 percent of the stock of his company to an outside buyer, suppose Mr. Johnson has his bank lend the company funds to enable the ESOP to purchase from him 60 percent of the outstanding stock of the company. Under Internal Revenue Code (IRC) Section 1042, he can defer the tax on the sale, which is the after-tax equivalent to his selling about 86 percent of the company to an outside buyer. Mr. Johnson could then make a gift to his son of the remaining 40 percent. Would this approach result in a gift tax of about half the value of the gift? No. Here is why.

By borrowing to acquire the 60 percent of Mr. Johnson's stock, the ESOP debt is reflected on the corporate balance sheet and, by displacing equity, reduces the value of the company from $10 million to $4 million. The value of the gift of 40 percent of the outstanding shares is not 40 percent of $10 million, or $4 million. It is 40 percent of $4 million, or $1.6 million. As a matter of fact, it is even less than that because after the sale to the ESOP, Mr. Johnson was left with a minority interest. This gift to Paul is thereby subject to a minority discount. The valuation firm might, for example, consider a 20 percent minority discount applicable in this situation, reducing the gift to $1.28 million. Because the son has no guaranteed market for the stock, a discount for lack of marketability might be added, such as, perhaps 25 percent, reducing the value of the gift to $960,000. This is substantially within the parents' combined unified credit. It should be noted that valuation firms differ in their approaches to minority and marketability discounts.

By reinvesting the $6 million proceeds in qualified replacement property, that is, securities of domestic corporations, Mr. Johnson defers the tax on the sale of the stock and, if he retains the replacement securities until he dies, they receive a step up in basis, thereby avoiding all capital gains tax.

24.2 USING MINORITY AND MARKETABILITY DISCOUNTS FOR A GIFT

By giving his son the remaining 40 percent of the outstanding stock, this had the effect of giving Paul effective control over the stock that is in the ESOP, as his stock represents 100 percent of all the shares outside of the ESOP trust. This arrangement would give Paul board control and operational control over the ESOP.

Mr. Johnson would therefore transfer effective control of the $10 million company to his son, incurring no gift tax liability in the process. The selling shareholder also bypasses capital gains tax, enabling him to receive an income on the full $6 million of stock he sold to the ESOP. The corporation deducts both the principal and interest payments it makes to the ESOP to service the debt for the purchase of Mr. Johnson's stock.

24.3 HOW TO MAXIMIZE NET INVESTMENT RETURN

It is possible for Mr. Johnson to increase his net yield from the qualified replacement property by sheltering the investment growth from taxes. He might want to give, say, $1 million of the replacement securities to a charitable remainder unitrust

(CRUT). This would give him a tax deduction based upon the present value of the remainder interest of the gift. He could carry over the tax deduction for six years, including the present year. Various private letter rulings (PLRs) indicate that the taxpayers who applied for the PLR would pay no capital gains tax on the transfer. The investment would accumulate tax free so that, if the investment grows, Mr. Johnson will receive a greater income than he would have received if the investment were in a taxable environment. The remainder at the death of Mr. and Mrs. Johnson will go to charities of their choice. As a result of this charitable transfer, the asset is not includable in the Johnsons' estate.

The only weakness in this strategy is the fact that the Johnsons' children are disinherited. To make the children whole, the parents can create a wealth replacement trust.

24.4 WEALTH REPLACEMENT TRUST

Mr. Johnson may elect to create an irrevocable life insurance trust (ILIT), often referred to as a wealth replacement trust (WRT), the purpose of which would be to hold a second-to-die insurance policy on the lives of Mr. and Mrs. Johnson with the children as beneficiaries. The death proceeds would come into the WRT income-tax-free and estate-tax-free, thereby replacing the value of the charitable gift and recovering for the children an amount equal to the amount that was donated to the CRUT.

24.5 ESOP—THE ALL-IN-ONE SUCCESSION PLANNING DEVICE

The ESOP is an all-in-one financial instrument for solving complex business succession problems. In the Johnson family scenario described above, Mr. Johnson achieved needed liquidity for retirement security for him and his wife with no tax erosion. He was able to pass operational control to his son with no gift tax. If the gift was larger and resulted in a gift tax, some or all of these taxes could be paid by the charitable tax saving and by the stream of income from the replacement securities or from the CRUT.

The corporation will be able to retire the debt for the stock purchase with pretax rather than after-tax dollars. The employees will feel a greater sense of job security and will also have an incentive to increase the value of the shares.

In the years ahead, if the corporation redeems shares from the ESOP as employees terminate, retire, or die, son Paul will gain a greater percentage of equity.

In summary, the ESOP is a vehicle that should be considered by profitable private companies where ownership transition is an issue.

CHAPTER TWENTY-FIVE

The Amazing Leveraged ESOPs

Capital formation for public and private companies is epitomized by the leveraged ESOP because of the tax advantages this unique plan brings to the corporate table.

Qualified plans other than ESOPs are precluded from borrowing. ESOPs are permitted to borrow from any commercial or noncommercial lender. They can even borrow from a party in interest such as the sponsoring employer or major stockholders. The terms of the loan must be on an arm's-length basis and just as favorable as would be the case between independent parties.

The loan can be in the form of a direct loan, a loan guarantee, or an installment sale. The ESOP may not pledge any collateral other than the stock that was acquired with the loan proceeds or stock that had been released as collateral for a previous loan as a result of the new loan proceeds. The ESOP's liability for servicing the loan interest and principal is limited to the cash contributions it receives from the employer or the earnings on those contributions. Dividends on the stock held by the ESOP can also be used to repay the loan and, under the 1986 Tax Reform Act, are tax deductible under IRC Section 404(k). The loan must not be a demand loan except where default is concerned and must be structured for repayment over a specified period of time.

Although the employer is not required to make contributions sufficient to service the ESOP loan, from a practical standpoint, lenders look to the corporation as their ultimate source of repayment. Creditors are therefore likely to stipulate that the corporation must make cash contributions at least equal to the amortization payments. ESOPs are considered by the regulations to be conduits of loan proceeds. Accordingly, they are treated in much the same manner as conventional borrowers. As a matter of practice, commercial lenders seldom make loans directly to

ESOPs. They lend to the corporation and the corporation, in turn, lends to the ESOP either as a mirror loan or under substantially different terms.

Independent lenders can accelerate the loan repayment in the event of default, while for parties-in-interest loans, only such assets as are required to cover the amount of the default may be transferred from the guarantor or from the sponsoring corporation itself.

The financed stock is allocated to the ESOP participants' accounts either as principal and interest is contributed by the corporation to the ESOP, or as principal only is amortized. There are stipulations that must be applied to the latter approach that preclude using this method for loans in excess of 10 years. A suspense account is created from which shares are released as the debt is paid.

25.1 THE ABCS OF A LEVERAGED ESOP TRANSACTION

The ESOP can acquire stock from two sources, namely, from the sponsoring corporation or from selling shareholders. The corporation can make tax-deductible contributions of authorized but unissued stock or it can sell stock to the ESOP. Here is an example of leveraged transactions:

(a) Purchase of Stock from the Corporation to Infuse Working Capital

- The corporation agrees to sell and the ESOP trustee agrees to buy from the employer a specific number of qualifying employer shares of stock at fair market value determined by an independent appraiser.

- A loan is arranged between the corporation and a lender for the purpose of purchasing the shares that are then pledged as collateral for the loan to be released for allocation to participants' accounts as the loan is amortized. The employer corporation will guarantee the loan.

- The corporation will then lend the loan proceeds to its ESOP.

- The ESOP trustee uses the loan proceeds to acquire newly issued stock from the employer corporation (to infuse working capital).

- The corporation will make tax-deductible cash contributions to the ESOP in an amount equal to the servicing requirement to pay principal and interest on the loan.

This is a typical leveraged ESOP procedure to enable the proceeds to be transferred from the bank to the employer to the ESOP and back to the employer. The loan would be paid with pretax dollars by corporate contributions using the ESOP as a conduit to the lender. As the loan is repaid, shares will be released from a suspense account and allocated to the ESOP participants.

(b) Result

The corporation obtains an infusion of working capital which can be used for any corporate purpose, such as purchasing equipment, building a warehouse, or making an acquisition. The fact that the corporation can deduct the principal payments allows it to repay the loan more rapidly than through a non-ESOP method. In the case of the purchase of equipment, the corporation will also be able to deduct depreciation.

(c) How to Do a Cashless Leveraged Transaction

The corporation could sell newly issued stock to the ESOP and instead of obtaining a loan from a bank, the corporation would take back a note from the ESOP. The company would make annual tax-deductible cash contributions to the ESOP in an amount that is equal to principal and interest. The ESOP would immediately pay these amounts of cash back to the corporation, thereby restoring the cash the company had contributed to the ESOP.

(d) Result

The corporation increased its working capital and cash flow by the taxes it saved in this transaction without any net out-of-pocket cash expenditure (see Exhibit 25.1).

25.2 HOW A LEVERAGED ESOP CAN CASH OUT A STOCKHOLDER

- The stockholder agrees to sell stock to the ESOP.
- The bank lends cash to the corporation.
- The corporation lends it to its ESOP.
- The ESOP pays cash to the stockholder for his stock.
- The corporation makes annual tax-deductible contributions to the ESOP in an amount that is equal to principal and interest.
- The ESOP pays it back to the corporation.
- The corporation then repays the bank.

Result: The ESOP acquired the stock from the stockholder with pretax dollars.

Exhibit 25.1

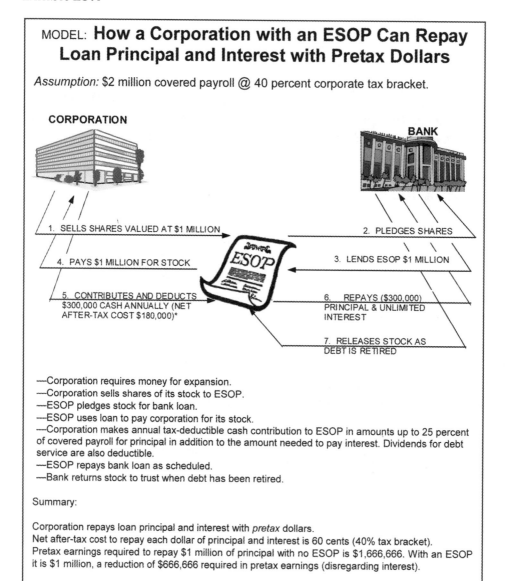

MODEL: **How a Corporation with an ESOP Can Repay Loan Principal and Interest with Pretax Dollars**

Assumption: $2 million covered payroll @ 40 percent corporate tax bracket.

CORPORATION

BANK

1. SELLS SHARES VALUED AT $1 MILLION

2. PLEDGES SHARES

4. PAYS $1 MILLION FOR STOCK

3. LENDS ESOP $1 MILLION

5. CONTRIBUTES AND DEDUCTS $300,000 CASH ANNUALLY (NET AFTER-TAX COST $180,000)*

6. REPAYS ($300,000) PRINCIPAL & UNLIMITED INTEREST

7. RELEASES STOCK AS DEBT IS RETIRED

—Corporation requires money for expansion.
—Corporation sells shares of its stock to ESOP.
—ESOP pledges stock for bank loan.
—ESOP uses loan to pay corporation for its stock.
—Corporation makes annual tax-deductible cash contribution to ESOP in amounts up to 25 percent of covered payroll for principal in addition to the amount needed to pay interest. Dividends for debt service are also deductible.
—ESOP repays bank loan as scheduled.
—Bank returns stock to trust when debt has been retired.

Summary:

Corporation repays loan principal and interest with *pretax* dollars.
Net after-tax cost to repay each dollar of principal and interest is 60 cents (40% tax bracket).
Pretax earnings required to repay $1 million of principal with no ESOP is $1,666,666. With an ESOP it is $1 million, a reduction of $666,666 required in pretax earnings (disregarding interest).

25.3 CORPORATE NON-ESOP LOAN COMPARED WITH A LEVERAGED ESOP LOAN

If a corporation with no ESOP borrows money directly, it cannot deduct principal payments but can deduct interest. If a corporation has an existing loan, the company can install an ESOP and can make annual tax-deductible contributions of stock to the trust in an amount equal to its principal payments to the bank. The after-tax effect is the same as though principal and interest were being deducted through an ESOP loan.

This route is less dilutionary than the ESOP loan transaction described above, whereby the corporation sells a large amount of newly issued stock to the ESOP. In the ESOP loan transaction, stock in the full amount of the loan is transferred immediately, whereas in the corporate loan scenario described above, the shares are contributed to the ESOP in an amount that is equal to principal payments annually. Stock goes into the ESOP gradually. If the stock will increase in value, fewer shares are required to accomplish the same end result over the years but with less dilution than putting the total amount of stock equal to the full loan amount into the ESOP up front.

25.4 THE COST EFFECTIVE ESOP LOAN

The cost of principal on an ESOP loan is reduced by the corporation's tax bracket. In a combined 40 percent corporate state and federal bracket, a $1 million loan to the ESOP requires $1 million of pretax earnings to pay $1 million of principal compared with $1.67 million of pretax earnings.

This should shorten the period for repaying the loan when compared with a direct corporate loan and would, in turn, reduce the dollar amount of interest that must be paid over the repayment period. One dollar of debt reduction means one dollar of added equity. The leveraged ESOP loan requires significantly less cash flow than does the direct or *naked* corporate loan where an ESOP is not involved. From an overall cost standpoint, one must factor in the requirement that in a leveraged ESOP transaction the corporation would transfer to the ESOP an amount of stock equal to the loan principal as collateral, which would be allocated to the employees' accounts as the debt is amortized.

If the ESOP contributions were in lieu of those to a pension or profit-sharing plan, the cost savings would be a partial offset to equity dilution, as would the productive use of the tax savings.

CHAPTER TWENTY-SIX

The Management Leveraged ESOP Buyout

26.1 SELLING A DIVISION TO THE EMPLOYEES THROUGH A LEVERAGED ESOP BUYOUT

Private corporations often have one or more divisions or subsidiaries, some of which could operate on a stand-alone basis. In some cases, they are run by a son or daughter of the founder or possibly by a nonfamily manager.

Founders of closely held companies who are at a stage at which they are thinking of retiring in a five- or ten-year horizon usually like the idea of starting to simplify their lives so that they can exit when their inner clock tells them to do so. One way this might be accomplished is by spinning off a division or subsidiary to the family heir or manager who has been doing a good job at operating the division and is likely to continue to do so.

The primary reason for wanting to sell divisions to the employees is that they have been loyal and know their jobs better than anyone else, and, if it is at all possible, it is the right thing to do.

One's child or managers seldom have sufficient cash with which to acquire the division being divested. The purchase would have to be done primarily with borrowed capital secured by the assets and cash flow of the division. Without an ESOP, the deal would depend upon adequate future earnings to service principal with after-tax dollars and interest with pretax dollars while leaving sufficient cash flow for corporate operations and possibly expansion.

Here is how the ESOP divestiture scenario can work. Let's assume that Mr. Brown, the founder and 100 percent stockholder of Brown, Inc. wishes to divest the company of a profitable division that can be made to stand alone.

The board of Brown, Inc. decides to give the first opportunity for purchasing the division to the management team that has demonstrated an ability to make the entity run at a profit. The managers can quite possibly acquire a different class of stock with a built-in incentive for achieving certain profit goals. Providing them with additional motivation can be better for the rank-and-file employees in the long run.

An independent appraisal determined the fair market value of the division on a restructured basis would be $6.8 million. It has experienced a 5 percent annual compounded growth in net worth over the previous five years, and this growth rate is projected for the next five-year period. The annual payroll is $2 million and is projected to increase at a rate of 6 percent annually over the next five years. Pretax earnings generated by the division for the prior year amounted to $1.8 million. The board agreed to sell the division for $6.8 million. The division's five senior executives had marginal net worth, but as a group they managed to borrow $800,000.

26.2 DOING THE DEAL

A new corporation, NEWCO, is created and implements an ESOP. The executives contribute $800,000 for the purchase of stock from NEWCO. A bank lends NEWCO $6 million. NEWCO, in turn, lends the $6 million to its ESOP.

The lender required that NEWCO stock be pledged as collateral and that NEWCO would agree to make annual cash contributions to its ESOP in amounts sufficient to service principal and interest.

NEWCO uses the $6 million of loan proceeds in addition to the $800,000 to purchase $6.8 million of assets from the parent corporation, pledging its stock as collateral. The bank will release the stock from the pledge as amortization payments are made. Those shares would then be allocated to the ESOP participants' accounts.

The corporation makes monthly tax-deductible contributions to the ESOP. The trustee will use these contributions to service principal and interest. The contribution is well within payroll limitation.

The executives anticipate that future growth of their stock will make the extra effort they put into the company over the next several years worthwhile, and will eventually make them quite wealthy.

The ESOP will acquire noncallable preferred stock that is convertible into the highest form of common at some future date. The management team, for $800,000, will acquire all of the common stock. Dividends will be paid to the ESOP's preferred but not to management's common stock. Therefore, the preferred will be assigned a higher value but will convert at the end of the term loan one share for one share. Management's 10 percent equity could increase by a factor of about 2.5 to 3.5 at the time of conversion. The employees not only will be able to look forward to reasonable compensation from their labor, but they can also anticipate the possibility of building equity as the loan is amortized and growth of the stock allocated to their ESOP accounts accelerates.

(a) Brown, Inc.'s ESOP

Brown, Inc., now flush with $6.8 million of cash from the divestiture, then implemented its own ESOP. An appraisal determined the value of the stock to be $30 million.

Mr. Brown decided that he would like to sell 30 percent of the outstanding stock of Brown, Inc. to the ESOP for $9 million under Code Section 1042. The ESOP was given an option to acquire at least 50 percent plus one share of stock within the succeeding four or five years. By doing this, though he sold a minority block of stock, no minority discount was applied to the sale.

Brown, Inc. loaned its ESOP $6 million of the $6.8 million it received from the divestiture and borrowed $3 million from its bank. Brown, Inc. also loaned that amount to the ESOP. The ESOP purchased $9 million of stock from Mr. Brown, who then invested the proceeds into a diversified equity portfolio. He bypassed capital gains taxes under Section 1042.

Mr. Brown was well on his way toward achieving his goal of cashing out his interest over the succeeding decade. He would plan upon selling another traunch of stock after the bank loan was essentially liquidated. Since the company was growing, he would sell his stock an increasingly higher prices.

He would groom certain members of his management team to stretch their talents so that one could assume the chief executive officer (CEO) position when Mr. Brown decided to relinquish that spot.

The ESOP made it possible for Mr. Brown to perpetuate his company and to signal ahead to his loyal employees that he did not intend to sell to outside interests. He would be able to sell out over time at ever-increasing prices and remain in control for as long as he would wish. The corporation would save huge amounts of taxes in the process by deducting the purchase costs. The employees were incentivized to grow the stock values in their ESOP accounts.

26.3 HOW ESOP DIVESTITURES CAN ENHANCE SUCCESSION PLANNING

Owners of privately held corporations can position themselves for succession planning by using an ESOP divestiture such as that described above. A corporation might create one or more divisions that are in different lines of business or in different geographical locations. These divisions can be structured to operate on a stand-alone basis and with their own capable managers.

The founder who is not quite ready to retire might want to position himself or herself for gradual succession planning by spinning off one or more of the company's divisions to those managers who would acquire the equity of the divisions through an ESOP leveraged buyout.

The founder could thereby reduce his or her area of responsibility, while at the same time putting the corporation into a more liquid position. Perhaps at a later date the founder might want to create an ESOP for the parent corporation and sell some stock to it.

The corporation could lend the proceeds of the earlier divestiture to the company's ESOP to purchase some stock from the founder under Section 1042. This strategy would reduce the need for bank financing or, alternatively, would allow the founder to sell a greater amount of stock to the ESOP.

26.4 MANAGEMENT GROUPS AS ACQUIRERS

Other corporations that wish to increase their market share might compete with management groups for acquiring the takeover target. More and more frequently, key executives who have been involved in the running of corporate departments, divisions, or subsidiaries have been purchasing these divestitures and continuing to operate the business as new companies.

Whole companies are often acquired by their management group. This is a relatively recent phenomenon and an exciting one. Public and private companies are eyed as challenges to management groups within those companies who feel that if they buy low, pare the company's staff to the bone, improve efficiency by streamlining manufacturing techniques, and develop a viable marketing plan, the company can be built to its full profitable potential. Such a corporation may be held permanently by the acquiring parties, sold for a substantial capital gain, or even taken public after having gone private.

Media attention is often directed at employee buyouts of failing companies. There are, however, numerous examples of highly successful public companies, the ownership of which were transformed from benefiting shareholders not directly involved with the company to enhancing the wealth of employees who devote their working careers toward improving corporate performance.

It is estimated that 98 percent of the ESOPs that have been implemented have been structured for profitable companies. Productivity has improved in many of those corporations as a direct result of employee equity ownership.

26.5 THE LEVERAGED ESOP DIVESTITURE

- A feasibility study is performed.

- The management group creates a new corporation, NEWCO.

- The managers put up whatever amount of cash they can muster and purchase some of NEWCO stock.

- NEWCO establishes an ESOP.

- NEWCO borrows sufficient cash from a lender, commercial or otherwise, or possibly from the parent corporation, which would take back a note. The funds would, quite possibly, come from a combination of sources. NEWCO would guarantee the loan, or possibly the parent corporation might agree to guarantee the loan.

- ESOP purchases stock from NEWCO.

- NEWCO acquires the assets of the division from the parent company.

- NEWCO would make annual tax-deductible cash contributions to the ESOP in an amount needed to enable the ESOP to service loan principal and interest.

- ESOP pays principal and interest to NEWCO.

- NEWCO then repays the bank.

- STOCK is allocated to the accounts of the employee participants as principal is amortized.

If the deal was right, the corporate earnings should be sufficient to service the obligation until the debt is retired. The note would be discharged with pretax dollars, cutting the cost of the acquisition substantially. When the loan has been amortized completely, the employee-participants of the ESOP will own the stock of NEWCO that is not owned by the managers. The managers will have effective control of most matters, however.

Quite often employees will take a reduction in their compensation to help with the repayment for the loan. The ESOP/LBO combination provides an ideal means for a corporation to divest itself of a unit.

Had the parent simply liquidated the unwanted division or sold its assets to another corporation in a different state, the executives and other employees would be on the labor market. They might be consuming the bounties of welfare instead of contributing to welfare as taxpayers. Wage earners support the many local businesses, which in turn pay more taxes. Subcontractors and suppliers will benefit from and pay taxes on the revenue they derive from the corporation's continued productivity. The multiple spinoff effects of a leveraged ESOP divestiture are enormous and lasting. A group of employees such as those of this ESOP corporation can someday be independent of the need for Social Security.

Leveraged ESOP takeovers often place 55 percent to 85 percent of the equity ownership in the ESOP for the benefit of the employees at the time of the implementation. The balance, or at least most of it, will be made available to key executives. Perhaps a modest amount of equity will be channeled to those who procure the financing or to the lenders themselves.

Leveraged ESOP transfers of ownership are for the most part friendly buyouts or takeovers. This is in the best interests of all concerned because the atmosphere is more conducive to getting off to a good emotional start with a free mind for production. Some of the larger leveraged ESOP buyouts have become classics. Many smaller company leveraged ESOP buyouts are also classic examples but are not newsworthy (see Exhibit 26.1).

Exhibit 26.1

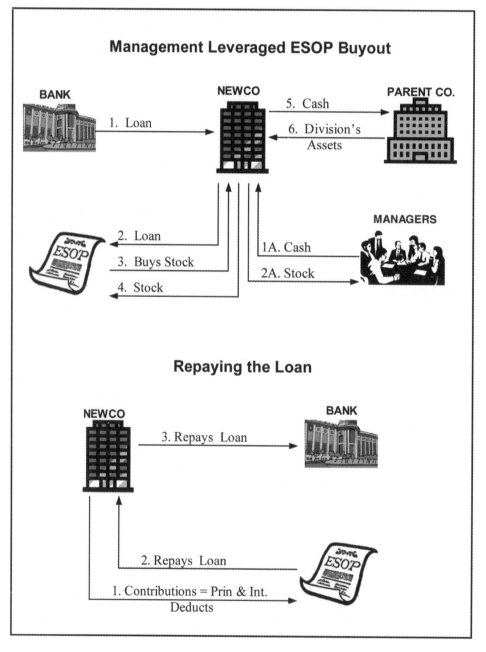

Management Leveraged ESOP Buyout

BANK
NEWCO
PARENT CO.

1. Loan
5. Cash
6. Division's Assets

MANAGERS

2. Loan
3. Buys Stock
4. Stock

1A. Cash
2A. Stock

Repaying the Loan

NEWCO
BANK

3. Repays Loan

2. Repays Loan
1. Contributions = Prin & Int. Deducts

ESOP Techniques to Acquire Competitors, Suppliers, and Other Corporations with Tax Benefits to Buyer and Seller

An ESOP can create various avenues for enabling a corporation or its ESOP to acquire another corporation with pretax dollars. Although a company cannot deduct the direct cost of acquiring another company, it can make corresponding deductible contributions to an ESOP that have the same tax effect as though the purchase were deductible. This is the basic tenet of the transaction. The degree of simplicity or complexity of the facts surrounding the components of the acquisition determines the magnitude of the sophistication that will exemplify the transaction.

The ESOP can be key to letting chief executive officers (CEOs) and chief financial officers (CFOs) of private corporations expand their companies horizontally by acquiring competitors, suppliers, and other companies at far less cost than other methodologies. The primary reason for this is that only through the use of ESOPs can principal payments for the acquisition be deducted. The tax savings increase the acquiring company's debt service capacity. This can be a huge advantage to the acquiring company.

The ESOP also frees up cash flow by replacing the need for other tax-qualified employee benefit plans, such as pension and profit-sharing plans. It can also offset the need for the acquiring company to make matching contributions to a 401(k) plan. Contributions to these plans sap equity from the corporation, thereby reducing the value of the outstanding shares of the company. Because ESOPs let employees participate in the equity growth of the company, they tend to become more speculative. The resulting added profitability helps the ESOP company accelerate the debt service, thereby paving the way for the next acquisition. The increased cash flow can increase the value of the company.

(a) The Acquirer

Widget, Inc., the acquirer, installs a combination ESOP covering 100 employees, the annual covered payroll of which is $3.5 million. The pretax earnings of the company are $1 million, and its fair market value has been determined by independent appraisal to be $6 million.

(b) The Target

Widget, Inc. has targeted Machine Co., Inc. for acquisition. Machine Co.'s stock has also been appraised at $6 million. To simplify matters, covered annual payroll is also $3.5 million. Machine Co. has a qualified profit-sharing plan to which it contributes $150,000. There are $1 million of assets in the trust. Pretax earnings after the profit-sharing contributions are $1 million. The firm's 68-year-old founder, Mr. Mashco, who owns 100 percent of Machine Co. stock, would like to retire. He has no heirs in the business nor does he have an executive whom he feels has all the talents required of a chief executive officer. A deal is struck. Mr. Mashco has indicated his willingness to sell his corporation to Widget, Inc. for $3 million.

(c) Buyout Strategies

This chapter provides four strategies that Widget, Inc. can use to structure the buyout of Mr. Mashco's stock.

27.1 ACQUISITION TECHNIQUE 1: BUYING TARGET, INC. STOCK OR ASSETS AND DEDUCTING THE COST

Widget, Inc. agrees to purchase the assets of Mashco, Inc. from Mr. Mashco for $6 million. Widget, Inc. borrows $6 million from a lender and purchases the assets of Mashco, Inc. from Mr. Mashco.

If Widget, Inc. purchases the stock or assets of Target, Inc. directly, it cannot deduct principal payment. Interest is, of course, always deductible.

Widget, Inc. is in the 41 percent combined federal and state income tax bracket. To repay $6 million of principal, ignoring interest, Widget, Inc. must earn $10.2 million, assuming it had no ESOP. If there were a way to deduct principal payments, ABC, Inc. would save $4.2 million in future pretax earnings. The company would also be able to accelerate the payment of principal, thereby reducing the amount of interest it would pay over the shorter loan period.

If ABC, Inc. could create a cashless deduction equal to the amount of principal payments the company will make, the effect is the same as though principal were being deducted. This is a matter of problem solving by going outside of the proverbial nine dots. This effect can be created by having ABC, Inc. make annual contributions of authorized but unissued stock, newly issued shares, to its newly created contribution stock bonus plan and money purchase ESOP in an amount equal to principal payments. ABC, Inc. would deduct these contributions just as though the company were contributing cash. Of course, the stock must be valued by an independent appraiser to determine fair market value. The valuation must be updated annually.

Assuming a $6 million, seven-year loan, the principal payments would be $857,142 annually. The corporation could make a tax-deductible contribution to the ESOP of authorized but unissued stock valued at $875,000. A deduction in the 40 percent combined tax bracket gives the corporation an annual tax savings of $350,000, or a total of $2.4 million over the seven-year term period. Interest payments are deductible in any event. This will make the company much stronger over the immediate and subsequent post-transaction years.

By reducing its cost of borrowing, the company will be able to use the tax savings to purchase equipment or increase its marketing budget to gain market share. Is it any wonder a large number of the companies on the *Inc.* magazine list of the top 500 private corporations in America have ESOPs?

This simple method of making an acquisition creates the following added benefits:

- The ESOP eliminates the need the company might otherwise have for a cash-draining form of qualified employee benefit plan, such as a pension plan, a profit-sharing plan, or matching contributions to a 401(k) plan.

- The stock contributed to the ESOP by Widget, Inc. accrues to the 30 percent threshold of stock that is required to be held by the ESOP for Mr. Widget to sell his stock to the ESOP at some future date in order for him to defer, or possibly avoid, capital gains tax without borrowing.

- Allocation of shares to the employees' accounts should increase productivity and profitability if the plan is communicated properly.

The method outlined here exposes the stockholders to little, if any, dilution because of the offsetting factors noted earlier in this chapter (see Exhibit 27.1).

27.2 ACQUISITION TECHNIQUE 2: POST-TRANSITION ESOP

Better late than never. Suppose Widget, Inc. had made an acquisition or bought out a stockholder's interest a few years ago. The company is servicing debt with after-tax dollars.

If Widget, Inc. installs an ESOP at this point in time, it is not too late to enjoy the tax savings and other benefits described in the previous section. The company can start contributing newly issued shares of company stock to the ESOP in an

Exhibit 27.1 Acquisition Technique #1

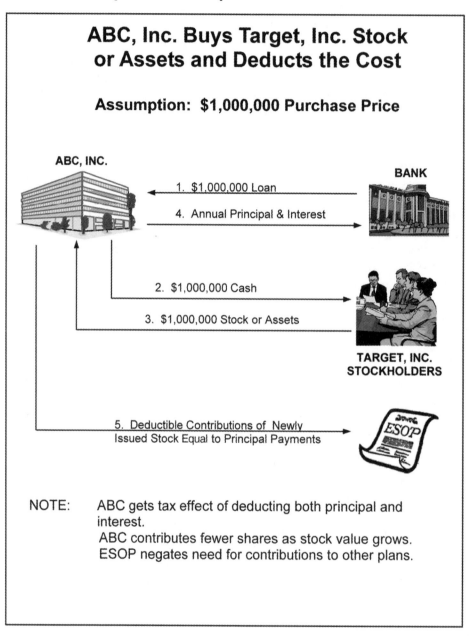

**ABC, Inc. Buys Target, Inc. Stock
or Assets and Deducts the Cost**

Assumption: $1,000,000 Purchase Price

ABC, INC.

BANK

1. $1,000,000 Loan

4. Annual Principal & Interest

2. $1,000,000 Cash

3. $1,000,000 Stock or Assets

TARGET, INC.
STOCKHOLDERS

5. Deductible Contributions of Newly
Issued Stock Equal to Principal Payments

ESOP

NOTE: ABC gets tax effect of deducting both principal and
interest.
ABC contributes fewer shares as stock value grows.
ESOP negates need for contributions to other plans.

amount equal to principal payments and shelter those and future payments from tax. If you wish to make up for the principal payments Widget, Inc. made but did not shelter, why not make contributions of new stock to the ESOP that exceed the amount of principal that must be paid currently? Play catch-up.

The effective use of the tax savings in the company can have a multiplier effect in increasing the value of the stock. The stockholders, as employees, would have the stock that is contributed to the ESOP allocated to their accounts.

To do this, the contributions to a combination ESOP must not exceed 25 percent of covered payroll. If the sponsoring corporation has a $3.5 million annual payroll, it can deduct up to an $875,000 annual contribution of new stock, saving about $350,000 of taxes, assuming the 40 percent tax bracket, with a zero cash outlay.

27.3 ACQUISITION TECHNIQUE 3: HOW TO ACQUIRE THE TARGET COMPANY WITH PRETAX DOLLARS AND GIVE TAX BENEFITS TO THE SELLER

Generally, profitable companies have tire-kickers galore knocking at their front doors, trying to see if they can pick up the company at a good price. Let's say two corporations of equal stature are competing with each other to acquire a company from its founder. Each has agreed to pay $10 million for the target company. All other factors being equal, the decision as to who will get the deal is a toss-up.

But what if one of the suitors comes up with an approach that will allow the founding seller to save more than $2 million in capital gains taxes? To the seller, the decision is a no-brainer. As a matter of fact, the winner of that competition might even be able to negotiate a lower price for the target company. Perhaps the seller would be willing to share half of his or her tax savings with the buyer by reducing the sales price. The seller would still have about $1million extra left to invest after taxes.

27.4 THE LOYALTY CARD

Many founders of successful private companies are reluctant to sell their companies because they do not want their loyal managers who helped them build the company to be left with nothing after the company is sold. The buyer can point out that if the founder sells to an ESOP, the employees are virtually assured that they will receive some equity. This logic should also put the would-be buyer in a more competitive position than others, because it eliminates the feeling of guilt on the seller's part.

27.5 STEPS TO THE ACQUISITION STRATEGY

One of the most appealing uses of an ESOP is to allow a selling shareholder to defer or possibly avoid taxes on the sale of his or her stock to the ESOP by adhering to the rules of Code Section 1042. To achieve nonrecognition of capital gains tax on such a sale, the stockholder must sell stock to the ESOP of his or her own corporation, not to the ESOP of another corporation. If, for example, the stockholder of XYZ, Inc. sells XYZ stock to the ESOP of ABC, Inc., the shareholder will not be able to defer the taxes under Section 1042.

Nonetheless, there is a strategy that will allow the owner of XYZ, Inc. to enjoy the tax advantage of Code Section 1042 when selling his or her company to another corporation that has an ESOP.

Let us assume that ABC, Inc. is valued at $10 million. ABC, Inc. has an ESOP. ABC, Inc. wants to acquire the stock of XYZ, Inc. from its founder, Mr. Jones. XYZ, Inc. has a fair market value of $5 million. This can be accomplished through a tax-free merger of the target company, XYZ, Inc. into the ABC, Inc., the acquiring company. Mr. Jones receives ABC, Inc. stock in exchange for his XYZ, Inc. stock.

Here are the steps that can result in giving Mr. Jones the tax benefits of Code Section 1042:

- ABC, Inc. borrows $5 million from the bank.

- ABC, Inc. lends the $5 million to its ESOP.

- Mr. Jones sells his ABC stock to the ESOP. The period for which he owned XYZ, Inc. stock tacks on to the ABC, Inc. stock he now owns. Because he held the original stock for more than three years, he qualifies for Section 1042.

- ABC, Inc. makes annual tax-deductible contributions to the ESOP in an amount that equals principal and interest on the loan.

- The ESOP pays principal and interest to ABC, Inc.

- ABC, Inc. pays the debt service to the bank.

- Mr. Jones pays no capital gains tax because he invests the $5 million in qualified replacement property (i.e., securities of domestic operating companies) within 12 months after the date of the transaction.

- The stock is allocated to the employees' accounts pro rata to their compensation as principal is amortized.

27.6 RESULT OF TRANSACTION

By engineering the acquisition in a creative manner, using an ESOP, ABC was able to acquire a company that it might otherwise not have been able to acquire. The selling shareholder was able to glean about $1.5 million more to invest than would have been the case otherwise.

ABC, Inc. could deduct the total acquisition cost. The taxes saved would make it possible for ABC to make another acquisition of nearly equivalent size.

ABC's employees received an equity stake in the combined company and were given the incentive to develop an ownership culture that would add value to the stock of the company.

The resultant company was able to reduce expenses by eliminating duplication of operating functions such as internal and external accounting, legal, human resources, and warehousing. The selling shareholder's compensation could also be used to service the acquisition debt.

If either ABC or XYZ had other qualified plans, their replacement by the ESOP put to better use the amounts of contributions that would otherwise have gone into those other plans. In this case, they would be used instead to service the new loan.

Investment bankers, attorneys, certified public accountants (CPAs), and financial planners should become familiar with these techniques or they should bring in a specialist in this environment. They might just be able to make a marginal deal become more viable. Certainly, the use of an ESOP in the right situation can make a company stronger than it would have been after an acquisition (see Exhibit 27.2).

27.7 ACQUISITION TECHNIQUE 4: HOW A SELLING STOCKHOLDER CAN ACQUIRE A CORPORATION WITH TAX-FREE DOLLARS

Mr. Adams and Ms. White are the sole and equal stockholders of ABC, Inc., a tool and die manufacturer. They decided to start diversifying their assets by selling an equal amount of their stock in XYZ, Inc. in accordance with the provisions of IRC Section 1042. They recognized that they could maintain effective voting power over any shares they sold to the ESOP, as discussed in Chapter 6.

The two selling shareholders planned upon continuing to run and build ABC, Inc. but wanted to start selling some of the equity that they had tied up in the business. Each shareholder had a different reason for wanting to do so. Mr. Adams planned to invest the proceeds of his sale of stock in a diversified portfolio of blue-chip stocks and simply hold them while operating ABC, Inc. He liked the idea of receiving an income that would supplement his salary.

Ms. White, in contrast, felt that she had plenty of extra time on her hands to spread her wings and explore other areas of interest. She was particularly intrigued by a start-up company that had created a state-of-the-art product that could capture a niche market in the telecommunications field. The young and promising company needed an infusion of capital. It also could derive great benefit by having seasoned executive talent in the person of Ms. White sit on its board.

In anticipation of this problem, Ms. White invested the proceeds of the sale of her ABC, Inc. stock in a 50-year floating rate note. She borrowed against the FRN, the bank lending 90 percent of the face value of the note at about a wash cost to Ms. White. She invested the borrowed amount in the stock of the telecommunications

Exhibit 27.2 Acquisition Technique #3

How to Make an Acquisition with Pretax Dollars and Give Tax Benefit to Seller

ABC, Inc. Wants to Acquire XYZ, Inc. Stock
from Mr. Jones, 100% Owner of XYZ, Inc.

- ABC, Inc. creates an ESOP
- XYZ, Inc. merges into ABC, Inc.
- Mr. Jones thereby owns ABC, Inc. stock and sells it to ABC, Inc.'s ESOP under Code Section 1042
- Bank lends cash to ABC's ESOP
- ESOP pays loan proceeds to Mr. Jones for his ABC stock
- ABC makes tax-deductible contributions to its ESOP equal to debt service
- ABC's ESOP repays the bank

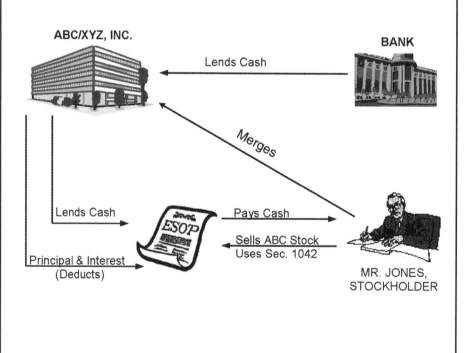

company, but she did not consider this to be a long-term investment. Therefore, when she sells the stock of that firm she would trigger a capital gains tax down to her original basis in ABC, Inc.

Ms. White decided to invest in the stock of the start-up company. It was not part of a control group with ABC, Inc. and, because it was an operating domestic corporation, the income of which was not more than 25 percent passive, the investment met the parameters of qualified replacement property under Section 1042. The new involvement gave Ms. White the intellectual challenge she needed. Before agreeing to invest in the new company, Ms. White stipulated that the owners must install an ESOP to be used as an exit vehicle for her investment in five years.

27.8 RESULT OF THE TRANSACTION

Mr. Adams satisfied his comfort level as to diversifying his assets without being required to give up his continued activity in and co-control of ABC, Inc.

Ms. White acquired her ownership in the start-up company with tax-free dollars, because she was able to bypass capital gains tax on the sale of her ABC, Inc. stock. ABC, Inc. deducted its contributions to service its ESOP loan that enabled the ESOP to purchase Ms. White's stock. The approach used here is a creative tax-advantaged method for an owner of stock in one company to acquire all or part of another company while still remaining involved in the original company.

The selling shareholders also liked the idea of providing their loyal employees with equity in the company so as to give them incentive to increase their productivity.

CHAPTER TWENTY-EIGHT

How an ESOP Can Help You Create a Miniconglomerate

If an owner of one ESOP company can acquire another corporation, bringing it under its ESOP umbrella, why should it not acquire others using the same tax-advantaged techniques described in the previous chapter?

A company has choices as to how it can expand more rapidly through the use of ESOPs as follows:

- Internally through the tax savings afforded by a nonleveraged ESOP. For every $100,000 of stock that the sponsoring corporation contributes to its ESOP, the company saves about $40,000 in taxes. If the company can use the tax savings to create or enlarge a profit center, this would be a significant offset to dilution. This method is more limited in its ability to produce a meaningful amount of expansion capital than is a leveraged ESOP.

- Internally or externally through a leveraged ESOP. This technique is useful for making greater capital infusion that can be used for such things as building a warehouse or purchasing heavy equipment. The corporation's enhanced financial capacity also lends itself to making acquisitions for other companies. This approach is limited only by payroll, earnings, and the size of the enterprise management is capable of governing.

An ESOP makes it possible for a corporation to acquire another company that is larger than itself. The selection of the company targeted for acquisition should factor in the likelihood that the fusion will produce an entity that is stronger than its two components. The restructured enterprise will reflect the efficiencies of being able to eliminate duplication of departments such as those of accounting, computer services, and warehousing. The talents of certain executives from the target firm can often be a key to making the deal really work, while others can be discharged due to duplication of effort in the two companies. Synergies of the firms will be conducive to greater cost effectiveness and income enhancements.

28.1 WHAT TO LOOK FOR IN SELECTING AN ESOP ACQUISITION TARGET

Here are some of the specifications to factor into the selection process in seeking a target for merger into, or acquisition by, an ESOP company:

- Of paramount importance is the fact that the target should fit in well with corporate development strategies of the acquiror and bring synergies to the transactions.

- The potential should exist for departmental consolidation to pare down overhead and bring increased value for the purchase price.

- Payroll intensity will increase the restructured company's ability to service a larger ESOP debt since the deduction of principal repayment is a function of eligible payroll.

- If the target company has a qualified employee benefit plan that can be converted to the restructured company's ESOP or replaced by it, this will allow contributions that had been going into those plans to be used toward debt service for the acquisition. It is conceivable that some or all of the target's profit-sharing plan's assets can be used to purchase the acquiror's stock. This would infuse interest-free capital into the company, thereby bringing added value for the purchase price. This approach must be tempered by the significant fiduciary risks.

- Targeting a competitor or a supplier for acquisition can provide obvious advantages to the marriage.

- The target should provide some good managers in order to prevent the possibility of spreading the acquiror's management too thin.

- It is essential that the pro forma demonstrate that the restructured company can service the debt and still be able to meet competition and grow.

28.2 WHAT PROSPECTIVE LENDERS LOOK FOR IN FINANCING AN ACQUISITION

A lender will look at the pro forma of the restructured combined entity to determine its willingness to finance the acquisition. Net worth and debt servicing capacity going forward are the two principal characteristics a bank will look for. If the assets are not sufficient, some lenders may seek personal guarantees. The corporation's ability to pay down the obligation is paramount since banks do not want to be in the business of liquidating assets of a borrower in order to come out whole.

If the lender is not willing to make the whole loan that is being sought, a mezzanine loan might be structured to take a subordinated position to the primary lender. Mezzanine financing is costly since the lender will not only charge much higher rates but may also require an equity position in the firm.

Bankers will extend credit to a company or to that firm's ESOP much more readily than it would lend to that corporation without an ESOP. Indeed, the bank would, in nearly all cases, lend to the corporation, which in turn would lend the proceeds to its ESOP. The ESOP could make the bank feel a bit more secure because the tax savings can pay down the debt more rapidly and with greater certainty.

28.3 HOW TO STRUCTURE SEQUENTIAL ESOP ACQUISITIONS

The post-transaction corporation will undergo a consolidation phase that will test the viability of the earlier projections. When the company is running at optimum efficiency, management can begin its search for a new target company to add to its stable of corporations.

(a) Acquisition Number One

Alpha Corp., a manufacturer of recreational vehicles, has 35 employees and an annual payroll of $1 million. Pretax earnings are $600,000 annually. Mr. Alpha owns 80 percent of the outstanding stock and Alpha's three-year-old ESOP owns 20 percent. The company's fair market value has been determined by independent appraisal to be $3 million and is growing at a 10 percent annual compounded rate. The company has decided to grow by acquisition.

Mr. Alpha met his competitor, Mr. Beta, at an industry conference and learned that Mr. Beta was interested in selling Beta Corp. and retiring. None of the managers have CEO capability. Beta Corp. is in the same field but manufactures a more luxurious vehicle. The corporation, whose net worth is $4 million, employs 100 people with an annual $3 million payroll. Annual pretax earnings are $1 million. Beta Corp. has a profit-sharing plan to which it generally contributes 10 percent of covered payroll and would contribute $300,000 in the current year. The plan has assets of $1.5 million invested conservatively at 8 percent average yield. Mr. Beta is willing to sell his company for $6 million.

Mr. Alpha and Mr. Beta related to one another instantly and eventually struck a deal for Alpha Corp. to acquire the stock of Beta Corp. for the asking price of $6 million after a feasibility study demonstrated that the restructured combined enterprise could support an ESOP debt of that magnitude. The pro forma of the fused corporations showed cost reductions of add-backs as follows:

Mr. Beta's salary, bonus, and perks	$ 200,000
Payroll duplication and elimination	$ 400,000
Warehouse consolidation	$ 100,000
Profit-sharing plan contribution	$ 300,000
	$1,000,000

The annual savings were added back into pretax earnings, increasing the combined projected pretax earnings to $2.6 million. The resultant payroll was $3.6 million.

A bank agreed to lend Alpha Corp. $6 million repayable over seven years at 1 percent above prime. Alpha Corp. then loaned the proceeds to its ESOP. The enhanced payroll permitted the corporation to service the $677,000 annual principal payments with pretax dollars since that amount fell below 25 percent of covered payroll. There was no cap on the amount of interest that Alpha Corp. could deduct. Had it needed additional leverage, it could have deducted dividends for debt service as well, using a different class of stock for the ESOP.

The ESOP exchanged Beta Corp. stock for Alpha Corp. stock. Alpha's net worth was increased by the net worth of Beta Corp. less the loan. Alpha Corp. made annual deductible contributions to its ESOP in an amount sufficient to service principal and interest. The bank held Alpha stock, releasing it to be allocated to the participant's accounts as the debt was amortized.

Result: Without an ESOP, Alpha Corp. would have had to earn $10 million to pay off $6 million of principal in the course of time. It therefore saved $4 million in pretax earnings. The below-market interest rate also increased Alpha's cash flow. Alpha's trustee also used $800,000 of the profit-sharing fund to buy authorized but unissued stock from Alpha Corp., thereby enabling the company to pay down its debt more rapidly.

The synergy of the corporate marriage made the transaction even more cost effective. Alpha's original accounting and servicing departments were adequate to service the new customer base, allowing the profit margins to increase. Alpha was able to accelerate principal payments, reducing the loan period by five years. Such acceleration generated a net savings equal to the gross interest for those years that were eliminated.

(b) Acquisition Number Two

After a consolidation phase, Alpha found that it was operating at peak efficiency and was ready to seek an additional acquisition. This time it targeted a supplier of parts used by Alpha in its manufacturing process. Delta Corp., the supplier, was valued by its owners at $10 million but the negotiated price resulted in a $9 million purchase by Alpha Corp.

The bank was impressed by Alpha's improved profitability as a result of the Beta acquisitions. The tax savings and other cost consolidations were more than sufficient to offset the cost of interest. Management proved that it was able to absorb its additional responsibilities and the debt pay down had been accelerated to the extent that only $2 million of the debt was still outstanding. A new feasibility study provided the bank with a comfort zone to enable it to lend the full $9 million to Alpha Corp., which the corporation then loaned to its ESOP.

Delta's reconstituted payroll of $2.5 million added to the leveraging capacity of the post-transaction company. Delta's pretax earnings of $2.7 million were enhanced by a paring down of expenses. This included the elimination of Delta's pension plan to which the company had been contributing approximately $300,000 annually. Delta's three active stockholders had been taking out $650,000 in compensation and perks, which were eliminated along with another $250,000 of compensation of others. Consolidation of professional, legal, and accounting services also enhanced the cost savings which totaled $1.2 million, bringing the Delta operation's pretax earnings to $3.8 million.

Alpha Corp. made annual deductible contributions to its ESOP in amounts equating principal and interest payments. The total debt including the $2 million of principal that remained from the Beta transaction brought the obligation to $11 million. Payroll was adequate to maximize the tax deduction for principal, saving $7.3 million in pretax earnings to pay principal. The increased earnings allowed an acceleration of debt service. The fact that a supplier was acquired added to the margins. The increased productivity brought about because of employee ownership further improved profitability.

The ESOP makes it possible for a company that does its homework through perception enforced by feasibility studies to create a miniconglomerate in a relatively short time frame. The basic concept is to add payroll in an amount needed to maximize the tax deductibility for principal.

The target should also be conducive to restructuring to the extent that the additional increment of profitability will give the post-transaction entity the ability to service debt and still grow to a significantly greater extent than it would have had it made no acquisition. Stockholders outside of the ESOP must be assured that their equity will be much greater than it would have without the ESOP/LBO, and the employees should benefit as well.

28.4 HOW TO SWEETEN THE ACQUISITION FOR THE SELLER

An acquisition technique that could give the selling stockholder the benefit of a Section 1042 nonrecognition of tax might result in putting the acquirer in a more competitive position to win the right to the target acquisition. It might reduce the price that the owner of the target company might accept.

The acquisition technique would have the seller sell his stock to the buyer for Buyer Corp.'s stock. Mr. Seller would be given an option to sell his stock to Buyer

Corp.'s ESOP after a three-year holding period under IRC Section 1042. By having the transaction structured in this way, the seller might reduce the selling price. In any event, it would put Seller Corp. ahead of other would-be acquirers. Buyer Corp. will also be able to delay the point at which it must start paying for the acquisition, meanwhile using those funds to expand the business. At the end of the third year, it would borrow funds to lend to its ESOP and service the acquisition debt with pretax dollars.

The seller would find it worthwhile to wait because of the tax savings. Meanwhile, he might receive a negotiated consulting fee. This should be done only with the advice of counsel.

CHAPTER TWENTY-NINE

Strategies for Investing the ESOP Rollover

A large percentage of ESOPs are implemented for privately held corporations to give the stockholders an opportunity to diversify their assets. For many owners of closely held companies, the stock of their corporation represents the major part of their total assets. This situation may be worrisome, because upon the owners' deaths, the estate tax, if any, will require liquidity which, in turn, might require a rapid sale of the family enterprise.

29.1 THE FLOATING RATE NOTE

Some financial institutions, hearing the clarion call, have designed a security that qualifies as QRP and offers owners great flexibility. They are typically 40- to 80-year floating notes that pay interest adjusted monthly or quarterly according to an index. The notes are callable in about 30 years.

The owner can borrow against these notes up to 90 percent of the face amount, paying interest to the issuer on the borrowed portion. The borrowed proceeds can be reinvested without recognition of tax on the original stock. The interest credited on the 60-year note is about a wash with the after-tax cost of the interest paid by the borrower.

Use of this technique permits the investor to trade securities and exercise judgment as to timing for going in and out of investments without concern as to being taxed down to his or her basis on the stock that was sold to the ESOP.

29.2 SELECTING THE PORTFOLIO

If the investor does not wish to use the floating rate note approach, several basic categorical decisions must be made, among them the fact that, to avoid the capital gains tax, the QRP cannot be sold.

With this fact in mind, stocks or bonds should not be callable. Bonds should be highly rated "A" quality at a minimum and have maturities that far exceed one's life expectancy so as not to trigger tax down to the original basis. The field of bonds that fit these prerequisites is quite limited.

Historically, stocks are more of a hedge against inflation but typically provide lower income than bonds do. The investor's age dictates the type of investment mix he or she will have in the QRP portfolio. A young investor whose salary negates the need for investment income can be more aggressive in selecting stocks of smaller capital companies and can endure the volatility that typifies those stocks with the hope of greater capital appreciation in the long run.

The older investor may need income that a bond portfolio can provide. To offset the impact of inflation, it might be prudent if one does not need to maximize current income to include some stocks that pay dividends and consider a mix of perhaps 70 percent bonds and 30 percent stock. Although this strategy would reduce current income, the portfolio would tend to track inflation.

The portfolio should be diversified and made up of businesses that have weathered the times and are likely to continue in that vein. The companies should demonstrate an ability to avoid problems of product obsolescence by diversification. If one holds onto the QRP portfolio until death, the securities get a step up in basis to then current value, and there will be no capital gains tax at all.

29.3 MAXIMIZING INCOME THE CHARITABLE WAY

The old saw, "charity begins at home," is consistent with charitable remainder trusts (CRT) because of the CRT's ability to maximize the income the creator of the trust receives during his or her lifetime and that of his or her spouse.

According to a private letter ruling, a selling stockholder was permitted to donate his QRP to a CRT without triggering the capital gains tax. The donor and spouse get a current tax deduction, the charity's remainder interest, for the gift, but the really important factor is that the creator of the trust, as trustee, can do all of the investing and trading without triggering any tax on dividends, interest, or capital gains.

This advantage means that the donor and his or her spouse, as lifetime beneficiaries, will receive lifetime incomes on 100 percent of the investment rather than a percentage reduced by capital gains tax. Because the investment gains, dividends, and interest are sheltered from tax, the donor will receive greater income than would be the case in a mutual fund with the same securities, because the income would not be sheltered.

As will be noted more extensively in Chapter 43, the amount left in the CRT will go to the charities of the donor's choice at death. An insured irrevocable trust can replace the amount given for the benefit of the children, but the gift will be eliminated from the donor's estate, saving the estate tax.

29.4 SUMMARY

There are many flexible choices for reinvesting the proceeds of a stock sale, including a combination of all of the approaches outlined in this chapter. One's selection will depend on one's stage in life considering age, state of health, lifestyle, and needs.

CHAPTER THIRTY

Seven Practical ESOP Exit Strategies

Mr. Jones, 100 percent owner of Jones, Inc., wants to sell stock and defer taxes but minimize leverage. Facts: Market value of Jones, Inc. is $10 million. Annual payroll is $2 million. As noted earlier, Internal Revenue Code (IRC) Section 1042 requires that, for the selling shareholder to defer taxes on the sale of stock to an ESOP, the transaction must result in the ESOP owning 30 percent of the outstanding stock of the company.

Mr. Jones feels that a $3 million loan to the ESOP would drain the financial resources of the Company and possibly retard growth. Here are some techniques for accomplishing his objective over a reasonably short time frame.

30.1 TECHNIQUE 1: PREFUNDING THE ESOP

The corporation could prefund the purchase of Mr. Jones's stock by making cash contributions of up to $500,000 (25 percent × $2 million payroll) to a combination ESOP. The annual amount of cash or stock that the corporation may deduct in a combination ESOP is 25 percent of covered annual payroll.

If, in year three, the ESOP has $1 million of employer stock, it would borrow the more tolerable amount of $2 million from a bank and purchase $3 million of stock from the stockholder. He would reinvest the proceeds in qualified replacement property within a year, recognizing no tax liability and would receive an income from those investments in addition to his corporate compensation.

30.2. TECHNIQUE 2: HOW TO SELL STOCK UNDER SECTION 1042 BUT AVOID LEVERAGE

Alternatively, the corporation can contribute authorized but unissued stock or a mix of new stock and cash to the combination ESOP equal to 25 percent of payroll, or $500,000, for two, three, or possibly four years. This would replace or eliminate the amount of cash flow that would be needed to fund the ESOP currently and would also reduce the amount the ESOP must eventually borrow to purchase a sufficient amount of stock from Mr. Jones to bring the ESOP to the 30 percent threshold.

If the corporation contributes stock to the ESOP in an amount that is equal to, say, 20 percent of the outstanding stock of the company, the ESOP would have to borrow an amount needed to purchase only another 10 percent of the stock from Mr. Jones if he wants to sell stock to the ESOP under Section 1042. This will reduce the amount of financing the ESOP will need but will also reduce the amount of cash the shareholder will receive. The technique may make it possible for him to start getting some liquidity into his hands under Section 1042 within several years, rather than being denied this opportunity. Meanwhile, the corporation would have saved a significant amount of taxes in the course of this time frame.

Mr. Jones would be a participant in the ESOP prior to his selling his stock under the 1042 election and, as such, some of the stock that the company contributes would be allocated to his ESOP account.

30.3 TECHNIQUE 3: SELF-BANKING THE STOCK SALE

If the corporation valued at $10 million, has, say, $1 million of cash in retained earnings, it could lend the $1 million to the ESOP on a two-year amortization schedule. The ESOP would purchase $1 million of new stock from the corporation. The ESOP pays the corporation the $1 million of cash that it borrowed. The corporation would then make deductible contributions of $500,000 for principal (25 percent of payroll), in addition to an amount equal to interest. It would do this for two years, thus paying off the $1 million loan. The corporation would then borrow $2 million from a bank and lend it to the ESOP, which would buy $2 million of stock from Mr. Jones. Because the ESOP's 30 percent threshold will have been reached, he can elect under Section 1042 to defer his taxes, although he receives only $2 million in this transaction. The corporation thereby was able to reduce the amount of bank leverage to $2 million instead of $3 million. Stock would be allocated to Mr. Jones's ESOP account on the first two year of contributions but not on the rest.

30.4 TECHNIQUE 4: THE CASHLESS TRANSACTION

This example is similar to Technique 3 but with an added dimension. Here, we also assume that the corporation whose fair market value is $10 million does not have a combination stock bonus plan and money purchase plan, but has only a standard stock bonus plan ESOP. We further assume that the corporation wants to reduce the amount the ESOP must borrow from outside sources to purchase stock from Mr. Jones under Section 1042.

The company would take back a note from the ESOP in the amount of $1 million. The ESOP would then purchase $1 million of newly issued stock from the corporation. The corporation will contribute $500,000, 25 percent of covered payroll, and an amount equal to interest to the ESOP to enable the plan to pay principal and interest on the note back to the corporation. The corporation recovers its outlay immediately, making it, in effect, a cashless transaction. This scenario is repeated in the following year.

The company deducts the contributions it makes to the ESOP covering principal and interest. In the 40 percent tax bracket, the company saves $400,000 on the principal portion of its contributions to the ESOP for the two annual contributions. It receives the principal repayment tax free.

Although it deducts interest, the repayment of interest by the ESOP is taxable; it is a "wash" effect as far as interest is concerned. The result is that not only is the transaction cashless, but it also actually increases working and cash flow by the taxes saved on the repayment of principal, namely, $400,000.

The ESOP has at this point $1 million of stock. It only needs to purchase $2 million from the stockholder to comply with the 30 percent threshold required for the Section 1042 tax treatment.

The company can lend the $400,000 of tax savings to the ESOP to be used to purchase $400,000 of stock from Mr. Jones. The company can simultaneously borrow $1.6 million from a bank, which would, in turn, lend it to the ESOP, bringing the ESOP's indebtedness to $2 million, of which $400,000 is owed to the corporation. The ESOP would then purchase $2 million of stock from Mr. Jones, bringing the amount of stock in the ESOP up to $3 million, or 30 percent of the outstanding shares. Actually, slightly more stock would have to go into the ESOP to make up for the issuance of new shares by the company.

The corporation would make annual tax-deductible contributions to the ESOP for principal and interest ($500,000 + interest), part of which is returned to the corporation and does not involve the bank.

Result: This technique reduces the bank leverage to only $1.6 million. Mr. Jones sells $2 million of his shares under Section 1042. He is a participant insofar as the shares are concerned on the newly issued stock sold to the ESOP. He is excluded as a participant only on the shares that he sold personally. Having met the Section 1042 requirements, the stockholder will be able to sell additional shares of stock to the ESOP without any further concern about achieving any specific level of stock.

30.5 TECHNIQUE 5: CORPORATION WANTS CASHLESS TAX DEDUCTION AND MINIMUM DILUTION

Facts: Raybar, Inc. is profitable and is growing at 15 percent annually. Fiscal and plan years end December 31. The annual covered payroll is $3 million. The appraised fair market value for the company is $10 million. Because the corporation is profitable, it would like to reduce the amount of taxes it will pay for the current tax year. It would like to minimize dilution as well.

The board has until it files its corporate taxes, including extensions, to make a contribution to its ESOP. The company files its automatic six-month extension in addition to the standard 75 days it has to file taxes, bringing the period up to September 15 of the following year to make its contribution for the previous year.

The board would plan on making a contribution of authorized but newly issued stock to the ESOP on August 31. The company employs a qualified appraiser in June or July to determine the fair market value of the stock so as to give it ample time to do its work. Based on interim financial statements, and assuming there were no changes that would affect the earlier valuation, the appraiser would provide the company with a firm value as of the date of the contribution. Assuming a steady monthly growth rate of 1.25 percent, the stock would have grown 10 percent since the end of the previous year for which taxes are to be paid. A contribution of newly issued stock to the ESOP would require 10 percent fewer shares to achieve the same deduction that would have been required as of the end of the prior year.

Example:
Fair market value as of December 31 of the current year is $10 million. The board plans to contribute stock in an amount equal to 15 percent of its $3 million covered payroll, i.e., the payroll as of December 31 of the current year. This would require a contribution of stock to the ESOP valued at $450,000. If, as of August 31 of the following year, the stock has grown 10 percent, the value of the company will have increased to $11 million.

A contribution of stock valued at $450,000 would represent 4.5 percent of the company's outstanding stock if the contribution were made as of December 31. By delaying the contribution until August 31 of the following year, the $450,000 contribution would represent only about 4.1 percent, a difference of 0.4 percent. If this technique were followed for several years, the antidilutionary effect would become meaningful.

This example does not take into effect the offsets to equity dilution created by tax savings, productivity gains, inclusion of stockholders in the ESOP having shares allocated to their accounts, and the elimination of contributions the company would otherwise make to other plans.

30.6 TECHNIQUE 6: HOW CONTRIBUTION OF REDEEMED SHARES CAN MINIMIZE DILUTION

If the stock of an ESOP company is appreciating in value, as in the prior example, it is advisable to consider the use of various stock contribution strategies which can result in a reduction of dilution.

The stock of the company in the preceding example is appreciating at a compounded annual 15 percent rate. As employees terminate, retire, or die, the corporation should consider redeeming the stock instead of making a tax-deductible cash contribution to the ESOP, which the ESOP trustee would use to purchase the stock that is allocated to the terminated employee's account.

If the corporation redeems the stock, it would do so with after-tax dollars. The stock comes back into treasury. The company can contribute those treasury shares to the ESOP and regain its tax deduction. However, if the company delays making the contribution until the next valuation, the same number of shares it redeemed will give the company a larger tax deduction because of the increase in the value of the shares. Conversely, fewer shares will have to be contributed to achieve the same deduction. This will, therefore, reduce the dilutionary effect.

30.7 TECHNIQUE 7: HOW TO DEDUCT PRINCIPAL ON AN EXISTING LOAN

Suppose your corporation is profitable and pays taxes in the 40 percent combined federal and state tax bracket. Further, assume that the company is paying off a $2 million long-term loan that has been paid down to $1 million. Perhaps the loan was incurred to acquire equipment, acquire a company, or redeem stock. Whatever the reason for the loan, principal payments cannot be deducted. The loan must be repaid with after-tax dollars. The company must earn $1.67 million to repay principal on the remaining debt. This ignores interest. The fact is that the corporation must earn more than the amount of the debt to retire the debt. This further reduces the value of the company and thereby dilutes the equity of the shareholders.

If principal were tax deductible, which it is not, the $1 million of remaining debt could be retired with only $1 million of pretax earnings, again ignoring interest. The company would retain the additional $667,000 of earnings, increasing the value of the company by a multiple of the annual amount of earnings saved. The corporation can achieve the same effect as though principal were deductible by making an annual tax-deductible contribution of newly issued stock in an amount equal to the annual payment of principal. The government is paying 40 percent of the loan principal.

If the tax savings are used to accelerate the loan payment, the company will pay less interest over the remaining term of the loan. Debt acceleration will increase the value of the corporation. The company is contributing a slice of a bigger pie to the employee trust, thereby, in great measure, offsetting the dilutionary effect.

30.8 THE FLIP SIDE OF ANTIDILUTION

The preceding techniques are to be considered from the viewpoint of the employer who wants to keep dilution at a minimum. However, many employers like the idea of letting the employees get the benefit of larger gains as a token of appreciation for the work they did to achieve the growth record. Moreover, employees who can reap the harvest of the full growth enjoyed by the owners of the stock outside of the ESOP are likely to become more productive. The increased productivity will result in greater profitability. This, in turn, will increase share value, the benefit of which will accrue to both the ESOP participants and the outside shareholders. In such an environment, both parties win.

CHAPTER THIRTY-ONE

How to Change Real Estate to Stock to Tax-Free Cash

In preparing for succession, one of the major objectives is to put oneself and his or her spouse into a more liquid position. Another objective is to reduce one's responsibilities and stress. Both ownership of real estate and ownership of stock in one's privately held company can be burdensome and stressful. It is possible to reduce both to cash, thereby enabling the owner to direct his or her attention to more relaxing pursuits.

It may be possible for a stockholder who owns real estate on certain other types of assets to exchange it for stock in an existing or a new corporation without recognizing a taxable gain, providing he or she has held the real estate for at least six months. The real challenge comes in finding a way to turn this nonliquid asset into a liquid form.

Mr. Diamond owned the building that he leased to the corporation of which he owned 70 percent of the stock. The real estate had appreciated in value over the years since he acquired it, and the company that he founded had grown dramatically through the years.

Mr. Diamond, who was in his mid sixties, had a burning desire to become more liquid. The bulk of his estate was in the real estate and in the stock of his private corporation. If he sold either, there would be a considerable tax to pay on the gain in value.

It was pointed out to him that he could exchange the real estate for stock in his company without incurring any tax under Code Section 351. This could be done because there was a valid business reason, an independent economic purpose, and the transferred property had an integral relationship to the business of the corporation. Moreover, the transaction would bring his holdings up to the 80 percent control ownership of the company. The real estate increased the value of the corporation.

The extent of the increase in value was determined by independent valuation. The greater the relationship and financial impact upon the corporation's cash flow, the greater the effect the valuation firm is likely to add to the stock's going concern value.

Mr. Diamond then had his company implement an ESOP. The corporation borrowed funds which it loaned to its ESOP. The period that Mr. Diamond had held the property was tacked onto the holding period of the stock, so that he was able to meet the three-year holding period requirement for a Section 1042 sale of his stock.

There had been no prior binding agreement, and the advisor stipulated that this transaction was not a sham. For this reason, he felt that no waiting period between the Section 351 and the Section 1042 transactions was required. Maintaining 80 percent of the corporate stock or control for any specified period of time after the Section 351 transaction is not required.

Mr. Diamond subsequently sold the stock to the ESOP under Section 1042 and invested the proceeds of the stock sale in a 60-year floating note. He borrowed approximately 90 percent of the face amount of the note using the note as collateral at about a wash cost. He then invested the loan proceeds in various investments and was able to switch in and out of investments without being taxed down to his original basis in either the real estate or the corporation.

Therefore, Mr. Diamond could sell the stock of the company to the ESOP and defer or possibly avoid all capital gains tax. This can be a major step toward succession planning. It must be stressed that no action of this nature should be consummated except under advice of competent counsel.

CHAPTER THIRTY-TWO

How Mr. Big Sold His Company Tax Free and Still Kept It

32.1 THE LOCKED-IN STOCK

Owners of private corporations must someday deal with the question of perpetuating the enterprise, selling it to another company or to individuals who will operate the company, or going public. A well-run privately held corporation can be a virtual money machine in that it provides the working owner with reasonable compensation and capital appreciation. Compensation is spendable, but capital becomes spendable only if all or part of the company is sold. It is most unusual for a founder to be able to sell a minority portion of a private company to an equity investor since the person putting up the cash would want to be able to call the shots. Unless he or she is able to purchase 51 percent, they are usually disinterested.

It is logical that the company's employees would be interested in purchasing stock of the company that employs them. This occurs commonly in public companies where there is a readily tradable market for the stock, but employees seldom purchase stock of a private company because they cannot afford to tie up their funds for an unknown time frame. They may feel that, absent dividends, their capital might be put to better use elsewhere. If they did purchase stock of their privately held employer, these employees may even look upon the investment as a loan to their employer. Finally, depending on the extent of their investment, they may even consider terminating their employment to recover their capital.

Taking the private corporation public as a means of getting capital out of the company is seldom a viable means of becoming liquid. Assuming the corporation is sufficiently charismatic to have a successful offering, it is difficult for a member of the control group to sell his or her own stock because of the stringent restrictions governing such shares. Selling large blocks of stock into a thin market through a secondary offering tends to depress the price and is not a very feasible means of cashing out.

Redemption of stock by the corporation also has its pitfalls. If the major stockholder sells a minor portion of his or her stock to the corporation, the transaction will be treated as a dividend. He or she will be taxed as though it were ordinary income and the purchase price is not deductible by the corporation.

Carrying stock to the grave as a last resort can create havoc. The downside effect of maintaining stock as a primary asset in one's estate is that the U.S. Treasury will not accept it as legal tender for paying estate taxes. The government wants cash, not stock. It is for this reason that families often sell or liquidate good going businesses at a distressed price. This opportunity is avidly sought by sharp-eyed vultures.

The ESOP is an alternative that can provide stockholders of private companies with the means of exchanging stock for cash without forfeiting control.

32.2 HOW TO CASH OUT THE PRIVATE COMPANY STOCK

The most practical means of selling stock in one's private C corporation without giving up one's avocation in life is through the ESOP cash out technique. Let's assume that Mr. Big owns 100 percent of the stock of his corporation but would like to have more cash to spend during his lifetime and more liquidity in the event of his death. Moreover, he does not care for the idea of taking in new stockholders who might interfere with his style of building the company, and he would consider selling the company only as a last resort. Here is what the owner can do to solve his problem under the ESOP provisions of the 1984 Deficit Reduction Act and the 1986 Tax Reform Act:

- He can sell part or virtually all of his stock to his company's ESOP and receive tax-deferred or possibly tax-free cash in the transaction.

- He can maintain effective control of his company.

- The corporation can deduct its payments for principal, interest, and dividends used to service ESOP debt.

- Mr. Big can implement a charitable ESOP (CHESOP). The charitable remainder trust can give him and his wife current tax deduction and a lifetime income without any loss of control.

32.3 THE CASHING OUT PROCEDURE

Here are some facts of the case:

- The corporation has established an ESOP for the current year.

- Covered annual payroll is $3 million.

- Pretax earnings are $1.5 million and are expected to grow at a 10 percent annual compounded rate.

- Fair market value has been determined to be $9 million. Mr. Big has offered to sell 51 percent to the ESOP under Code Section 1042. He conveyed the offer to the ESOP Administrative Committee and it was agreed that if suitable financing could be obtained, the ESOP trustee would be instructed to proceed with the purchase of the shares for $4.59 million.

32.4 LEVERAGING THE TRANSACTION

The ESOP Committee negotiated a seven-year, $4.59 million loan for the corporation. The corporation loaned the $4.59 million to its ESOP. The corporation agreed to make annual contributions to the ESOP in amounts sufficient to enable the ESOP to service principal and interest, deducting both.

The principal payments are well within the 25 percent of payroll limitation for the deductible contribution of principal. There is no limit on the amount of interest the company can deduct.

32.5 THE TAX-DEFERRED (POSSIBLY TAX-FREE) ROLLOUT

The $1.5 million pretax earnings would offer a cash flow comfort zone to the company with respect to its contributions to the ESOP. Mr. Big proceeded to invest in a portfolio of qualified domestic company stocks and bonds within 12 months from the time of the sale of his stock. Under the terms of Code Section 1042, he was able to defer his taxes on the sale of his stock.

By continuing to own all of the outstanding stock not held by the ESOP, Mr. Big maintained active and effective control of the company since voting rights are not passed through to the participants except on those grave corporate issues such as mergers or consolidation, recapitalization, reclassification, dissolution, or sale of substantially all of the assets. The limited vote pass-through to the participants would pertain only to those shares that had been released by the bank as the note is amortized. The trustee would vote the unallocated shares. In any event, it would still be a few years before the allocation of Mr. Big's stock to participants' ESOP accounts exceeded 51 percent of the outstanding stock. It might be noted that some ESOP corporations pass voting rights through to the participants on the unallocated shares as well as those that are allocated.

If the company felt the need to do so, it could have declared dividends. Those that were to be paid on the ESOP shares to service debt would be tax deductible. If the terms of the loan agreement permitted, the corporation could pass some of the dividends to the participants based upon the shares that were allocated to their ESOP accounts and deduct those as well. This would be a direct reflection of the employees' productivity and should serve as an additional incentive to them. Improved productivity would make Mr. Big's remaining 49 percent more valuable.

The arrangement was far better than an outright sale of the company from the standpoint of Mr. Big and the employees. Mr. Big continued to run the company as he always had, and the employees were delighted because there were no dislocations or relocations of management or rank-and-file employees. Moreover, the employees were destined to own the equity of the company without putting up a dime. They continued to receive compensation for their labor and a pass-through dividend as well.

There would be no pressure brought to bear to sell the company upon Mr. Big's death because the sale of his stock to the ESOP made his estate quite liquid. Upon his death, the qualified replacement property receives a step up in basis and there will never be a capital gains tax on these assets. The 51 percent that Mr. Big sold to the ESOP netted him as much after tax as he would have had he sold approximately 68 percent of the company to outsiders. He continued to receive his usual compensation in addition to the dividends and interest he received from his qualified replacement portfolio of stocks and bonds. The investment income was on the total investment since there was no tax erosion on the principal. The stock he did not sell to the ESOP will enable him to participate in the growth of the company. It is important to note that a selling shareholder cannot have shares of stock that he or she sells in a tax-deferred rollout allocated to his or her account or to that of certain family members.

Although the government helped tremendously with tax relief, the perpetuation of the corporation and continued expansion resulted in the hiring of many more people who would pay more and more in taxes just as the corporation itself would. The U.S. Treasury was destined to make a recovery of deferred revenue in the many years ahead. The community at large would not lose the enterprise to outsiders.

CHAPTER THIRTY-THREE

What Lenders Look for in an ESOP Loan

33.1 LENDER'S CRITERIA

Historically, banks not only are willing to lend money, they are anxious to do so. The conditions for their actually writing the check often create frustrations on the part of borrowers, but in the long run, borrowers who are successful at obtaining bank financing usually agree—if reluctantly—that the lender has irrefutable logic on its side.

When a loan is sought, the presence of an ESOP often requires a bit of explanation, because many bankers do not run into ESOP transactions on a routine basis. Some bankers actually say their bank will not lend to ESOPs, which is often a factual statement. When the seeker of financing explains that the loan is really to the corporation followed by a mirror loan from the company to the ESOP so that principal can be deducted, the lending officer is quick to grasp the fact that an ESOP actually improves the corporation's cash flow and debt-paying capacity, affording greater security for the bank.

The banker wants to do due diligence on the character of the borrowers and their credit history. If the other factors are good but the character of the principals in the company do not measure up, the banker will shun the transaction.

The history of the corporation, usually going back over the reviewed financials for five years, is one of the primary factors in evaluating the company's creditworthiness. The bank wants to see historical revenue and profitability trends to assess the credibility of the projections of the company's debt service capabilities and the likelihood that the company's working capital will be adequate to continue the growth pattern in spite of the leverage.

The lender will, in most cases, require that the loan be collateralized by the corporation, or if that is insufficient, it will look to the shareholders, or possibly both. Service companies generally have only accounts receivable and possible real estate available as collateral, while distributors or manufacturers have accounts receivable, inventory, and the company-owned building. In addition to those assets, manufacturers have equipment.

The loan officer will examine the quality of these unencumbered assets to ascertain the amount that it finds acceptable as collateral for a loan. For some or possibly all of the shortfall, the banker may look to a personal guarantee from the principals. If the transaction involves the purchase of the major stockholder's stock under Internal Revenue Code (IRC) Section 1042, the selling shareholder may put up the replacement securities as collateral. The bank generally will release the personal collateral on a dollar-for-dollar basis as principal is amortized.

The lending bank officer will require the potential borrower to state his or her future plans. Assuming the loan's purpose is for cashing out the founders, will the selling shareholder responsible for the company's profitability be retiring during the five- or seven-year term loan period?

To what extent is there managerial backup? Will the shareholder reduce his or her salary and bonus to create add-backs on the pro forma?

Will the profit-sharing plan be converted to the ESOP so that cash contributions that formerly went off the balance sheet can be used henceforth to service the ESOP loan? Will existing long-term debt be refinanced through the ESOP to deduct the repayment? What is the possibility of product obsolescence? What are the company's plans for increasing market share and profitability? These are some of the areas the bank will explore in addition to key historical and projected ratios. The better management's presentation, the greater the likelihood of procuring financing.

As noted, in leveraged ESOP transactions, the lender can lend to the corporation which, in turn, makes a mirror loan to the ESOP. The corporation secures the loan with its assets. As an alternative, the lender can lend directly to the ESOP trust with the loan being guaranteed by the corporation. Banks generally feel more secure with direct access to the collateral in the event of default. For this reason, the loan to the corporation is the approach most often used.

If a loan is sought for a leveraged ESOP transaction of a private corporation, the bank should know that the valuation was performed by a firm that is totally independent, reputable, experienced in doing ESOP valuations, and that regularly performs appraisals of companies. The bank must feel satisfied that the ESOP does not pay more than adequate consideration for the stock it acquires in the transaction. Therefore, the ESOP loan amount may not exceed fair market value for the stock being purchased.

33.2 ANALYZE THE DOCUMENTS

The lender should analyze the ESOP plan and trust documents to determine if they provide information such as when distributions must be made to terminating participants. For example, does the ESOP allow a delay in making distributions and redeeming the shares until the loan is fully paid? This would lend comfort to the bank.

33.3 FRAUDULENT CONVEYANCE

The bank should be assured that fraudulent conveyance is not involved; such a problem could, in the event of bankruptcy, cause the security for the loan to go under attack and wind up satisfying other creditors' claims. Such an attack would occur under the provisions of the Fraudulent Conveyance Act, the Uniform Fraudulent Transfer Act, and the United States Bankruptcy Code.

This issue tends to be of concern primarily where the corporation is highly leveraged. To alleviate that concern, the bank may require the borrowing entity to provide an opinion letter from an independent expert outlining the fact that there is a reasonable expectation that cash flow will allow the company to service debt and note the margin by which assets exceed liabilities.

33.4 REPURCHASE LIABILITY STUDY

ESOPs contain an option that permits participants to put the stock in their accounts to the corporation upon the contingencies of death, retirement, disability, or termination for other causes. ESOP law permits the employer to delay these payments under prescribed limitations as defined in the ESOP document.

Some plan designs, coupled with employer practice as to timing of distributions, are more liberal than others. As noted *supra,* the experienced lender will want complete clarification of the plan's distribution provisions.

Moreover, the lender will frequently require the borrowing entity to provide a repurchase liability study to determine the expected timing as to when distributions are likely to occur and a quantitative cash flow analysis to denote the amount of cash the company will need in order to cash out the participants. The lender, of course, wants to see what effect this might have on the company's ability to service debt.

Even though the study would undoubtedly show that the major part of the distribution stream will not commence until the loan is fully discharged, the bank may want to know that the company will have sufficient liquidity to meet the obligation to cash out the employees in the future, starting after the loan is paid off. A properly designed sinking fund is appropriate for consideration.

For the most part, the bank will look at the ESOP loan as it would a non-ESOP loan for the corporation with certain differences. The bank that lends to an ESOP has recourse only to the company stock that is pledged as collateral in the ESOP; it has no recourse to any other assets in the ESOP.

The ESOP stock is released from the collateral pledge as the debt is paid down. The lender will, therefore, want the company to provide a security guarantee as well as a guarantee that it will contribute an amount equal to principal and interest to the ESOP to enable it to service its obligation to the bank. In addition, the loan document will require that other provisions of the Employee Retirement Income Security Act of 1974 (ERISA) as well as other pertinent tax laws are observed.

For example, the lender will stipulate (1) that a proper valuation will occur annually; (2) that the loan may not be payable on demand; and (3) that the term loan will be used only to acquire stock of the employer and to cover expenses of procuring the financing and ESOP implementation fees.

The loan document will provide numerous references to ERISA and Department of Labor (DOL) requirements, such as the exemption from prohibited transactions and loan structuring rules and a warrantee that the borrower is in full compliance with the pertinent code sections. There will be additional documents regarding company-owned real estate, various guarantees, security agreements, and counsel's opinion that the ESOP is in full compliance with the law.

CHAPTER THIRTY-FOUR

How to Obtain Financing for the ESOP

34.1 WHO PROVIDES THE FINANCING?

If the ESOP transaction involves a management buyout, equity investing by the managers is the basic building block of the financing pyramid. The extent to which this is available determines the amount of additional financing that must be sought for the proposed ESOP transaction.

Senior debt is the next layer of the pyramid and ideally the last. This is obtained from banks, savings and loans, insurance companies, individuals including stockholders, and from the company itself. Interest charged on this level of debt is typically in the range of one-half to three-and-one-half percent above prime assuming the borrower is not a *Fortune* 1000 company. A commitment fee (points) may be levied in addition. ESOP debt financing can be structured on a secured or on an unsecured basis. In the former instance, corporate cash and/or personal collateral can be used. The lender looks to the corporation's ability to service the debt through cash flow.

If the combined management equity investment and senior debt is inadequate, mezzanine financing may be needed to make up the shortfall. This debt is subordinated or junior to the senior debt. It is customarily designed to yield a high fixed compound rate of 18 to 40 percent, including warrants or whatever other equity kicker may have been required. Buyout funds, insurance companies, and pension funds are sources of mezzanine financing.

Venture capital is the source of last resort since these investors demand 50 to 60 percent of the company in the form of common stock. The ESOP can serve as an excellent exit vehicle for their block of stock at some appropriate future date.

34.2 HOW A LENDER EVALUATES THE LOAN

The more complete and professionally prepared the financing package, the greater the likelihood of obtaining a rapid and favorable response from a prospective lender. The simpler the transaction structure, the better the chances of negotiating a loan.

The bank's deliberations will factor in the nature of the transaction. An ESOP loan to increase working capital affords the lender more security than one that is used to purchase the owner's stock.

The bank will want five years of balance sheets, income statements, and cash flow summaries as well as those of any acquisition targets and a pro forma for the restructured enterprise showing the use and effect of the proposed loan in the detailed assumptions on which the pro forma is based.

The bank will analyze the sources of collateral coverage, including the itemization of inventory, recent appraisals of equipment, accounts receivable aging, and real estate appraisals. It will take into consideration the value of patents, royalty streams, and potential litigation against the firm.

The management team will be of great importance to the lender. This is particularly true if the founder and/or chief executive officer (CEO) is selling his stock and moving out of the company. Unless he or she is pledging personal collateral, the lender must rely solely upon the dedication, capability, and staying power of the managers and successor CEO. If those individuals have purchased an equity stake and have a great deal to lose, so much the better.

The ESOP can pay no more than fair market value for the stock and the bank will be partially guided by the value determined by independent appraisal. The appraiser's report will include valuable information on the company's market share as well as shadows on the horizon.

34.3 OTHER FACTORS FOR ANALYSIS

The lender will be more wary of a high growth company's continued ability to service debt because of its insatiable need for new capital attended by debt. A stagnant company is even less desirable. The labor intensive company more readily adapts to an ESOP loan since principal payments are limited to 25 percent of covered payroll. The bank will want to analyze the corporation's existing debt structure, including any covenants not to incur additional debt as well as prepayment penalties. Some lenders may seek the advice of those knowledgeable in the technical aspects of ESOPs to help arrive at the most advantageous structure. A repurchase liability study to determine the amount required to cash out ESOP participants will dispel much of the mystique and help the bank see how the ESOP will function going forward.

The fact that principal can be paid with pretax dollars and dividends can be deducted for ESOP paybacks is an advantage of great magnitude since a dollar of earnings will go farther in servicing debt. The lender will expend considerable thought in pricing out the loan based on all of the foregoing. Competition with other lenders will undoubtedly color its decision.

A feasibility study will enhance the banker's ability to assess the viability of the transaction and move the process along much more rapidly. Upon cursory review, a lender might conclude that a corporation with a very small covered payroll does not fit the parameters for ESOP financing. It should be brought to the lender's attention that reasonable dividends on ESOP stock can be deducted, in addition to the limits imposed by Code Sections 404 and 415, if they are used to repay ESOP debt. The company can create a super common or a noncallable convertible preferred class of stock to which it will pay dividends. It is the stock that would be sold to the ESOP. Dividends would not be paid to the stock that is outside of the ESOP because they would not be deductible. Interest is also deductible on an unlimited basis unrelated to the Code Sections 404 and 415 limits so long as the interest rate is reasonable.

There are many small profitable companies with limited payroll intensity to which this might be applicable.

34.4 REAL VALUE VERSUS COSMETIC EFFECT

An ESOP brings tax savings to the table. Tax savings increase corporate cash flow and debt service capacity. It obviously accomplishes this by reducing taxable income and after-tax profits.

Which is more important to a lender? The answer depends upon the lender's knowledge of ESOP financing and degree of sophistication. It is therefore important to determine in advance of seeking financing whether the banker understands the beneficial effect the ESOP has in protecting the bank's interest. The ESOP makes the lender more secure by allowing the corporation to deduct principal, thereby putting the lender in a senior position to the IRS on the payback of principal. It also lets the bank deduct interest under certain circumstances.

CHAPTER THIRTY-FIVE

How to Recover Taxes Paid in Prior Years with No Cash Expenditures

ESOPs can be used in a way that is useful for recovering corporate taxes or creating a loss to be carried forward for future years. A corporation can make contributions to an ESOP even in years when there is no profit. Moreover, the contribution to the ESOP need not be made in cash.

Corporate losses in C corporations can be carried back two years and forward 20 years. Let's assume a corporation has paid taxes in each of the prior two years but has a current year of no earnings—a flat year.

The corporation could make a tax-deductible contribution of newly issued stock to its ESOP this year, thereby creating a loss that can be carried back two prior tax-paying years. The current contribution to the ESOP would offset the taxable income of the earliest of the two years and then the most recent year sequentially. The taxes that had been paid in those years could then be recovered with no cash contribution using this methodology.

A variation of this technique can also be used where loss carry forwards (NOLS) exist. By contributing stock to the ESOP, the corporation would extend the number of years into the future at which time taxes would be payable. This is a form of tax money in the bank.

A recovery of taxes is an interest-free infusion of cash at a time of lean earnings and therefore most useful to the corporation (see Exhibit 35.1).

Exhibit 35.1

MODEL: How an ESOP May Make It Possible to Obtain a Tax Refund

Year	Taxable Income	Contribution to ESOP (Installed 2001)	Federal Taxes Paid
1999	$250,000	-0-	$80,750
2000	200,000	-0-	61,000
SUBTOTALS	$450,000	-0-	$141,750
2001	-0- (A)	$450,000 (B)	($141,750) (C)

(A) Corporation breaks even in 2001.

(B) Corporation installed an ESOP in 2001 to which it contributed 15% of its $3 million payroll or $450,000 in cash or stock.

(C) Corporation is entitled by the Internal Revenue Code to a refund of federal taxes paid for two years preceding because the ESOP contribution in 2001, a break-even year, offset the taxable income in those years. The refund in this model is $141,750.

CHAPTER THIRTY-SIX

Valuing Leveraged ESOP Stock

The book value of a corporation is reduced by the amount of its debt. The economic value or fair market value, whether it be an ESOP or a non-ESOP company, will be reduced, but not necessarily dollar for dollar. A leveraged ESOP brings tax advantages to the company which add to its economic value. These benefits include the tax savings available to qualified lenders that are passed on to the corporation in the form of below-prime loans. Deductions for principal servicing and for dividends used to discharge ESOP debt are other tax benefits supplied by the ESOP. The fact that the corporation will pay fewer taxes means that the debt servicing period may be reduced by two or three years. This will result in a reduction of gross interest as well. The tax advantages of a leveraged ESOP transaction could eventually increase the market value of the company as much as 20 to 35 percent of the debt involved as compared with a leveraged buyout (LBO) without an ESOP.

By using the tax savings to expand the company or increase market share, other factors that may affect the valuation of stock in a leveraged ESOP corporation include employee wage concessions, the replacement of pension or profit-sharing plans, the likelihood of improved productivity, and the repurchase liability.

36.1 VALUATION IN A MANAGEMENT BUYOUT

Valuation is impacted by what the various investors bring to the leveraged ESOP transaction. For example, consider the management buyout of a $10 million company. The managers invest $1 million in the form of cash for 100 percent of the common stock. The ESOP borrows $9 million from the bank for which it receives noncallable convertible preferred stock. On the transaction date the manager's equity is valued at $1 million and the ESOP's equity is valued at $9 million. Management starts out with 10 percent of the equity and the ESOP owns 90 percent.

The debt is serviced by tax-deductible contributions for servicing principal, subject to the 25 percent of payroll limitation, in addition to the unlimited contribution for interest. The corporation also pays tax-deductible dividends to the ESOP stock for debt service. The ESOP receives all of the dividends and the managers receive none. Moreover, the dividends are contractual, and preferred stock receives preferential treatment in the event of liquidation, thereby reducing the ESOP's risk. This would seem to be unfair to the managers unless there is a tradeoff. The equalizer lies in the fact that the common stock owned by the managers will receive a larger amount of the equity growth at such time as the ESOP's shares are converted to common. This occurs as a result of the fact that the convertible preferred stock is designed with a conversion ratio, which will result in shares of the preferred being converted at the end of the term period into fewer shares of common. This will result in the common getting greater growth than the preferred.

36.2 EXAMPLE

The result of owning growth stock can be seen in the example that follows:

- The managers, as noted earlier, invest $1 million cash for 100,000 shares of common stock. The ESOP acquires 900,000 shares of callable convertible preferred stock with a 10 percent dividend paid annually, valued at $9 million.

- At the end of the tenth year, the ESOP's 900,000 shares are exchanged for, or converted into, 692,308 shares of common, increasing the manager's ownership from 10 percent to 31 percent of the equity. The company, at the time of the original transaction, was valued by independent appraisal at $10 million. If the company increases in value at an average of 7 percent per annum, the company's equity value in 10 years would approximate $19.5 million. Accordingly, the original common investors' shares would increase from $1 million to $6 million. The preferred investors' shares increase from $9 million to $13.5 million. In the interim, they have received $9 million in dividends, a total of $22.5 million. The dividends were used to pay principal on the loan.

- The ownership at the outset for the managers was 10 percent, and for the ESOP, 90 percent. At the point of conversion, the ratio changed from 10 percent/90 percent to 31 percent/69 percent. At any rate, this is one very competent appraiser's way of analyzing the relative values of the classes of stock on a pre- and post-transaction basis in this generic example with its sketchy fact content. Some valuation firms might disagree with this conclusion.

- As the ESOP debt is amortized, the shares released by the lender to the ESOP participants' accounts increase their equity rapidly. The employees come out well since management's chartered course enabled the company to discharge the note obligation. The managers will have done well because their performance exceeded the debt service requirement.

- The appraiser feels justified in valuing the stock to reflect this changing equity relationship because of what each investor brings to the transaction. The economic reality of the transaction must take into consideration the return an investment banker or venture capital group would reasonably require in financing the buyout. The return should not be abusive but can be in accordance with businesslike performance incentives. The rate of return for an incentivized management buyout group can exceed the normal yield on a straight hands-off money investment. It should be noted that the downside risk should be consistent with the upside potential. Throughout the security design and structuring of the transaction, the Employee Retirement Income Security Act (ERISA) requirements must be adhered to by the fiduciaries. The ESOP must pay no more than adequate consideration and the investment must be solely in the interest of the plan participants and beneficiaries.

The security allocation can be the converse of the foregoing example. The ESOP can own the common with its downside risk commensurate with its upside potential and the non-ESOP investors can invest in the convertible preferred with its dividend stream and safety net, but this is unlikely. Alternatively, the outside investors could receive a subordinated debt security coupled with an equity kicker to be received after the ESOP perceives a reasonable return on its common stock. This format is not as practical as the converse since ESOP participants are generally perceived is a group that should be protected on the downside and the outside investors as being more sophisticated and imbued with a predisposition toward chance taking.

The valuation of the securities takes into consideration an assessment of the degree of risk. The value of a security in which there is not risk would differ from one that has substantial risk.

36.3 ESOP TRANSACTIONS INVOLVING MULTI-INVESTORS

Complex ESOP transactions sometimes involve several categories of investors, each with a different set of objectives and varying degrees of risk tolerance. A form of security might be designed to conform with the various characteristics.

The investors might include the management group, outside equity investors, and the ESOP. The selling shareholder retains some stock in the company. Typically, both the management group and the outside equity investors would have common stock. The equity investors would probably have kickers such as warrants in addition to the stock. They would likely subordinate their position to that of the others in order to justify their greater reward. The ESOP would most likely have preferred stock that pays dividends and is convertible to voting common at the end of the term period.

This type of structure demands a great deal of expertise on the part of the financial advisor so as to assure that each party to the transaction is treated fairly. In multiple-investor ESOP buyouts, a fairness opinion should be rendered and adequate consideration should be assured for each class of security.

CHAPTER THIRTY-SEVEN

Issues in Selecting
a Valuation Firm

In considering the criteria for selecting a firm to value the stock of a corporation for purposes of an ESOP transaction, it is essential to keep in mind the guiding Employee Retirement Income Security Act (ERISA) principle: that the ESOP cannot pay more than fair market value for the stock it acquires and that distributees must receive fair market value for shares allocated to their accounts.

The administrative committee members or the trustees are responsible for the ESOP's adhering to this principle. They are treated as fiduciaries of the ESOP, and as such see to it that the ESOP obtains an independent and quality appraisal.

37.1 FIDUCIARIES SELECT THE VALUATION FIRM

Because of their responsibility, it is the fiduciaries who select and engage the appraiser on behalf of the ESOP, and it is the fiduciaries—not the sponsoring corporation—to whom the appraiser submits the report; otherwise, the appraiser is not deemed to be independent.

The fiduciaries not only must attest to the quality of the appraiser's work, but also must be assured of the total independence of the appraiser.

The Tax Reform Act of 1986 mandated that the appraisal be done by a firm that is totally independent. Prior to that time, no such legal requirement existed. The act also requires that the appraisal firm be a reputable one that regularly performs appraisals of businesses and is experienced in performing calculations for ESOP purposes.

This act requires that the stock in the ESOP be valued annually and that the IRS be notified as to the appraised fair market value by means of a form signed by the appraiser of the stock. Although a formula for buy-sell agreements is used quite commonly, forms are inadequate for purposes of arriving at fair market value for ESOP transactions. In the complex world of business, there are far too many variables that must be weighed in determining adequate consideration or fair market value.

A formula simply will not retain its ability to remain fair to all parties after awhile. Valuation methodologies tend to be relatively consistent from year to year, but there may be reasons to change the approach used in prior years due to significant factors affecting the business.

37.2 FREQUENCY OF APPRAISALS

Many advisors feel that it is appropriate to require the appraiser to provide the fiduciaries with a letter as of the date of any stock transaction to the effect that the appraiser is unaware of anything of significance that would change the value of the stock since the last valuation or to provide a new valuation figure if there have been significant events in the interim.

37.3 MULTISTOCK TRANSACTIONS

The valuation firm must advise the fiduciaries as to whether the valuation reflects a minority discount or a control premium. The firm must be prepared also to deal with various classes of stock such as convertible preferred or super common shares.

If, for example, the owner of a company sells convertible preferred stock or super common stock to the ESOP, the valuation will be affected by the amount of the dividend and the period for which it is paid on a cumulative basis. The features of the stock and the conversion ratio are factors that can have a profound effect on the value of the stock.

The valuation firm must understand the nature of the ESOP and how the value of the stock can be affected by the impending transaction. If the transaction is for less than 50 percent of the shares outstanding, the appraisal firm will apply a minority discount to the stock. If the valuation firm determines that the ESOP has an option to acquire more than 50 percent of the stock over the next four or five years under independent control, it will quite likely be willing to apply a control premium.

37.4 DUE DILIGENCE IN SELECTING A VALUATION FIRM

The ESOP committee, in selecting the valuation firm, should ask for a sample appraisal to evaluate the quality of the firm's work and the degree of its professionalism.

It is important to review the firm's history, the vitae of the principals, and the credentials of the firm itself. It is crucial that the fiduciaries satisfy themselves in the selection process that the appraisal firm being considered has had considerable experience in valuing stock for purposes of ESOP transactions. Has the firm had experience in representing clients in court or before the Internal Revenue Service (IRS)? It should.

The Department of Labor (DOL) has set forth procedural requirements that must be followed by the valuation firm. The DOL requires that the methodologies as well as the conclusions arrived at in the valuation report can be supported. If this turns out not to be the case, the whole transaction might be unwound and the parties in interest could be subject to penalties.

The valuation must hold up to the potential scrutiny of the IRS and the DOL. The former is concerned with being certain the sponsoring corporation does not take an excessive tax deduction. The latter wants assurance that the employee trust, the ESOP, pays no more than fair market value.

If a problem occurs, it is quite likely to occur in connection with the determination of fair market value. For this reason, the ESOP fiduciary should exercise adequate due diligence in the selection process.

The fiduciaries should, at the very least, determine that the valuation firm has thorough knowledge of the proposed "Regulation Relating to the Definition of Adequate Consideration" (25 C.F.R. Part 2510). The proposed regulations, though withdrawn, are, for all practical purposes, treated as though they are final regulations by the IRS, the DOL, and knowledgeable practitioners.

37.5 WHAT A BUSINESS VALUATION REPORT SHOULD COVER

Business valuation reports should contain the items set forth by the American Society of Appraisers (ASA) as follows:

1. **Signature and Certifications.** All of the individual appraisers who did any meaningful amount of work on, or took any responsibility for, the appraisal report must sign the report and be identified. A statement of certification must be included in the report attesting to the accuracy and truthfulness of the contents, the absence of personal interest on the appraiser's part in the subject of the appraisal, the fact that the appraiser's compensation is not contingent on the result of the appraisal, the fact that no one who is not mentioned in the report provided significant assistance in its preparation, and that the report was prepared in accordance with the Uniform Standards of Professional Appraisal Practice.

2. **Assumptions and Limiting Conditions.** The report must contain assumptions generally attesting to the validity of statements as to the ownership of the business and assets thereof.

3. **Definition of the Valuation Assignment.** The report prepared by the appraiser should define precisely what is being appraised and what standard of

value is being determined—that is, market value, investment value, fair market value, economic value, or some other value standard, and as of what date the report was prepared and for what date the value applies. The report should also state whether the purpose is for an ESOP, gift or estate tax, divorce, sale, or other reasons.

4. **Business Description.** The report should state whether the business is a sole proprietorship, partnership, or corporation. It should outline pertinent facts about the nature of its operations, including its products, market base, market share, extent of diversification of customers, history, and future outlook for the company as well as for the industry as a whole and how the economy might affect the business. The report should indicate whether or not the company is dependent upon one operational person or has a complete backup management team, and any other information that might affect the valuation.

5. **Financial Analysis.** The balance sheet, income sheets, and pro forma projections—including assumptions on which the pro forma is based—should be made a part of the appraisal report and analyzed.

6. **Valuation Methodology.** The methodologies used by the appraiser must be identified and satisfied as to the reasons for their being used by the appraisers. The report must disclose whether minority discounts, marketability discounts, or control premiums were used by the appraiser.

7. **Full Written Report Format.** The report must be in writing and must provide a logical progression for clear communication of pertinent information, valuation methods, and conclusions, and must incorporate the other specific requirements of this standard, including the signature and certification provisions, according to ASA standards.

8. **Confidentiality of the Report.** Unless the client permits otherwise, the client should be the only recipient of the appraisal.

37.6 SUMMARY

An acceptable valuation report must contain no less than the information discussed herein. The better the backup, report quality, and rationale for the conclusion, the greater the likelihood the conclusion will withstand scrutiny by the IRS and the DOL.

CHAPTER THIRTY-EIGHT

Cashing Out Through a Nonleveraged ESOP

A nonleveraged ESOP combined with creative planning can be an ideal vehicle to enable an owner of a private company to unleash his or her nonspendable stock asset and transform it into cash without relinquishing corporate control or burdening the company with debt. This win–win combination can also serve to assist in the gradual and orderly transition of ultimate control of the company, placing it in the hands of the owner's children who have demonstrated an aptitude and desire to carry on the family tradition. Key executives might also fall into a similar category.

Mr. Big is the 100 percent owner of Big Enterprises, Inc., a profitable C corporation. He wishes to perpetuate the firm and wants to find a means whereby he can reward the employees for their loyalty while at the same time giving them an incentive to continue to build the company. He wants to eventually place control in the hands of his two children, both of whom are active in the business. He cannot afford to give his stock away, since it represents his only significant asset. Above all, he has a strong feeling about retaining control of the company until he is assured of two things:

1. His children can run the company.

2. He has accumulated a sufficient nest egg for a secure retirement for himself and Mrs. Big.

38.1 HOW MR. BIG CAN REMOVE HIS CAPITAL, RETAIN CONTROL, AND PERPETUATE THE COMPANY

The corporation can rearrange its capital structure by creating a new class of stock, class B nonvoting common. The corporation will declare a stock dividend of, say, nine shares of class B nonvoting common stock for each share of stock outstanding. This means that 100 percent of the voting capacity rests in 10 percent of the equity, namely, in the class A voting stock. Mr. Big recognizes that his children have insufficient cash to buy out his interest in the business. Yet, he cannot afford simply to give the stock to his children or, for that matter, to executives.

He solves the problem by selling his class B stock to the nonleveraged ESOP. The corporation will make deductible cash contributions to the plan which the trustees will use to purchase class B nonvoting stock from Mr. Big. This process will continue indefinitely, since the amount he sells each year roughly parallels the annual appreciation of the stock he continues to own. Mr. Big and his two children will have stock allocated to their ESOP accounts pro rata to their compensation. This will possibly offset his inability to defer his capital gains tax. However, he will be taxed on the appreciation that will have occurred in the value of the stock he sells above its cost basis since this approach does not qualify for tax deferral treatment under Code Section 1042.

This technique involves a nonleveraged ESOP rather than a leveraged ESOP. The annual deductible corporate contribution is limited to 15 percent of covered payroll, which is a limiting factor. This can be increased to 25 percent by simply adding a money purchase pension plan component to the plan. On the plus side, the corporation will not have to struggle to meet annual debt servicing payments or make interest payments.

In addition to selling stock to the ESOP, Mr. Big can make gifts of some of the class B shares to his children as he sees fit as long as he does so within the gift tax exclusion.

A stock purchase agreement is structured so as to provide that the children who are in the business will purchase the class A voting stock from the executor of Mr. Big's estate. The class A stock would have a very small value relative to the total value of the company. This purchase will be funded by insurance owned by the children on Mr. Big's life. The balance of the class B stock that is not sold during his lifetime could be redeemed over time by the ESOP, assuming the trustees deem the purchase to be prudent. Corporate deductible dollars would be used to accomplish this.

The end result coincides with Mr. Big's goals:

- The stock will be reduced to liquid form so that he will be able to enjoy the diversification that cash brings.

- He will be able to maintain control for the duration of his lifetime.

- The children will acquire ultimate control at very little cost, since the life insurance premiums will be bonused to them by the corporation.

- The employees will gain a lion's share of equity, which will be destined to give them the incentive to become more productive.

- The family, the executives, and the rank-and-file employees will have greater peace of mind in knowing that the company's perpetuation will be assured and dislocations of employees will not occur.

- Mr. Big and his children, who are employees, will also be participants of the ESOP and have a pro rata amount of the stock that he would to the ESOP allocated to his ESOP account since stockholders are not selling stock under Code Section 1042.

38.2 HOW TO FEEL LOVED AND NEEDED AFTER SELLING THE COMPANY—KEEP CONTROL

Control can be everything. This has become a cliche because it has a basis in fact. Equity is important, but with control, equity frequently follows. This downside of equity in the form of private company stock is that it is, in a practical sense, a liability. It triggers a governmental invoice demanding as much as 55 cents of cash for each $1 of nonspendable paper held in the estate at the time of death. It is this fact that drives owners of private companies to seek ways of transforming their paper into cash. Such owners might consider a nonleveraged ESOP as a means of permitting themselves to cash out as they see fit without losing control. In this way, they could have their cake and eat it too. A sidelight, not to be discounted, is the self-assurance that accompanies control. Whether one is loved and adored matters little so long as he or she owns the precious commodity of control.

CHAPTER THIRTY-NINE

Strategies for Selling an ESOP Company to Outsiders

In considering whether or not to sell one's private corporation, an owner must first establish his or her ultimate objectives. Does the owner wish to retire immediately or over a gradual phasing out period? One's age, state of health, and alternative interests must be factored into the retirement decision.

If the owner is young and eager to conquer new vistas, the objective might be to fatten the company for a sale and use the proceeds to found or acquire another company. In any event, the ESOP should be considered as a means to further these goals.

An ever-increasing number of public and private companies are discovering and focusing on the ESOP as an ideal means of placing corporate equity into the hands of employees to reward and promote loyalty and productivity.

An ESOP can have a salutary effect on a corporation that may be considering purchasing the ESOP company. There are many scenarios that might be pertinent. Let's look at a few.

Scenario 1: A private company, Buyer Corp., acquires Seller Corp., a private corporation that has an ESOP which holds some Seller Corp. stock. Buyer Corp. purchases the stock of the stockholders other than that held by the ESOP trustee. Buyer Corp. establishes an ESOP. The stock held by the seller's ESOP is rolled into Buyer Corp.'s new or existing ESOP and is exchanged for Buyer Corp.'s stock of equivalent value. This reduces the amount of cash needed by Buyer Corp. for the transaction, since it had to cash out only the non-ESOP stockholders.

Scenario 2: Public Corp. buys privately controlled Seller Corp. Seller Corp. has an ESOP. Whether the acquisition is for cash or stock of Public Corp., the ESOP can be terminated and both the non-ESOP stockholders and the ESOP trustees can be cashed out and the account balances distributed. Alternatively, the ESOP account balances can be exchanged for Public Corp. stock and rolled into another qualified plan of Public Corp. such as an ESOP, a profit-sharing plan, or a 401(k). If the transition involves a sale of Seller Corp.'s stock, the ESOP participants do not have the right to vote on the deal. If it is a merger, the vote must be passed through to the employee participants.

Scenario 3: Mr. Seller, who owns 100 percent of Seller Corp. stock, wishes to retire but also wants to protect the jobs of the loyal company employees. Seller Corp. has good middle management but has no one individual who is endowed with CEO capabilities. Mr. Seller thinks it would be in his employees' best interest if he would sell the company to his friendly competitor, Buyer Corp.

He would also like to take advantage of the tax-deferred rollout available to those owners of private companies who sell their stock to their own company's ESOP. Here is what can be done to achieve both objectives. Seller Corp. implements an ESOP. Mr. Seller sells at least 30 percent of his stock to the Seller Corp. ESOP. Buyer Corp. establishes an ESOP. Buyer Corp. acquires Mr. Seller's remaining stock.

Seller's ESOP is then merged into an ESOP which Buyer Corp. establishes. Mr. Seller invests the proceeds of his sale to the ESOP in qualified replacement property (i.e., securities of domestic companies). The more he sells to his ESOP, the greater the tax advantage. Mr. Seller might be willing to share some of the tax savings with Buyer Corp. in the form of a reduced price. A consulting agreement might be implemented with a nonqualified deferred compensation plan as an element of the package. Buyer Corp. will have a say as to the percentage of the company it wants to own outright.

Scenario 4: Same facts as Scenario 3 but the strategy is different. In this approach, Seller Corp. is merged into Buyer Corp., a C corporation that has an ESOP. Mr. Seller receives stock of Buyer Corp. income tax-free, Code Section 368.

Mr. Seller then sells his Buyer Corp. stock to Buyer Corp.'s ESOP. Under Code Section 1042, Mr. Seller can bypass capital gains tax if he purchases qualified replacement property within 12 months of termination.

CHAPTER FORTY

The Mature ESOP Company

An ESOP can carry its sponsoring company into a new dimension of experiences that might not have been available had there been no ESOP. However, the mere presence of an ESOP will not have much of an effect on the corporation, its employees, or its outside shareholders unless the following things happen:

- The ESOP is used to fulfill a specific corporate, stockholder, or employee objective.

- The ESOP's presence, workings, objectives, and status of objective fulfillment are communicated to the employee-owners.

- The employee-owners are made to recognize the advantages that can accrue to them if the value of the stock in their ESOP achieves its potential.

- The employee-owners are educated as to how their actions can affect stock value.

- The employee-owners are motivated to think like owners, strive to create stock value, and, in fact, do so.

- The ESOP is managed or governed properly.

Ideally, the ESOP company will have done its homework prior to and during installation of the plan. It is generally not too late to implement training and communication procedures years after the ESOP is installed. If these components are not present in an ESOP company, the underlying cause often lies in the fact that the founding stockholder or chief executive officer (CEO) did not have a thorough understanding of either the potential of the ESOP or how to go about achieving it.

The ESOP is a flexible financial instrument that can be pointed in many directions. For example, the ESOP's sponsor's original stated objective might have been to acquire stock from the major stockholder or from other stockholders for the ESOP. Perhaps its primary objective was to purchase the stock or assets of a competitor, infusing working capital for internal expansion. A two-pronged objective may have been one as simple as waiting to control taxes while increasing employee incentive to maximize productivity.

If the original objective of management was to use the ESOP for acquiring a block of stock from a retiring shareholder, the surviving stockholders might want to increase their equity in the years ahead. They can accomplish this by having the corporation redeem some of the shares of stock that are allocated to participants' accounts and that must be cashed out when the employees terminate, retire, become disabled, or die. In this way, the company reduces the number of shares that are outstanding, thereby increasing the equity value of the stock held by the outside shareholders in proportion to their ownership. This is an alternative to having the ESOP cash out the ESOP participants, in which case the stock is allocated to the participants' accounts, thereby remaining in the ESOP.

A large number of ESOPs have reached an age at which the ESOP that was incurred to purchase a block of stock from a selling shareholder has fully amortized the loan. Now it is time to consider having the ESOP buy an additional block of his or her stock. It is hoped that the company has prospered and that the appraised value of the company has increased substantially. Although the selling shareholder will receive a greater amount for his or her remaining stock, the company's increased cash flow will make it easier to service a larger debt. Although the company is undoubtedly relieved to have gotten the debt paid off, the corporation may possibly have become accustomed to sheltering its taxes by servicing the ESOP debt during the first block purchases. Although it is invariably a pleasant experience to be debt free, there can be ambivalent reactions. The fiscal managers of the company might even breathe a sigh of relief when new financing is arranged to buy another block of stock. The audible sigh occurs because of the company's being able to deduct principal and interest and avoid writing so big a check to the IRS. The company can use the tax savings to accelerate the fulfillment of its obligation to cash out the stockholder or other stockholders who may have been waiting patiently to sell their shares.

40.1 GIVING A PIECE OF THE PIE TO NEW EMPLOYEES

Suppose new employees are hired after the loan to acquire stock has been fully amortized and allocated to the accounts of the existing participants. Such employees will not have stock allocated to their accounts and will feel that they are being disenfranchised. To avoid this, here are some things the company can do:

- Although the outside loan from the bank to the corporation may be, say, five years, make the term of the inside loan from the corporation to the ESOP a longer period, such as, perhaps, 15 years. By doing so, the stock will continue to be allocated to the new employees who become eligible to participate in the plan after the outside loan has been amortized. The problem with this approach is that the corporation will have to wait a longer time for its tax deductions to equal the amount of the loan.

- After the loan has been amortized and fully allocated, the company can continue to make contributions of cash and/or newly issued stock to the ESOP. This will enable the newer employees to have stock allocated to their accounts.

40.2 PLANNING FOR REPURCHASE LIABILITY

In some instances, mature ESOP corporations have been sold because of the cost of cashing out the ESOP participants when they terminate, retire, become disabled, or die. These companies did not do their homework and address their repurchase liability while the plan was still in its early years and it was possible to do so fairly easily. By so doing, a company can diffuse the problem and transform it into virtually a nonissue.

Even in a mature ESOP company, it is imperative to review the effect of the ESOP's repurchase obligation on valuation of the stock. The review should also consider how the problem might be mitigated by instituting a funding program that will get the company started on a path to stabilize and ultimately reverse the decline.

40.3 THE STAGNATING COMPANY

Some maturing ESOP companies are in declining industries. The upside potential may, therefore, be limited. This will tend to retard the growth of the stock. The employee-owners will soon conclude that their heroic efforts to improve productivity are inadequate to overcome the effects of a dying industry. The ESOP can be used to solve such a dilemma.

Management can initiate a program of diversification by using the ESOP to acquire one or more companies in an industry that is enjoying an upward spiral. There should be a fit so that the acquirer's existing personnel and physical plant can be used to maximum effectiveness. In a well-conceived acquisition, restructuring can occur, and duplication of support personnel, warehousing, management, and whole departments can often be eliminated. These savings go to the bottom line, as do the tax savings that can be created by the ESOP.

Many dead-end companies have accumulated significant amounts of cash that the business cannot use to increase profits. The company could lend this cash to the ESOP to be used to make a synergistic acquisition of a growing company in a growing industry. It could thereby reduce or eliminate the need for outside leverage. The one-dimensional company that had been facing a dead end can thus become multidimensional and change its declining fortunes into an upward growth curve.

40.4 PARTICIPATIVE MANAGEMENT

We have observed that many companies that have ESOPs gradually change from a philosophical approach that insulates the employees from financial information pertaining to their company, to an open-book management style. This usually occurs as the companies gain experience with the ESOP environment. Over time, top management often gains confidence in the employees' ability to use profit-and-loss information in a positive manner for the benefit of the company and its non-ESOP owners as well as the ESOP equity owners.

ESOP companies that practice participative management often find that the employee-owners work harder as a team to reverse a downward trend. When profits are high, they are motivated to maintain the high lead or to try to accelerate the growth of profits. Achieving a high level of motivation among ESOP participants depends upon how information is disseminated to the employees and how they are being taught that they can affect the destiny of the company and their own stock value.

The open-book management style is gaining momentum. It is not uncommon for corporations to engage consultants to conduct a course on how to understand a balance sheet and profit-and-loss statement. In some cases, only management-level employees are invited to attend. Some companies make the opportunity available at no charge to all employees who wish to learn these accounting basics. Such a course has little value in getting these employees to apply this knowledge fruitfully, though, unless the company makes sales and profit figures available to them. Participative management coupled with meaningful ESOP equity ownership and an effective communications program have been found to pay off in productivity gains for the company, its stockholders, its employees, and for the community at large. Companies that have had ESOPs for about a decade often have very active employee-run ESOP advisory committees. The employees that make up the committees make recommendations to management, bringing their individual areas of expertise to bear. This takes place in a creative atmosphere that is conducive to adding profit to the company's financial statements and added value to the ESOP stock accounts. This is but one area of governance that will have been refined over the years for the mature ESOP company.

40.5 COOPERATIVE GOVERNANCE ISSUES IN ESOP COMPANIES

Corporate governance involves coordination of the roles to be played by the ESOP's administrative committee, the ESOP trustee, the sponsoring corporation's management and board, and stockholders outside of the ESOP.

Corporate governance is reflective of whether control lies in the ESOP or in the hands of shareholders outside of the ESOP. It is also modified by the percentage of the company's outstanding shares that are held by the ESOP, the percentage that the company's board intends to go into the ESOP, and the amount of annual stock or cash contribution the company is currently making to the ESOP.

The way corporate governance is handled is affected by the success of the company (or lack thereof) and by industry trends. It is also impacted by the annual stock appraisal (assuming it is a private company) and the trend of the company's stock value.

Corporate governance must take into account whether selling shareholders plan to sell additional blocks of stock to the ESOP and over what time frame.

Whether there is more than one class of stock in the corporate structure and whether dividends are funneled into the ESOP will affect the governance aspects of the company and its ESOP. If, for example, the ESOP holds a dividend-paying stock, such as convertible preferred or a supercommon, the ESOP committee might decide to pass some of the dividends through the ESOP to the participants or directly to them. The dividends would be based upon the shares allocated to participants and would be deductible by the corporation. Dividends are not subject to FICA. They therefore have considerably more purchasing power than do equivalent amounts of bonuses. They also have a positive impact on the participants' understanding and appreciation of stock ownership.

ESOP design factors, such as vesting schedules, stock allocation methods, determination of eligibility, and distribution requirements, are important to governance. Governance is also affected by whether the employees are covered by other qualified employee benefit plans, such as 401(k) plans, and the proportion of corporate contributions that goes into each. How the company intends to handle the cash flow demands imposed upon it by the diversification requirements when participants reach ages 55, 60, and 65 is an important point to be considered in corporate governance.

The age of the ESOP will affect the many components of corporate governance. The corporation will tend to develop a mindset so that major transactional decisions will take into consideration how the ESOP might enhance the transaction. The ESOP should have its own counsel. Its counsel should not also be corporate counsel or counsel to the major outside stockholder.

Although the CEO of the sponsoring corporation can be the trustee for the ESOP, he or she must act in a completely independent manner. Even if this is done, the appearance of partiality is sometimes present. Certainly this is true during a transaction in which the major stockholder is selling shares to the ESOP. In these instances, it may be advisable to have an independent corporate trustee. After such a transaction has been finalized, many companies are content to use the majority stockholder as trustee, to eliminate the fee that would otherwise be charged for this service. The trustee takes direction from the ESOP committee. The trustee can resign if it objects to the instructions it receives. A successor trustee can be appointed. Some trustees make a practice of being available for singular transactions.

The ESOP committee can be comprised of one person or many. Typically there are two to four committee members in small to medium-sized companies, but more in larger ESOP companies. Third-party administrators are generally used to perform the duties such as annual filing of the appropriate forms with the IRS, record-keeping, allocation of stock and other assets to the participants' accounts, and issuance of reports to the ESOP committee.

Good corporate governance requires that repurchase liability studies be performed periodically to see if the company is on pace as to its ability to redeem the stock when the participants exercise their put options or have the ESOP repurchase the stock. The ESOP committee should also maintain a grasp on the future trends of the company, to enable it to exercise good judgment in its handling of the ESOP. It should be aware of sales and expense projections, market share positioning, and the need for acquisitions. As the ESOP ages, the expanded experience level tends to make the board members, stockholders, corporate officers, ESOP committee members, the ESOP trustee, and the ESOP participants more comfortable with their understanding of the interactions that should occur among themselves.

Because of the benefits and the motivational aspects indigenous to ESOPs, they should make a corporation stronger than it would otherwise be if it were undertaking an equivalent transaction in any other way.

CHAPTER FORTY-ONE

How and Why to Keep, Freeze, or Terminate an ESOP

Sponsoring corporations install ESOPs with the idea that the plan will be used effectively forever. In line with the adage "Nothing is forever," some ESOP companies decide that they want to stop making contributions to their plans, thereby freezing them. There are numerous reasons why some companies arrive at this decision, but, for the most part, a decision to freeze the plan comes about because the decision makers and their advisors are unfamiliar with the creative uses to which their ESOP can be put. Agreed, there may be situations wherein freezing the ESOP or even terminating it might be advisable. Nevertheless, this conclusion should be reached only after a great deal of research as to possible alternatives and much soul-searching have occurred.

Many ESOP sponsors initiate the plan with a single transaction in mind. This might involve the sale of newly issued stock to the ESOP by the corporation in order to save taxes and to infuse capital, or the ESOP's purchase of stock from one or more stockholders under Internal Revenue Code (IRC) Section 1042. Perhaps the sponsors did not think past the initial transaction as to what function, if any, the ESOP might have in the post-transaction environment. They may have planned to use the ESOP to amortize the debt and, once that was accomplished, to "wind down the ESOP" (whatever that might have meant), and carry on business as usual. After the initial loan has been fully amortized, "winding down the ESOP" probably means one of three things:

1. Continuing to make contributions of cash or authorized but unissued stock to the ESOP, but at a reduced level

2. Discontinuing all contributions to the ESOP (i.e., freezing it)

3. Terminating the ESOP

41.1 REASONS TO KEEP THE ESOP ACTIVE

If the sponsoring company goes into an irreversible funk and its days of profitability are a thing of the past, an ESOP will be of no help. The value of the shares held by the ESOP, as well as those held outside of the ESOP, will continue to erode and ESOP tax benefits will give no advantage to the corporation. The company will be forced to either freeze or terminate the ESOP.

Conversely, if the company continues to enjoy profitability, the corporation could start contributing newly issued stock to the ESOP and save taxes while enhancing the accounts of the participants and, it is hoped, increase productivity. The ESOP would also preclude the need to install a different form of tax-qualified plan that, unlike ESOPs, requires cash outlays.

The sponsoring corporation might use the ESOP to cash out additional blocks of stock from the stockholder or from other stockholders who have aged to some extent since the original ESOP loan was initiated and might be ready to diversify their holdings. Perhaps the sponsors should become more acquainted with ways in which the ESOP can enhance their ability to expand by acquisition.

41.2 FREEZING THE ESOP

Freezing the ESOP means that the ESOP sponsor has decided to make no further contributions to the plan. The IRS must be notified of this course of action (or future inaction) because of the Employee Retirement Income Security Act (ERISA) requirement that the company make "continuing and reoccurring" contributions to the plan. Unless proper documentation is given to IRS, the plan will become disqualified.

Freezing a plan does not change the operational rules at all. For example, as participants terminate, retire, die, or become disabled, they become entitled to receive distributions in accordance with the terms of the ESOP.

Because the corporation is not contributing cash to the ESOP, it must purchase the shares with after-tax dollars and bring the shares back into treasury, thereby removing them from circulation.

The plan activities continue as they had been prior to the freezing of the plan. The reporting and other administration requirements are not affected by the freezing of contributions.

The vesting status of the ESOP participants remains unchanged. The stock in the plan must continue to undergo annual valuation updates and the fiduciaries of the ESOP must avoid decisions that are inconsistent with the best interests of the participants.

41.3 TERMINATING THE ESOP

The third of the preceding courses of action that the sponsoring company might adopt is to terminate the ESOP. Terminating an ESOP is generally quite simple, but under certain circumstances it can become a relatively involved procedure.

Unlike freezing, termination triggers 100 percent vesting of all participants' accounts. The ESOP must commence making distributions within 12 months of the termination date, either in a lump sum or on a five-year installment basis, in equal payments, with adequate security other than employer stock.

The company can distribute cash or stock subject to the right of the participants to demand stock. The need to distribute stock can be avoided if the corporate articles or bylaws stipulate that employees must own substantially all of the stock of the company. This article or bylaw amendment takes precedence over ERISA.

The participants can be given a choice as to whether to receive the proceeds in hand or roll their plan accounts into a profit-sharing plan, 401(k) account, or an individual retirement account (IRA). It is within the sponsor's province to require the participants to roll their plan assets over into another plan.

If a selling shareholder had sold stock to the ESOP and elected to defer taxes under Code Section 1042, the stock he or she sold must remain in the ESOP for a period of three years after the sale. If a disposition occurs under which the stock leaves the plan prior to that time, the corporation will be assessed a 10 percent excise penalty tax. Accordingly, the timing of the termination is important. It should not be done prematurely.

When an ESOP is terminated, an arm's-length determination as to the price of the stock is of critical importance from a fiduciary standpoint.

An in-depth analysis of the termination procedure and related issues is beyond the scope of this book. As noted earlier, no action should be taken except under guidance by knowledgeable counsel.

CHAPTER FORTY-TWO

The Emerging Repurchase Liability

42.1 HOW THE PUT OPTION AFFECTS REPURCHASE LIABILITY

Private corporations or their ESOP trustees must be prepared to repurchase the stock allocated to the accounts of their ESOP participants when they terminate, retire, or die. The put option applies to stock acquired by stock bonus plans after the end of 1986 and to post-1979 stock acquisitions by nonleveraged ESOPs. The put rule applies to stock acquired by leveraged ESOPs after September 30, 1976. But, even if these rules had not been mandated by legislation, private companies would have almost invariably instituted a procedure for cashing out participants.

The put is the obligation of the corporation. There is no put against the ESOP, although the ESOP is frequently the entity that in fact purchases the stock from the terminated employee or from his or her account. It is this obligation to cash out ESOP participants that is referred to as the repurchase liability. Although the repurchase liability does not have to be reflected on the sponsoring company's financial statement, it is nonetheless a liability.

Private corporations seldom want former employees to own stock in their companies. There is always the possibility of minority derivative suits. Moreover, if too many ex-employees own shares, the company may have to register its stock with the Securities and Exchange Commission (SEC). From a morale standpoint, employees want to know there is a market for their shares, not only because they will be taxed on the distribution, but for their long-term security. If the employees know they can count upon the fact that the stock can be translated eventually into cash, they will tend to make the shares more valuable during their careers through greater productivity.

The corporation can distribute cash or stock subject, however, to the terminated employee's right to receive stock. This right or demand can be tempered by an article or a bylaw change restricting stock ownership substantially (probably 85 percent) to employees or to a qualified employee trust (e.g., ESOP).

ESOPs of public corporations for which there is a readily tradeable market are not subject to a put option. This chapter, therefore, will be devoted to ESOPs of private companies, although public companies whose stock is thinly traded might be wise to consider adopting a funding strategy since large block sales by terminating participants might have a disruptive effect on the market price of the stock.

42.2 HOW THE REPURCHASE LIABILITY AFFECTS VALUATION

The good news is the company is growing. The bad news is the more the stock grows in value, the more money will be needed to cash out the participants. There is a paradoxical effect in that as the ESOP repurchase liability increases and greater amounts of cash are contributed to the ESOP to cash out the participants, the growth in the value of the stock will tend to be retarded. Cash will vacate the corporate balance sheets and the valuation may reflect an ever increasing discount for lack of marketability, thereby reducing the price of the stock.

This is somewhat akin to an unfunded defined-benefit pension plan. The sales price the seller of a company will receive will be reduced by an amount equal to the unfunded liability of the pension plan.

By the same token, if the ESOP company does poorly, its stock will be valued at a lower level. One might observe that this will reduce the amount of the repurchase liability. But, the poor earnings might make it even more difficult for the company to come up with the cash needed to cash out the participants even at that lower stock price. Moreover, the employees will be less than euphoric if this scenario were to unfold. A company with future prospects of failure should not adopt an ESOP. However, one whose pro forma smacks of success should strongly consider adopting such a plan.

A funding program that is designed actuarially in such a way as to offset the repurchase liability will correct the valuation slide problem that accompanies the discount for lack of marketability. It will add strength to the company's financial statements and credibility to the ESOP. This will, in turn, have a positive effect on employee morale and productivity.

Distribution strategies are often designed to delay the need for cashing out the participants, but they do not eliminate the need to come up with the cash someday.

42.3 REPURCHASING THE STOCK

If the ex-employee's stock is to be repurchased by the corporation, it will have to be done with after-tax dollars because a corporate redemption is not a deductible transaction. On the flip side, this technique is counterdilutionary since it reduces the number of shares outstanding and held by the ESOP. If stock is to be redeemed by the trustee, it will be done with pretax dollars that the corporation contributes to the ESOP, thereby reducing the net cash flow cost. Purchase of the terminating participants' stock by the ESOP trustee results in no reduction of the number of shares held by the ESOP. It merely recycles the shares.

42.4 WHETHER TO REDEEM OR RECYCLE THE SHARES

Two methods are available for cashing out the shares of the ESOP participants. They are:

- Corporate redemption, in which case the company will purchase the stock from the ESOP participant. The company cannot deduct the redemption.

This has the effect of retiring the shares from circulation, thereby reducing the number of outstanding shares. By doing this, the value of each share is increased. This has a counter-dilutive effect since it reduces the percentage ownership of the ESOP. Each of the ESOP participants have fewer shares so that there will be fewer shares to repurchase in the future.

- Recirculating the shares in the ESOP, in which case the corporation would contribute cash to the ESOP and deduct the contribution, although in the case of an S corporation the deduction is passed through to the stockholder. The ESOP trustee would use the cash to cash out the ESOP participant by paying him or her an amount of cash that is equal to the value of the stock that is in the participant's account.

This has the effect of leaving the number of shares in the ESOP unchanged and its percentage ownership of the outstanding shares unchanged as well. The value of each share is lower than in the case of the corporate redemption, resulting in there being a greater number of shares in each participant's account that must be cashed out in the future.

Recirculating the shares might have a bit of an edge over redemption because:

- The contributions to the ESOP are deductible and

- The contributions constitute an ongoing plan benefit to the employees. Were they not continuing to be made, the company would feel compelled to contribute to an alternate plan such as a 401(k) or profit-sharing plan.

- If the company redeems the shares, the employees may feel that equity is being taken away from then as the number of shares in the trust declines. This perception can be important to consider.

42.5 A FUNDING PROGRAM THAT WON'T WORK

The problem of redeeming the participant's stock is frequently, albeit inadequately, addressed by making cash contributions to the ESOP and maintaining an amount of cash in the trust that will anticipate the repurchase requirements for several succeeding years. The amount of cash to be contributed is determined by projecting near-term retirements. This technique does not adequately address the long-range repurchase liability issue.

As the corporation grows, it will be in a better position to provide the cash for repurchasing stock from terminating participants. The corporation can keep the stock repurchase problem in check so long as its cash flow continues to increase. However, when the corporation contributes cash to the ESOP, its working capital and cash flow will be reduced. This can have the effect of retarding the growth in the value of the stock, which, in turn, might mitigate the employees' enthusiasm for the ESOP. The timing for making distributions to terminating employees is irregular and cannot easily be anticipated. This is not conducive to good financial planning.

Cash contributions to a sinking fund in the ESOP is, in essence, a profit-sharing plan contribution. The cash that is contributed to the trust is allocated to the participants' accounts and adds to their value. It must be distributed to the participants someday just as the shares of stock or their cash equivalent must be distributed. The sinking fund in the ESOP does not address the long-range obligation to buy back the shares of the corporation that are owned by the employee trust.

42.6 THE REPURCHASE LIABILITY STUDY

In order to solve the emerging repurchase liability problem on a long-term basis, the corporation should have a repurchase liability study performed. The study, ideally, should be done at the time the ESOP is being implemented so that the management can anticipate the cash needs of the corporation. During the first decade the problem of cashing out ESOP participants is not generally burdensome. However, the second decade usually requires considerable cash flow to cope with the distributions. The study is an actuarial report that factors in the amount of cash and stock to be contributed over the next 20 years or so, the growth of the per-share value of the stock, turnover, morbidity, mortality, and other factors.

The report should consider the likelihood of major transactions that management may be considering. These might include sales of stock by shareholders who own stock outside of the ESOP, sales of stock by the corporation in order to infuse working capital, and the likelihood of making acquisitions using ESOP techniques. The study must cover the need to have funds on hand to meet the 1986 Tax Reform Act's diversification requirements so that liquidity is at hand when needed. It should also analyze techniques that will maximize flexibility in distributing account balances to the participants. A simple actuarial study of the kind used for pension plans will not address the total financial interrelationship between the corporation, the ESOP, the stockholders, and the employees. The repurchase liability study should also provide recommendations as to how to fund for the liability if it is to be of real value to the plan sponsor.

42.7 A FUNDING PROGRAM THAT WILL WORK

As noted earlier, the valuation will eventually reflect the unfunded repurchase liability. This is another reason why a farsighted funding program should be adopted that will create capital on the corporate balance sheet that will be adequate to meet the amount that is projected to be needed according to the repurchase liability study. The study should project the company's cash needs over a minimum period of two decades. This funding will offset the liability and will permit the corporation to maintain the integrity of the growth curve it currently projects for the future. If such a program is implemented, the owners of the company will be more apt to use the ESOP to its greater capital-formation potential. A well-designed repurchase liability funding program can also enable the corporation to redeem the stock to counteract the effect of dilution.

The diversification rules applicable to post-1986 contributions have served to make the repurchase liability problem more visible at an earlier stage. This legislation requires the trustee to make other investment choices for participants who have been in the ESOP 10 years and who reach ages 55, 60, and 65. This means that the corporation must have ample liquidity on hand to conform with this requirement, and makes funding more important than ever.

The distribution rules do allow considerable leeway in distributing account balances. This is particularly true in the case of leveraged ESOPs because the distribution to employees who terminate for reasons other than retirement or death can be delayed for up to 10 years if an ESOP loan is outstanding.

The design of a funding program to cope with the ESOP's emerging repurchase liability is one of the most important elements that must be dealt with by companies that are considering the implementation of an ESOP. It is of particular importance for those that have had a plan in effect for some years.

The problem is insidious in that there is relatively little in the way of repurchase obligation during the first eight or ten years. The obligations can quite easily be handled out of corporate cash flow during that period. Yet, this is the time when the funding program should be effectuated, since it will be far less costly than when the barn is afire.

42.8 METHODS OF FUNDING THE REPURCHASE LIABILITY

- Cash flow is the most commonly used method that is used for cashing out ESOP participants who terminate, retire, die, or become disabled. As cash leaves the corporate balance sheet it reduces the net earnings of the company, thereby tending to lower the value of the stock.

- Creating a sinking fund in the ESOP is an oft-used method of funding the ESOP. The corporation can deduct the cash contributions that are made to the ESOP but the cash must be allocated to the accounts of the ESOP participants. This, in the long run, will add to the value of their account balances, exacerbating the repurchase liability.

- By going public, the company can possibly rid itself of the repurchase liability. Relatively few companies can count upon creating a readily tradable market for their stock in this manner, but if the initial public offering (IPO) is successful the public market will relieve the corporation of the obligation to cash out the ESOP participants.

- Borrowing to finance the obligation to cash out the employees is rather draconian and costly because of the layer of interest that must be paid.

- Internal markets can be created whereby the employees can purchase the stock from each other. This can become unwieldy and impractical in all but a very small minority of companies. The employee would have to come up with the purchase price with after-tax dollars. At some point, if too many stockholders are created, the stock of the corporation may have to become registered with the SEC.

- Creating a sinking fund in the corporation as a balance sheet item. Corporate-owned life insurance (COLI) can be a practical way to create such a fund since the cash will accumulate tax free and, by using some of the equity-based products that are on the market, this approach can be very cost effective.

42.9 SUMMARY

The ESOP, unlike a pension plan, is not a fund-as-you-go plan. Pension plans are funded in advance while ESOPs are funded in arrears. This is why capital can be created with an ESOP but not with a pension plan. The ESOP is of a different breed and should possibly be funded accordingly, with an approach that will not usurp its basic capital-formation characteristics.

A properly designed funding program will offset the discount for lack of marketability that an appraiser might assign the stock due to an unfunded repurchase liability that would otherwise loom ahead. This is a problem that is quite easily solvable if addressed early and with a long-range viewpoint in mind.

CHAPTER FORTY-THREE

The Charitable ESOP— How to Get a 200 Percent Personal and Corporate Tax Deduction on Your Charitable Gift and Other Strategies

Founders of privately held corporations frequently try to factor favorite charities into their thinking when mapping out their strategy for transitioning ownership to a younger generation. They often feel that payback time has arrived. All too often, their primary asset is the stock of their company for which there is no readily tradable market.

The ESOP can perform wonders in changing this nonliquid asset to one that is highly liquid. The ESOP can generate tax deductions that can actually exceed the value of the stock being donated.

Tax deductions that exceed the value of your gift? Yes, but only through a charitable ESOP (CHESOP). (Please see Exhibits 43.1 and 43.2.)

A CHESOP can help you help your college, hospital, church, temple, or other favorite charitable organization—and yourself.

If you are a stockholder, you can donate shares of your appreciated stock to a qualified public charity, Code Section 501(c)(3), and get a tax deduction equal to the current value of the gift. If you have held your appreciated stock long enough for it to be considered long-term gain property, your limit for the deduction under most circumstances is 30 percent of your adjusted gross income. The limit for cash gifts is 50 percent of the adjusted gross income. Excess amounts can be carried over for five years plus the current year. The gift eliminates the tax on the appreciation over the base cost of the stock. The charitable act also serves to reduce one's taxable estate.

If the security that is given to the charitable institution is publicly traded stock, the recipient, such as a college, usually sells it in the open market to convert the gift

Exhibit 43.1

Model: CHESOP

How to Get Personal and Corporation Tax Deductions That Exceed The Value of Your Gift to an IRS-Qualified Public Charity

- Donor gives public or private corporation appreciated stock, which he or she owns, to a qualified public charity. Value of stock is $100,000.
- Corporation whose stock is gifted has an ESOP, which purchases the stock from the charity.
- Corporation contributes $100,000 in cash to ESOP, which deducts it from taxable income.

Income Tax Deductions:

DONOR'S DEDUCTION	
(For contribution to charity)	$100,000
CORPORATION'S DEDUCTION	
(For contribution to ESOP)	100,000
TOTAL DEDUCTIONS	$200,000

NOTE: Donor reduces gross estate by $100,000.

Estate tax savings: $55,000
(55% estate tax bracket)

Income Tax Savings:

DONOR (35% tax bracket)*	$ 35,000
CORPORATION (40% bracket)	40,000
COMBINED INCOME TAX SAVINGS	$ 75,000

Summary:	
Value of gift	$100,000
Total income tax deductions	$200,000
Total income tax savings*	$ 75,000
Estate tax savings	$ 55,000
Donor's current cash outlay	ZERO
Corporation's gross cash outlay	$100,000

*Assumptions: 35 percent personal tax bracket.
40 percent corporate federal and state tax bracket.

Exhibit 43.2

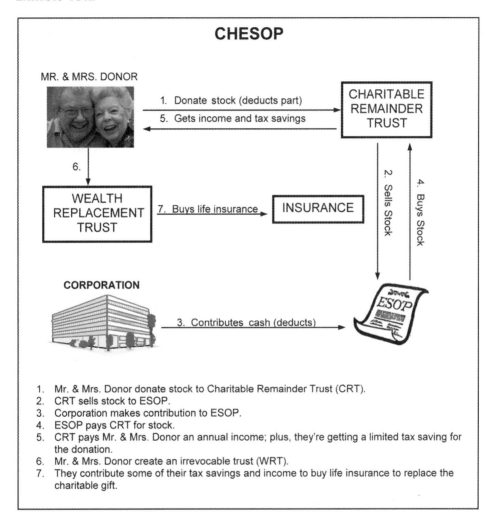

CHESOP

MR. & MRS. DONOR

1. Donate stock (deducts part)
5. Gets income and tax savings

CHARITABLE REMAINDER TRUST

6.

WEALTH REPLACEMENT TRUST

7. Buys life insurance

INSURANCE

2. Sells Stock

4. Buys Stock

CORPORATION

3. Contributes cash (deducts)

ESOP

1. Mr. & Mrs. Donor donate stock to Charitable Remainder Trust (CRT).
2. CRT sells stock to ESOP.
3. Corporation makes contribution to ESOP.
4. ESOP pays CRT for stock.
5. CRT pays Mr. & Mrs. Donor an annual income; plus, they're getting a limited tax saving for the donation.
6. Mr. & Mrs. Donor create an irrevocable trust (WRT).
7. They contribute some of their tax savings and income to buy life insurance to replace the charitable gift.

to usable cash. If the stock is thinly traded, it may be difficult to sell a significant block of stock without adversely affecting the stock's price.

A donation of a minority interest in a nonpublic company is all but useless to a charitable organization, since there is virtually no market for the stock. The charity needs cash—not just a vote as a minority stockholder.

A gift of voting or nonvoting stock may be made in such a way that it is essentially the equivalent of cash from the charity's point of view. Let's assume that the donor is the controlling stockholder in a closely held corporation that installs an ESOP. By donating some personally owned stock to a favorite tax-qualified university, the donor is entitled to a federal income tax deduction on the gift of up to 30 percent of his or her adjusted gross income for the current year plus five years of carryovers. The donor pays no capital gains tax on any appreciation in value above the base price.

The university may then sell the stock to the ESOP, a logical marketplace. The ESOP pays the university an amount of cash equal to the appraised value of the securities. It is assumed here that the ESOP has no prearranged obligation to purchase the stock.

The corporation could contribute cash to the ESOP and deduct this amount if it does not exceed 15 percent or, if applicable, 25 percent of covered payroll.

43.1 TAX EFFECT ON THE DONOR

The donor receives a 100 percent income tax deduction for the current value of the gift. Though the donated stock may have cost only $2,000 and is currently valued at $100,000, the donor is entitled to an income tax deduction on the appreciated value. Moreover, the donor will also avoid recognition of capital gains for tax purposes. If the donor is in the 35 percent federal and state tax bracket, he or she will save $35,000 in income taxes on the gift to a qualified public charity, possibly saving about $20,000 or more in capital gains tax. The estate tax is also reduced by the removal of this asset from the estate. Appreciated stock makes a better charitable gift than does cash from the donor's viewpoint because had he or she sold the stock, the gain would have been taxed, leaving the donor only the net after-tax amount of cash to give to charity. The donor gets a larger deduction and the charity receives a larger gift—all starting with an equivalent amount of stock.

43.2 TAX EFFECT ON THE CORPORATION

The corporation contributes $100,000 of cash to the ESOP, thus providing the liquidity with which the trust can pay for the shares. If the company is in the 40 percent federal and state combined tax bracket, it saves $40,000 in taxes.

The tax effects can be summarized as follows:

- The combined personal and corporate income tax deductions are 200 percent of the value of the gift.

- The combined income tax savings are approximately 75 percent of the gift.

- The estate tax savings, assuming donor is in the 50 percent estate tax bracket, are $50,000.

- The donor avoids the capital gains tax on any appreciation in the stock's value in connection with the transaction.

- The public charity gets $100,000 worth of stock that it can sell to the ESOP for $100,000 in cash, assuming the ESOP trustees are willing to buy the shares.

The procedure can be referred to as a CHESOP.

43.3 THE CHARITABLE REMAINDER TRUST CHESOP

The shareholder might want to kill two birds with a single stone by creating a charitable remainder trust (CRT). He or she can help the charity of choice while getting the benefit of a lifetime income stream.

The stockholder can donate voting or nonvoting stock in a private corporation to a CRT and receive a tax deduction, calculated in accordance with actuarial factors. The CRT will then seek a buyer of the stock which may be the ESOP. The corporation would make tax-deductible contributions of cash to its ESOP to enable it to cash out the charity. The unitrust can give the donor a stated income of not less than 5 percent of the value of the gift on each trust annual valuation date for life. The charity, as remainderman, can receive the amount remaining at the donor's death, thereby reducing estate taxes.

Since the stock is donated rather than sold to the unitrust, the donor pays no tax on the appreciation. Thus, there is a greater trust corpus from which to receive a larger income. The donor can use the tax savings toward the purchase of life insurance in an amount that is equal to the value of the gift. The insurance can be owned by an irrevocable trust, naming his or her children as beneficiaries so that they eventually receive the full value of the gift. Upon death, the insurance proceeds come into the irrevocable trust income tax free and are not includable in the insured's estate, thereby avoiding estate taxes.

It is possible to design the CRT and its form of investments in such a way as to not receive any income since income currently may not be needed. This can be done by designing the CRT as a net income makeup charitable unitrust (NIMCRUT). This allows the charitable trust to retain a greater amount of the investment to accumulate tax free. This will enable the donor to have a greater income stream in later years when more may be needed. The remainder goes to the charity of the donor's choice. The choices can be changed at will right up until the donor is on his or her deathbed.

Some public charities exist that have no specific charitable cause of their own, such as cancer, heart disease, etc. They merely serve as a conduit—an umbrella charity. Community foundations that exist in most medium to large cities have such charitable organizations. A donor who directs the charity as to where the funds should go from year to year is not locked into any single charity but can still get an immediate write-off since it is a public 501(c)(3) charity.

Though these charities will accept cash, real estate, or other property, private company stock is generally ideal from the donor's standpoint. Since it seldom pays a dividend to the donor, he or she would be forfeiting no current income. The stock can also be nonvoting. Taxable gains on appreciation can be eliminated.

The advantages can be summarized as follows:

- Current income tax savings for the donor

- Current income tax deduction for the corporation

- No capital gains tax on the gift; transforming a nonliquid asset into an income stream

- Probably greater lifetime income

- Reduction of estate tax

- No loss of company control

- A cost-effective benefit for the employees

- An eventual tax-free exit vehicle for the company owner

- All without disinheriting the family

- A cash benefit for the charity

43.4 CHARITABLE GIFT ANNUITY CHESOP

Charities often create gift annuities whereby donors can receive an income for a prescribed period or for life. The donor could contribute stock of his or her corporation to the charity in a single transaction or in annual installments, earmarking part of the contribution as a gift and part as a purchase of an annuity from the charity. As the charitable institution is able to obtain cash from the ESOP as payment for stock, the charity pays, at a predetermined rate, a monthly or annual lifetime income to the annuitant. Such payments can be treated partially as return of capital, part as ordinary income, and a portion as capital gains.

Any part of the contribution that was not used as an annuity purchase will constitute a deductible donation within prescribed limits. The gift remainder portion could be calculated so that the deduction would offset the income tax on the annuity. The donor also bypasses capital gains tax and estate tax.

43.5 POOLED INCOME FUND BUYOUT ARRANGEMENT

Some charities create funds that result from the pooling together of smaller donations. These are referred to as pooled income funds. Donors receive a variable income depending on investment results. The donor's income is based on the number of units allocated to his or her account in the fund. If private company stock donated to the charity is placed into a pooled income fund which sells it to an ESOP, the donor will receive a current tax deduction, an ongoing income, and an estate exclusion.

43.6 CHARITABLE LEAD TRUST ESOP BUYOUT

One who gives to a charitable lead trust provides an income to the charity for a pre-determined number of years, at the end of which time the corpus of the gift will revert to the donor or to the donor's named beneficiary with beneficial gift, income, and estate tax consequences.

If the donor gives stock of his or her private corporation, it could be sold by the charity to the donor's corporation's ESOP and the investment yield would provide an income to the charity for the pre-stated time span.

Let's assume that the donor, Bill Big, Sr., wishes to transfer the control of his corporation to his son, Bill Jr., who is being groomed by his dad to become the future chief executive officer (CEO). Big, Sr., could make annual gifts of company stock to Bill Jr. of up to $20,000 annually with the consent of his wife without incurring any gift taxes.

Dad can also make a substantial gift of nonvoting stock to the charity. The charity would sell it to the corporation's ESOP. The charity would receive an income from the sale proceeds for a stated number of years. At the end of that time, the corpus would revert to Bill Jr. essentially tax free. Mr. and Mrs. Big, Sr. would give $1.35 million of their remaining stock to Bill Jr., which at that time was their lifetime gift tax-free exemption. Dad could sell his remaining stock to the ESOP on a tax-deferred arrangement under Code Section 1043.

Result: The charity would receive a much needed income. Dad would be able to transfer stock tax-free to his son whom he will have been grooming to replace himself as CEO. Bill Jr. will have effective control since he would own all of the stock outside of the ESOP and would control the board. Dad would have the corpus of the gift and the proceeds of the tax-deferred sale to the ESOP.

As an alternative, the donor's corporation can purchase the stock from the charity and sell it to the ESOP to recoup its outlay. The company would make deductible contributions to the ESOP to enable the ESOP to buy the stock. It is even possible to subsequently arrange a buy–sell agreement between a future buyer and the charity, to be triggered by the donor's death. Thus, the corporation or the stockholder's grandchildren could agree after the fact that the stock will be purchased from the charity when the stockholder-donor dies. The ESOP could be given an option to buy if the others do not. Insurance on the donor's life funded by the tax savings can fund the various arrangements.

CHAPTER FORTY-FOUR

Mixing and Matching ESOPs with Other Qualified Plans

The ESOP is an ideal stand-alone plan, but it is also a good mixer with either qualified or nonqualified employee benefit plans. A corporation can have a money purchase pension plan, a defined benefit pension plan, a profit-sharing plan, a 401(k) plan, and an ESOP. It would be unusual, confusing, and probably inadvisable, but possible to have all of these simultaneously.

44.1 CONTRIBUTION LIMITS

Code Section 404 imposes a tax-deductible corporate contribution limit of 15 percent of covered payroll for any combination of profit-sharing plans, 401(k) plans (both the employer's contribution and the employees' contribution count), and non-leveraged ESOP or stock bonus plans individually or in combination with one another. 401(k) plans have their own guidelines within this framework. The use of any one of these detracts from the contribution limit available for any other qualified plan.

The maximum contribution for a money-purchase pension plan is, by definition, set in concrete and cannot vary from year to year. The plan may define the level annual contribution amount in a range of from 1 percent to 10 percent of annual covered payroll.

A company might have a defined-contribution pension plan requiring an annual contribution of 10 percent of covered payroll and an ESOP into which it can make contributions of from 1 percent to 15 percent of covered payroll as determined annually by the board of directors. The combination of these two plans in this example permits a deductible contribution of from 11 percent to 25 percent of payroll as decided by the corporation from year to year.

Defined-benefit pension plans have a more complicated limit, which is governed by formula. These plans require that contributions be calculated annually so that the trust will have the precise amount of funds allocated to the participants' account to provide the promised benefit at retirement. The actuary makes assumptions as to turnover, mortality, and investment yield on growth to retirement age. The employer is at risk if the investment performance falls short of the ultimate requirement, in which case the corporation must increase its annual contributions. Conversely, if the plan becomes overfunded, contributions must be reduced or suspended, thereby depriving the corporation of a tax deduction until such time as the overfunding is corrected. Overfunding can also result in the payment of an excise tax.

Profit-sharing plans have the same deductible contribution limit as nonleveraged ESOPs or stock bonus plans, namely 15 percent of covered payroll. Both are flexible contribution plans and the employer is permitted to vary the ratio of the contribution between the plans so long as the total going into the plans does not exceed 15 percent of total compensation.

44.2 PLAN CHARACTERISTIC DIFFERENCES

Typical pension and profit-sharing plans must be diversified and are precluded from investing more than 10 percent of their assets in employer company securities. ESOPs, however, are mandated to invest primarily in such stock. Defined-contribution pension plans and profit-sharing plans can be structured as independent account plans, thereby permitting all assets to be invested in stock of the sponsoring employer. One should exercise caution in using those plans to buy company stock because of the significantly greater fiduciary problems in doing this than are associated with ESOPs. The ESOP is mandated to invest primarily in employer stock, while pension and profit-sharing plans are not relieved of the requirement that they achieve a reasonable return on their investments.

In earlier times, combination stock bonus plans and money-purchase pension plans designed to invest in employer stock were used fairly commonly so that the employer could contribute up to 25 percent of covered payroll, all of it to be invested in employer stock. The 1981 Tax Act allowed corporations to increase their deductible contributions into leveraged ESOPs from 15 percent to in excess of 25 percent of includable payroll, making the combination plan unnecessary.

Neither profit-sharing plans nor stock bonus plans can borrow. Moreover, they cannot afford selling shareholders the opportunity of using the tax-deferred rollout. Profit-sharing plans are exempt from the put option requirements, but stock bonus plans are not. Profit-sharing plans, of course, do not come under the 1986 age 55, 60, and 65 diversification rules since they are already diversified.

44.3 HOW THE 401(K) WORKS WITH AN ESOP

A 401(k) plan is a tax-qualified employee benefit plan that permits employees to defer taxes on compensation. This is accomplished by having the employer reduce the employees' compensation so that it may be contributed to the 401(k) and invested in various investments. The amount that can be deferred is subject to a cap that is adjusted periodically.

The invested funds accumulate in the employees' accounts income tax-free. They are taxed when they are distributed to the employees. Antidiscrimination rules determine the amounts that can be deferred by highly compensated employees. The average percentage of compensation that this segment of the employee population can defer cannot be more than one and one quarter times the average deferred by the lower compensated sector.

An alternative test is provided under the antidiscrimination rules. This limits the deferral of highly compensated employees to an amount that cannot be greater than twice the deferral of the lower compensated employees. If the lower compensated employees contributed, say, 2 percent, the highly compensated group could defer a maximum of 4 percent. Any greater amount would be discriminatory.

(a) The Employer 401(k) Match

It often turns out that an insufficient number of the lower paid employees feel they can afford to defer any of their income. This reduces the amount that the highly paid group can defer. The employer need not match the employees' contributions. In order to increase the level of contribution to the 401(k) plan by the lower-paid group, the employer often matches the employees' contributions by a designated percentage such as, for example, 25 percent of the first 3 percent of pay contributed by the employee. Perhaps the matching amount might be 50 percent of 6 percent or some other formula.

In any event, this can become rather costly for the corporation. Employers sometimes resent the fact that they must use their cash to entice someone to save. They must be on constant alert not to let the ratio of lower paid to higher paid slip below the required percentage, otherwise the highly paid group might have to have their contributions returned to them and taxed. When it appears that this might occur, the employer may feel pressured into increasing the amount it must match. This can be a drain on working capital that can be uncomfortable for a number of companies. The KSOP may be an answer.

(b) The 401(k) ESOP (KSOP)

The ESOP can provide the corporation with a means whereby it can match the employee contribution with employer stock. The company generally feels it can afford to be more generous to the employee by contributing stock rather than cash, while at the same time getting the employee involved in equity ownership of the company. The ESOP can be designed with a 401(k) provision, making the plan a 401(k) ESOP (KSOP).

The maximum amount that can be contributed to the ESOP and to the 401(k) by the employer cannot exceed 25 percent of covered payroll. Leveraged ESOPs are an exception in that interest payable by the corporation to the ESOP for debt service can be deducted in an unlimited amount so long as the ESOP contribution allocations to highly compensated employees do not exceed one third of the total allocations to all employee accounts.

The definition of highly compensated employees relates to a compensation figure that changes periodically and is $85,000 at the time this is being written. Dividends payable by the corporation to the ESOP can also be allocated to the employees' accounts over and beyond the aforementioned 25 percent cap, since dividends are not considered to be compensation.

A nonleveraged ESOP limits the company to a deductible contribution to the ESOP of 15 percent of covered payroll, unless it is a combination stock bonus plan and money-purchase plan, in which case the contribution limit to the ESOP is 25 percent reduced by contributions to the 401(k).

The leveraged ESOP allows the corporation to kill two birds with a single stone by allowing the corporation to deduct up to 25 percent of payroll plus dividends for principal paydown plus unlimited interest on a loan to infuse capital or purchase stock from a stockholder.

The usual situation for a company that is sufficiently healthy to procure financing is that its stock is appreciating in value. In the leveraged ESOP situation, where the stock price is growing each year, the company would be using the stock's annual appreciation to match the employee contribution in the 401(k).

Since the corporation is committed to making annual payments to the ESOP to service debt, the employees have the security of knowing that the company must continue to make its ongoing matching payments. If the stock rises meanwhile, the employees will also benefit from the appreciation.

(c) Administering the ESOP, the 401(k), or the KSOP

The plan must be administered with considerable care, since the sponsoring employer of contribution plans must adhere to strict sets of discrimination rules. The actual deferral percentage (ADP), and actual contribution percentage (ACP), unless the sponsoring employer agrees to contribute 3 percent or more of compensation prior to December of that year plus certain other distribution, vesting and notice procedures, in which case the testing rules will not apply. There is also an overall limit that governs the amount that can be allocated to the totality of all plans. The IRS has issued a private letter ruling, PLR 8828009, dated March 1988, that precludes companies from combining ESOPs with 401(k) plans in determining if both plans are nondiscriminatory. This applies to post-1988 plans. Each plan must stand on its own two feet in meeting the test.

If a company has more than one plan, they should all have the same year in order to simplify the utilization and the administration of both plans. Fortunately, most corporations do not administer their own plans. They rely on outside administrators to cope with the rules.

CHAPTER FORTY-FIVE

ESOPs as an Executive Benefit in Combination with Nonqualified Non-Equity Incentive Plans

In designing a succession planning strategy, a founder often comes to grips with the decision as to how to incentivise selected individuals such as certain managers on whom the owner will rely to build the company in the years ahead.

The simplest form of compensation is, of course, salary. Fringe benefits and perquisites average in excess of 35 percent of base salary. The top layer of super executives in major corporations receive nonvisible perquisites, plus bonuses that often go as high as 150 percent of base salary. Corporations must bear in mind reasonableness of compensation, which has proven to be quite subjective from the viewpoint of the Internal Revenue Service (IRS), the corporation, and the employees. Unreasonable compensation is treated as a dividend and, as such, is not deductible by the corporation.

Merit salary raises, while still in vogue for the lower echelons of white collar and lower supervisory employees, are losing their appeal for the higher echelon executive. Merit increases subject the employee to the possibility of the raise hinging upon personality, or whether there are conflicts with the individual who decides whether the merit increases are granted. For employees below the executive level, the job description is becoming popular as a means of determining eligibility for automatic increases. An employee who graduates to the next higher category on the job description list is entitled to a specific and often publicized salary level.

45.1 DESIGNING THE INCENTIVE PLAN

The real challenge comes in the design of an incentive package that would make a significant difference in corporate earnings. Management by objective has become a way of life in corporate compensation design.

In designing such a package, corporate objectives must be borne in mind. An incentive for an executive to attain a goal that is not in line with that of the company becomes counterproductive. The design of the executive inducement must keep this possibility in mind. Further, the compensation package must be tailor-made for each corporation. There is no compensation standard that will pass the test for every company.

In determining how to increase productivity, the corporation must bear in mind that no two executives are alike and that each is motivated in different ways. Certain proven incentives for some executives are not for others. Management should explore the differences before wasting a lot of time and money on the wrong concept. If, for example, executive Bill Jones is compelled to function 180 degrees off of his norm, he may well develop an ulcer, a breakdown, or become a terminating executive. Executive Mary Smith, on the other hand, may blossom with the new productivity challenges.

Beware of open-ended obligations. Be certain the incentive compensation does not:

- Run both parties into an unreasonable compensation problem

- Create too great a distinction among executives in terms of compensation

- Bankrupt the corporation

Each increment of incentive compensation must be related to the additional increment of pretax earnings which, without the incentive compensation, probably would not exist. Feasibility studies should be made to determine the cost, incremental pretax earnings, and effect on the financial statement under simulated production achievements by the executive or executives under consideration. The best plan is one that is easy to understand. It is free of ambiguities and is straightforward as to its reason for existence. It must be communicated in writing to the executives as well as to staff members who will be involved in administering the plan.

Counsel must pass judgment on the plan to avoid Securities and Exchange Commission (SEC) problems or lawsuits. The accountant must review the impact the plan or plans might have on the financial statements.

Plans must be reviewed each year to see whether they are fulfilling their purpose as employee incentives. Compensation is more effective and generally less costly if the corporation beats the executive to the punch and anticipates the need for enhancement before the executive is forced to request it. Things are never quite the same if the employee is put into the position of requesting improved benefits.

One of the virtues of nonqualified plans is that they do not interfere with the contribution limits of an ESOP as do pension or profit-sharing plans.

Nonqualified incentive plans can be discriminatory, unlike ESOPs, which are nondiscriminatory and broad based. There are a variety of nonqualified plans that can be designed to complement ESOPs. Although an ESOP must be nondiscriminatory to meet ERISA requirements, the plan can indeed provide greater benefits for the more highly paid employees. Since the ESOP is almost invariably noncontributory, it requires no burdensome near-term or long-term capital outlay by the executive. This is quite different from a stock option plan wherein, if the stock appreciates, the executives will have to come up with a bundle of cash in order to take full advantage of the appreciation. An ESOP participant can look forward to receiving the ultimate distribution of benefits with no coinciding monetary obligation except for paying taxes at that time. Those taxes can be deferred still further by rolling the distribution over into another qualified plan such as an IRA.

In spite of the nondiscrimination rules, the highly compensated management group will also receive a greater portion of the forfeitures of those who terminate. This makes their participation in the ESOP even more meaningful. The executive will receive ESOP participation statements at the end of each year showing ever-increasing values due to new employer contributions, forfeitures, and valuation changes, assuming the stock valuation has not declined sufficiently to offset the quantity of shares added to his or her account. The maximum amount of an employee's annual compensation that can be considered for allocation purposes in an ESOP is $175,000 at the time this is being written. This figure is adjusted periodically. Allocations of dividends, forfeitures, and interest can be added over and beyond this if not more than one third of the contribution is allocated to highly compensated employees.

The incentive characteristic of an ESOP varies somewhat in proportion to the valuation of the stock. Noting that greater earnings increase the value of the stock, the executive will be predisposed to enhance the value of his or her account through greater productivity. The management group might go so far as to keep a weather eye out for those employees who do not carry their weight, thereby leveraging the productivity factor.

One will also think long and hard before terminating employment, an act that would trigger forfeiture of the nonvested interest in the trust. It is quite common for the plan to be designed so as to provide for deferring larger distributions and spreading them over a five-year period in the event of preretirement terminations. This provides a further deterrent for leaving. The extended payment approach also gives the corporation the benefit of preparing for the liquidity needed for distributions.

By contrast, other types of incentive programs such as phantom stock option plans or stock appreciation rights tend to tie up corporate cash on a near-term basis, since the measurement point is usually short-range.

The corporation normally prefers an incentive program that has long-range retention goals. The executive, by contrast, tends to like the idea of as much cash up front as possible, but also has a natural desire for postretirement security. The ideal incentive package is one that can satisfy the needs of the corporation and the executive.

A combination of an ESOP and, say, a participating units plan (discussed in the following chapter) might be an example of such a combination. The latter provides the sweet smell of cash and the ability to use it in the not-too-distant future. The deferred aspect of the ESOP gives the executive greater freedom to spend and enjoy the fruits of the more current distributable awards under the participating units plan.

A current cash distribution plan brings with it current tax payments and, for one who is in the top tax echelon, the resulting erosion of purchasing power detracts from its glamour in the year received. The stock in the ESOP helps offset this since it grows unencumbered by taxes.

(a) Phantom Stock Plan

This is really a form of deferred compensation whereby the company agrees to pay selected executives an amount of cash in the future equal to the value of a determined amount of stock in the company, including dividends that would have been paid on that block of stock. The stock, however, is not distributed to the employee. Thus, it has sometimes been referred to as *phantom stock*.

Job performance criteria generally govern the number of phantom stock units to be awarded the employee. One unit might equal one share of stock. A vesting schedule can be included. Cash payout can be in the form of a lump sum, but it is more likely to be doled out in annual installments beginning at the end of the deferral period.

Young companies with little track record and with a young executive staff quite frequently have a short deferral period of just a few years, whereas older companies with older executives tend toward normal retirement age maturities.

The executive is not taxed until he or she receives cash payments, at which time the payout is considered earned income for tax purposes. The corporation takes a tax deduction in the year of the payout to the employee. The expense is accrued annually and the income statement is charged based on the year-end value of the phantom stock units allocated to the employee. Nonvested forfeitures are credited since those amounts had been expensed out previously. At payout time, the income statement is not affected because the charge had already been made.

One of the advantages that this form of compensation package has over stock options is that this is truly a cash transaction. Security regulations are not applicable to phantom stock, whereas they do apply to stock options.

(b) Stock Appreciation Rights Plan (SARs)

Stock appreciation rights are identical in essentially every respect to phantom stock—with the exception that the former are based upon the increase in stock price plus dividend equivalents, whereas the latter is based upon the full stock value plus the dividend equivalents. In this regard, SARs are a less costly increment to compensation than phantom stock. Both are taken into consideration by the IRS in determining the reasonableness of compensation. Neither creates stock dilution as do nonqualified stock option plans. They do, however, require concern as to maintenance of liquidity in order to avoid fiscal surprises in the event executives who are partially or fully vested terminate. Liquidity can be maintained on a reasonably sound basis by using turnover and mortality factors in anticipating requirements. SARs work well with ESOPs.

(c) Performance Share Plan

This is merely a form of stock bonus plan wherein units are granted in accordance with executive performance as measured by a predetermined method. It is used as an incentive for the executive to achieve greater heights.

The shares are granted after the performance objective has been achieved and are not taxed to the executive until he or she actually receives them. The plan is identical in all other respects to the nonqualified stock bonus plan as described earlier. Performance share plans, like any other bonus type of program, has no relationship to ESOPs other than the fact that they provide a *now* benefit—cash in hand. Of course, the dividend pass-through can also provide current cash to ESOP participants.

(d) Participating Units Plan

One of the shortcomings of stock-oriented incentive programs is that the executive has little control over the fair market value of the shares. The participating units plan contemplates a bonus in the form of cash to be delivered to the executive at a future date, in accordance with a formula conceived with corporate growth objectives in mind.

Each unit can have a zero value at the base period or a starting value of, say, one dollar or ten dollars. The unit increases or decreases in value in proportion to the executive's success in meeting the assigned goal. The goal can be contained within a section or a division, or it can encompass the whole company. The change in unit value is measured from the date of award to the end of the deferral period, which can be any number of years such as two, three, four, or five.

Vesting can be utilized, and part or all of the vesting amount can be distributed in the form of cash from year to year, at which time it is received as earned income by the executive and expensed out by the corporation. The amount accrued for the executive at the end of the deferral period can be paid in installments, thereby enhancing the company's working capital.

Units start out with a new base value each year and achieve their own new value during the deferral period. The unit value at the end of each year is accrued on the corporate books, and the income statement is charged for the unit values as they are allocated rather than being charged at the time of cash distribution to the executive.

Since stock is not involved, SEC regulations are not applicable. The corporation must, nevertheless, be diligent in arriving at a formula that will limit its additional compensation costs to the extent that it is prudent from a fiscal standpoint, and reasonable as to compensation from the standpoint of both the corporation and the employee. The plan can provide great incentive for achievement, and is primarily popular in medium and large corporations. The concept is conducive to improving tenure among executives who are reluctant to forfeit nonvested benefits.

(e) Supplemental Executive Retirement Plans (SERPs)

The inadequacy of retirement benefits has become quite apparent in our society. It is highly visible among executives who are accustomed to high living standards and find themselves incapable of setting aside an amount sufficient—after taxes—to provide adequate income at retirement. This is particularly true when one considers the impact of inflation on retirees who rely on fixed income plans.

A supplemental executive retirement plan (SERP) provides an income over and above the amount that can be provided under qualified pension plans, profit sharing plans, or ESOPs. Qualified plans must be nondiscriminatory. SERPs can discriminate in favor of the prohibited group (highly compensated executives).

The various tax acts that have been enacted have left the nonqualified compensation plan, or SERP, attractive and unscathed. Under this concept, the corporation agrees that if the executive continues to be employed by the corporation for a stated number of years (generally to normal retirement age), the corporation will, commencing upon fulfillment of his or her service obligation, pay to the executive an annual income for a defined period. In the event the executive dies prior to receiving all due benefits, the income that he/she would have received would be payable to the surviving spouse or other named beneficiary.

In order that the income not be taxed to the executive until the money is actually received, there must be a reasonable element of forfeiture on the executive's part. An example of this is the forfeiture that would occur if creditors had the prior right to corporate assets and earnings that might otherwise be used to pay the executive. Thus, in the event of the company's bankruptcy, the executive might be left out in the cold with no income.

The SERP is technically unfunded in order that the funds not be construed as belonging to the executive. Any funds that the corporation will have retained for general corporate purposes are accumulated with after-tax dollars; however, the payout to the executive is treated as a deductible compensation expense to the company and is taxed to the executive or to the surviving spouse as earnings in the year the income is received. This is true even if a so-called *Rabbi Trust* is used. The Rabbi Trust ensures that the corporation will not squander the funds before the employee receives them. The deferred-compensation or SERP package is subject to IRS scrutiny in terms of reasonableness, along with all other compensation. This form of benefit can be more cost effective than the others.

45.2 PROVIDING THE CASH TO THE CORPORATION FOR A SERP

There are numerous ways in which the corporation can make provisions to have the funds on hand at the time they are needed. One of the more common ways is by obtaining insurance on the executive's life and making itself owner, beneficiary, and premium payer. The policy ownership should be structured in a manner that makes it unrelated to the employee's benefit so as to avoid constructive receipt.

The cash values which accrue as company surplus on a tax-favored basis provide a substantial corporate balance sheet offset against premium outlay. Alternatively, they can be borrowed, subject to certain tax restrictions, to enhance corporate cash flow. The policy can be paid up at the executive's retirement, and at the time of death, the insurance proceeds go into corporate surplus essentially tax-free, subject only to the alternative minimum tax, enabling the corporation to meet the deductible payments to the executive's surviving spouse.

The cash value can also be used in the event of the executive's retirement. The corporation can pay out $1.66 of deductible compensation (assuming the company is in the 40 percent tax bracket) for each dollar of cash reserve. Or the company could meet its payout obligation out of then current cash flow. The company would retain the policy, which will have been paid up prior to retirement. At the executive's subsequent death, the policy's proceeds will flow into corporate surplus on a tax-favored basis to enable the company to recover the cost of the compensation program.

A vesting schedule can be included or, if preferable, the plan can be entirely forfeitable as a *golden handcuff.* A nonqualified deferred-compensation plan is useful as an incentive tool in that it is flexible in design, simple to administer, free of SEC problems, and requires no prior IRS letter of determination. The executive finds it appealing since it is tailored to his or her individual needs. This program makes a splendid fit with an ESOP.

45.3 THE ESOP AS A COMPENSATION PLAN

The ESOP, as an incentive program, has a great deal going for it. It fulfills many of the corporation's nonaltruistic needs, such as increasing working capital and cash flow, buying owner's stock, or helping the company gain market share through acquisitions while giving a long-term beneficial interest in the company to the employees. In order to meet the costs of some of the other compensation packages, the corporation might consider the ESOP as a means of reducing the after-tax cash outlay by simply making contributions of newly issued stock to the ESOP in an amount equal to those costs—thereby letting the tax savings reduce the net after-tax cash outlay to zero.

Let's assume that the corporation has granted phantom stock options to an executive. Upon exercise, the corporation makes a cash payment to him or her in an amount equal to the spread between the grant price and the strike price (i.e., the growth of the underlying stock).

The company can offset the after-tax cost of the cash it pays to the executive by making a contribution of newly issued stock to its ESOP in an amount that will create a tax saving that is equal to the after-tax cost of the phantom stock cash outlay.

Example

Corporation's cash outlay upon exercise of phantom stock option	$10,000
Less taxes saved (40% T.B.)	<$ 4,000>
Net after-tax outlay (decrease in working capital)	$ 6,000
Corporation's stock contribution to ESOP (zero cash outlay)	$15,000
Taxes saved (increase in working capital)	$ 6,000

Result: The after-tax cash outlay for the exercise of the phantom stock is offset by the taxes saved by the contribution of stock to the ESOP. The executive also benefits as a participant in the ESOP. An employer might want to get a partial tax offset by contributing a smaller amount of stock to the ESOP.

ESOPs afford those employees who like to invest their own funds an opportunity to do so. The plans may be designed so as to permit employees to make voluntary contributions to an ESOP with after-tax dollars. The investment yield accumulates tax-free. One's contributions must not exceed 10 percent of compensation. If the employee's contributions are invested in employer stock, the transaction will be considered a sale of stock to the employees. In this event, the stock may have to be registered on a Form S-8 under Section 2(3) of the Securities Act of 1933 unless it falls under the SEC exemptions stated in Sections 701, 702, and 703.

If the employees' voluntary contributions are invested in money market instruments in the stock of other companies, the transaction will be exempt from the 1933 Securities Act.

ESOPs tie in with long-term objectives while bonuses and some forms of nonqualified plans are geared to short-term incentives. By placing its emphasis on long-term objectives rather than on bonuses, the corporation will reduce its compensation expense in connection with those employees who are not destined to remain for a long duration with the company. It will reward those who stay with the corporation and help it grow in the years ahead. This will enhance corporate profitability and its competitive position.

CHAPTER FORTY-SIX

Equity Participation Planning

46.1 INTRODUCTION

Employers are rightly concerned with their ability to attract good, high-quality, effective managers and to retain them. They also give considerable thought to ways to give these managers incentive to improve productivity and enhance the bottom line.

ESOPs have been proven to work well, by themselves or in tandem with other forms of equity plans, as an incentive to those on whom the benefits are bestowed. It is also only natural that executives and other managers who are employed by, or who are considering becoming employees of, a privately held company are concerned with their abilities to share in any successes that their efforts might bring about. They are all too aware of the relatively short time they have before retirement, at which time money at work will be needed to replace man at work.

Private companies carry a great deal of uncertainty as to their disposition when their owners decide to call it quits. How will the company survive? Will it be sold to outside strategic buyers, go public, or be transferred to family members or to the executives? Executives and other managers would like the security of knowing that whatever happens to the corporation, they will own a piece of the equity.

Aside from cash incentives, there are five primary stock-sharing methodologies that should be considered by companies that recognize the importance of sharing not only the vision, but also the equity in the employer's stock. These methods are:

1. Stock options:

   - Incentive stock option plan (ISO)
   - Nonqualified stock option plan (NSO)

2. Direct stock purchase programs

3. Stock purchase plans under Code Section 423

4. Nonqualified stock bonus plans

5. ESOPs

6. Restricted Stock

These six primary equity-sharing approaches, in no particular order, can be used independently or in combination with one another. The decision as to their use lies in an understanding of their characteristics.

46.2 STOCK OPTIONS

Stock options are commonly used in connection with publicly traded corporations. They are starting to be used for privately held companies as well. Stock options granted by employers provide certain employees with the right to buy a specific number of shares of company stock (typically at that day's price) by some later specified date.

Stock options are cashless and tax neutral at the time the employer grants them, from the perspectives of both the employer and the employee. When the stock options are exercised by the employee, though, there will be a tax consequence. ISOs entitle the employee to preferential tax treatment and, because of this, must conform to a number of conditions specified by the IRS. NSOs, in contrast, do not afford special tax treatment to the employee and can be designed with virtually no restrictions.

Both forms of options share a few common objectives. They are used to give selected employees an opportunity to share in the growth of the company without using any corporate cash. The employees are thereby motivated to make the shares grow in value, so that when they exercise their options at the lower grant price, they can realize the profit. In granting stock options, the corporation does not invade its working capital or cash flow.

The creating of stock options does not inhibit the company's ability to grow. This increases the grantee's potential for greater stock appreciation.

Stock option plans are used as a recruiting device to attract good executives to the company. They also serve as a "golden handcuff" to retain them. This can be accomplished by designing the plan with a vesting provision that restricts the employee from exercising the option for a certain number of years after the date of grant. Restriction periods of three, four, or five years are common. Vesting periods often overlap. For instance, one year after a number of options are granted with a three-year vesting period, the company might grant another set of options with a new three-year period, thereby keeping the carrot dangling for two additional years. The "golden handcuff" is very effective if the stock price moves higher. If, however, it does not go beyond the grant price, or declines below that price, the "handcuffs" become ineffectual.

46.3 INCENTIVE STOCK OPTION PLAN

The ISO has certain tax advantages for the employee because it lets him or her defer taxation from the date the option is exercised until the stock is sold, at which time the employee is taxed on the gain over the price of grant. The gain is taxed at capital gains tax, rather than ordinary income tax, rates.

Eligibility for ISOs is determined by the sponsoring corporation's board of directors. ISOs can be limited to specific management levels or groups. Alternatively, the ISO allotment can be spread among all employees. If desired, the options can be doled out to the employees in accordance with their salaries, as a factor of corporate profitability, or by other selection formats.

These are the seven requirements set forth by the Internal Revenue Service (IRS) for this favorable tax treatment:

1. There must have been a written plan document approved by the corporation's stockholders. The plan must recite the class of employees that is eligible to receive options and the number of shares that can be issued under the option plan.

2. The options must be granted within 10 years of the date the plan is adopted.

3. The employee to whom the option was granted must keep the stock for a minimum of one year after the date of exercise and two years after the date the option was granted.

4. No more than $100,000 worth of stock options can become exercisable in any year.

5. Only employees can be given incentive stock options.

6. The exercise price must be at least 100 percent of the market price of the underlying stock as of the grant date.

7. If the employee owns more than 10 percent of the voting power of all of the outstanding shares at the time of the grant, the exercise price must be at least 110 percent of the market value of the stock on the date of the grant, and the option may not be exercisable more than five years from the grant date.

46.4 ISO TAX TREATMENT

There is no tax deduction available to the corporate plan sponsor if the employee exercises the option prior to the end of the holding period. However, the employee can use capital gains tax rates on the spread between option grant price and exercise price, as opposed to using ordinary income rates.

If the employee exercises the option without meeting the holding period requirement, the spread will be subject to ordinary income taxation, rather than capital gains taxation, on the part of the employee, and the amount of the spread can be deductible to the corporation.

46.5 NONQUALIFIED STOCK OPTION PLAN

In contrast to the ISO, an NSO has virtually no restrictions. The sponsoring corporation can design the plan to suit its objectives because there are no tax advantages for the employees.

46.6 NSO TAX TREATMENT

The employee optionee will be subject to paying tax, at the ordinary income rate on the gain at the time of exercise above the price at the time of the grant. The corporation will be entitled to an income tax deduction on that same spread between grant price and exercise price.

46.7 STOCK OPTIONS—AN EMPLOYEE WIN/NO LOSE DEAL

Stock options are a win/no lose deal for employees. Once they have the option, it is strictly up to them as to whether and when to exercise the option. If the value of the stock declines after the option has been granted, they simply do nothing and allow the exercise date to expire.

If, by contrast, the stock increases in value after the date of grant, the employee will, of course, purchase the stock at the price that was fixed as of the date the employee was granted the option. It is a win/no lose deal for the participating employees if the options are granted in addition to, rather than in lieu of, another form of benefit.

Assume, for example, that Widget Company grants an option to an employee that will permit him or her to purchase 1,000 shares of Widget Company stock within a three-year period from the date the option was granted, at the $2 price that existed as of the grant date. Further assume that the value of the stock doubles in two years to $4 per share. The employee will most likely either exercise the option for a $2-per-share profit (rather than take a chance that the stock will drift back down) or wait a bit longer in the hope the stock will continue to rise.

In the case of an ISO, the person who exercised the option must continue to retain the shares of stock that he or she acquired in the ISO process for a period of two years after the date of the grant and one year after the date the option was exercised. The employee will, therefore, be at risk for a period of one year, assuming the option was exercised after two years. Moreover, in the case of an NSO, the optionee will face a cash outlay for the tax incurred as a result of exercising the option.

46.8 VESTING OF THE OPTIONS

A great deal of latitude is permissible in designing a vesting schedule for both ISOs and NSOs. They can be designed to be fully vested at the time of grant; more often they are subject to gradual vesting, such as 33⅓ percent per year for three years or 20 percent annually for five years. Alternatively, they can be designed with zero vesting for three, four, or five years and 100 percent at the end of those periods. A new grant and vesting period would begin before the vesting period of a prior grant has been completed. If the new options are granted each year, a new vesting period applies to each new option grant, thereby creating a rolling vesting effect. As noted in Section 46.2, this is a form of "golden handcuff" because the employee would forfeit some options if he or she left during the vesting period.

46.9 STOCK OPTIONS FOR EMPLOYEES OF CLOSELY HELD COMPANIES

Stock option plans are available to privately held corporations, but are used far less frequently in nonpublic companies than in public corporations although the gap is closing rapidly.

Privately held companies most often are run in an entrepreneurial style. Such companies generally have a scant handful of stockholders, and often only one or two. Bringing others into the inner sanctum as potential outright stockholders can, in many cases, require a culture change on the part of the founders.

Granting employees an option to acquire stock is quite different from affording them equity ownership in an ESOP, wherein their status is that of having a beneficial interest in the ESOP trust. The only direct stockholder pursuant to an ESOP is the trustee. If the stock option plan covers too many employees, a securities registration may be required before the stock is purchased by the employees.

46.10 DETERMINING STOCK VALUE FOR PRIVATE COMPANY OPTIONS

A decision must also be made as to how the stock is to be valued; unlike a publicly traded company, the stock of a private company has no readily tradable market. For purposes of the stock option plan, the stock can be valued by formula, or the value can simply be book value. Alternatively, the value can be determined by an independent valuation firm. If the sponsoring company has an ESOP, the valuation for the ESOP can be used for the stock option plan as well.

When a stock option is exercised by the employee, it will dilute the ownership of the other shareholders, including the ESOP, assuming the company has one.

Stock option plans for closely held corporations are more practical in situations wherein the founder wants to groom one or perhaps several employees to accede to a top position as a future chief executive officer (CEO) or chief operations officer (COO). The owner might want to demonstrate faith in those employees and give them tangible evidence that they have the potential to succeed the owner someday. The owner may prefer to do this rather than create new stockholders immediately.

46.11 PROS AND CONS FOR STOCK OPTIONS IN PRIVATE COMPANIES

(a) Cons

Founders of closely held companies are entrepreneurial by nature and usually prefer to make and pay for their own mistakes without having to report to others. It is partially for this reason that they might be reticent about creating new minority stockholders by making available to certain employees stock options—which will, of course, eventually result in those employees' becoming actual stockholders.

ESOPs in private companies need not create any new stockholders among the employees, even though all of the employees may possibly become participants. The reason for this is that the trustee, who might be the founder, is often the sole outside stockholder other than the founder. The employees accumulate equity without full shareholder rights.

(b) Pros

Stock options can allow the employee who is concerned with succession planning a means of testing whether one or more specific promising employees will someday be able to succeed the founder. The vesting schedule will help the owner weed out employees who are not likely to work out.

The options can provide some managers who might become a buyout team with a block of equity ownership at a favorable price that can eventually become the nucleus of the buyout.

Stock options can also be used as a means of providing incentives to specific managers to start thinking more like owners and strive to increase the underlying value of their options. Options can work well in concert with an ESOP.

46.12 DIRECT STOCK PURCHASE PROGRAMS

If the corporation's objective is to make stock available to one or more employees, it can do so in a variety of ways. It can disseminate stock according to a formal, structured program or one that has little or no uniformity. The direct purchase program falls into the latter category. The sponsor simply offers the employees the chance to buy its stock, generally on a payroll deduction basis.

If the company is not publicly held, it must be mindful of securities laws that might apply if the firm makes offers to more than a certain number of persons to purchase stock.

If the company is public, some of these securities issues will have already been addressed, although there may still be registration requirements. With this in mind, a corporation can sweeten its offers to selected employees by granting stock options to those who also purchase stock.

Corporations frequently offer employees the opportunity to buy a certain number of shares of the stock at a discount and may even lend the employee the funds to acquire the stock. The discount is deductible by the employer. Although the discount is unlimited, the employee is taxed on the discount at the time it is granted.

46.13 STOCK PURCHASE PLANS UNDER CODE SECTION 423

Stock purchase plans that are structured to comply with Code Section 423 are generally designed to permit all full-time employees who meet tenure requirements to participate. Those who own an amount of stock equal to or greater than 5 percent of the outstanding stock are ineligible to participate. These plans afford eligible employees the right to buy stock at a discount. The offering price can be as low as, but no lower than, 85 percent of the fair market value.

To be eligible, an employee must work at least five months of the current calendar year at least 20 hours a week and must have been employed by the company for two or more years.

The employee will not be subject to any taxation on the discount until he or she sells the stock. At that time, the discount is taxed to the employee as ordinary income.

Stock acquired under a Section 423 program is subject to certain holding requirements for purposes of the tax treatment when the stock is sold. If the stock is sold two or more years after the date the purchase right was granted, or after one year of the date the employee purchased the stock, the total gain will be taxed to the employee at capital gains tax rates. If the employee sells the stock prior to those time frames, the discount will be taxed to the employee as ordinary income. An employee can deduct the discount from taxation only if the employee sells the Section 423 stock before the end of the holding period noted earlier.

Stock purchase plans can be used as a means of instilling an ownership culture in employees, because the participants actually invest their own cash in the company. This plan also infuses working capital into the sponsoring corporation, although this does not usually appear to be the driving force in the decision to adopt this type of plan.

46.14 SECURITIES ISSUES

As noted in Section 46.13, the sponsoring corporation must be cognizant of the myriad of securities laws at both the federal and state levels. There is a great deal of variance among the states. A number of factors must be considered to determine whether a particular type of stock dissemination program will require that the company register its stock. There are exceptions that might be applicable, having to do with the amount of stock being sold and the number of individuals being invited to participate. It is of utmost importance to consult informed counsel on this subject.

46.15 THE NONQUALIFIED STOCK BONUS PLAN

Nonqualified stock bonus plans, not to be confused with qualified stock bonus plans, are relatively common fringe benefits used primarily in large public companies, but they are useful in a number of private companies as well. For public companies, the stock market price usually governs the fair market price. For private companies, valuation is in accordance with a formula such as book value or fair market value as established by independent appraisal.

Actual shares are granted by the corporation to the executive with no monetary contribution on his or her part. The nonqualified stock bonus plan need not be submitted to the IRS for special tax treatment since there is none. The allocation of shares can be based upon performance or simply on the basis of position so long as the element of compensation reasonableness is maintained.

The shares can be granted outright or placed on a vesting schedule, the latter being popular when employee retention is a goal. An executive will think long and hard about leaving the firm if he or she must suffer substantial forfeitures under the program. The stock bonus plan is something used to recruit prime candidates who are looking for a piece of the action. It is used more often, however, as an incentive, tied into the executive's performance and the achievement of certain production or profit goals.

The corporation deducts an amount equal to the market value in the case of a public company, or fair market value when used in privately owned companies. The tax deduction takes place in the tax year in which the shares are granted to the employee. The executive receives earned income tax treatment based on the market value as the shares are granted, and is taxed on the gain at the time of sale of the shares.

The shares are unrestricted. The executive can sell them at any time without putting up any capital to acquire the shares, as would have to be done in the case of options. For this reason, an outright bonus is more meaningful to the executive than options that may prove worthless. With actual shares of stock, the executive is assured of market value, which is subject to fluctuation.

A stock bonus plan in a public company offers a marketplace in which executives can sell their stock. Such a plan for a privately owned company would be likely to include a right of first refusal of the corporation to buy the stock from the executive at the agreed upon formula or price. The owner of a closely held corporation may not be enamored at the prospect of having to accept a minority shareholder, and for this reason is not nearly so likely to adopt a stock bonus plan as is a public company.

From an accounting standpoint, the compensation liability is accrued as are dividend equivalents credited from the point of grant. The statement reflects a compensation cost as the shares are accrued.

As the stock is issued, the accrued compensation expense is credited to capital stock. The issuance of the stock under the stock bonus plan is dilutionary and does not bring capital into the corporation. It is discriminatory, which adds to its appeal from the owner's standpoint.

Shareholder approval is required and the shares must be registered. The owners of the stock are subject to Securities and Exchange Commission (SEC) rules relating to insider trading.

46.16 RESTRICTED STOCK PLAN

A popular way to transfer actual stock of the sponsoring corporation to selected executives is by means of restricted stock. Under this program an employee is granted stock of the company subject to substantial rights of forfeitures as well as restrictions as to transferability.

These substantial risks of forfeiture will lapse if the employee remains an employee of the company for a stated period of time after the stock was granted to the employee. In the event of forfeiture, the shares will revert back to the corporation.

It is not uncommon to require that at such time as the employee eventually terminates employment subsequently to their becoming unrestricted, the employer is given a right to purchase the stock at its then current value. There would also be the requirement that the employee sell the stock to the corporation.

The employee will not recognize any income at the time the restricted stock is granted but will be taxed on the value of the stock at the time the restrictions lapse. The company will receive a corresponding compensation tax deduction at that time [Code Section 83(a)], unless he or she files a Code Section 83(b) election to be taxed at the time of grant as ordinary income. The employee's gain at the time of sale would be subject to capital gains tax.

Because of the restrictions, the value of the stock being valued would be subject to a significant discount for lack of marketability. If the restricted stock is granted after the company has leveraged itself, such as in connection with a leveraged ESOP, the per-share value of the stock will be reduced. This would be advantageous to the recipient of the grant since the gain upon the stock's sale would be greater.

46.17 EMPLOYEE STOCK OWNERSHIP PLANS

It is estimated that about 13 million employees are accumulating equity in their companies as participants of ESOPs.

Unlike the other stock-related plans discussed in this chapter, ESOPs do not require or even permit cash outlay on the part of the employees for the acquisition of stock in their ESOP trust accounts, or for the payment of taxes, because the ESOP is a tax-qualified plan. The ESOP can be used in conjunction with the other categories of stock plans, serving typically as the underlying plan that includes virtually all employees other than those who are in excluded categories.

Although ESOPs can be used simply as a means of getting stock-based equity into the employees' accounts, they have unique financing characteristics that create added value for the sponsoring corporation and its shareholders.

Except in fairly rare instances, ESOPs do not require registration of the stock involved. This is unlike some other programs that are designed to enable a broad spectrum of employees to acquire stock of their employer. ESOPs are the only plans discussed in this chapter that fall under the requirements of the Employee Retirement Income Security Act (ERISA).

46.18 SUMMARY

This chapter provided an overview of some of the more popular types of programs that can provide employees with a means to acquire equity in the employer company. An in-depth discussion of these programs is beyond the scope of this chapter.

There are many nonqualified plans such as stock appreciation rights and phantom stock options that are incentive-driven programs; these are described in the main volume. These plans do not actually put stock into the employees' hands but are related to stock appreciation.

CHAPTER FORTY-SEVEN

Profiles of Likely Candidates for ESOPs

A profile of likely candidates provides an overview of firms that should explore an ESOP's possibilities. The ESOP is not for every company. It is especially important to determine the basic goals of those who control the corporation being evaluated as an ESOP candidate. The strength, structure, and earning capacity of a company must be considered as well.

Specific characteristics to consider before matching a company with an ESOP:

- C corporations should be in the top income tax bracket, with the likelihood of remaining profitable in order to enjoy the tax advantages of an ESOP.

- Subchapter S corporations that have significant, steady, and sustainable earnings, although they are not taxed at the corporate level, should consider an ESOP.

- The company must be a domestic corporation and only its domestic employees can be participants in the ESOP.

- The corporation may be privately or publicly owned.

- The company must have ample coverable payroll, that is, full-time domestic employees who are not part of a collective bargaining unit, unless the corporation wishes to include union employees in order to achieve the tax savings to justify the cost of implementing the ESOP.

- It may be acquisition oriented. The corporation can make acquisitions with pre-tax dollars using ESOP methodologies.

- It may be seeking to make a divestiture. The corporation can facilitate this by making it possible for buyers to purchase the division with pretax dollars.

- If it is a private corporation, it may have major or minor stockholders who wish to cash out either immediately or over a period of time. The ESOP provides a private pretax method for accomplishing this.

- A corporation whose stockholders are of different ages with different exiting timeframes.

- A stockholder who wants to diversify assets by selling part of the company.

- A management group wants to buy the company or a division of the company. This can be more readily accomplished with an ESOP than through a conventional leveraged buyout.

- It may be a public corporation wishing to avoid a takeover. An ESOP can tender for shares with pretax dollars and serve as a friendly voting block.

- A company that has major stockholders who desire creative and tax-advantageous methods of providing liquidity in their estate planning.

- It may be looking for ways to service debt for future financing or refinancing existing debt. Principal and interest can be serviced with pretax dollars through an ESOP.

- The corporation may have a profit-sharing plan. It may be possible to convert it to an ESOP, thereby possibly using some or all the assets to buy company stock.

- The company wishes to increase working capital and cash flow.

- A company whose owner wants to make way for successor management, such as working heirs or other key executives, fits the profile of an ESOP candidate.

- In many cases, the owner simply wishes to transfer ownership to the employees tax free in lieu of other employee benefits.

- The corporation is a profitable public company that feels its stock price on the open market does not reflect its true value, or management is convinced that it would be more advantageous to be goal oriented for long-term results than quarterly profits that are demanded by outside stockholders. Such a company might want to go private through a leveraged ESOP buyout.

- The corporation is failing, and the employees, who face imminent unemployment wish to acquire the company so as to preserve their jobs and turn the company around and are receptive to wage concessions.

- The corporation may want to thwart unionization of its employees.

- The corporation, for altruistic reasons, wants to have the employees own a greater piece of the action. This has become more and more commonplace.

CHAPTER FORTY-EIGHT

Security Law and the ESOP

It is seldom that private corporations that have ESOPs face a securities issue, but one should be aware of possible situations wherein securities law might come into play relative to the sale of stock other than to an ESOP.

The Securities and Exchange Act of 1933 (SA'33) requires the registration of offerings of securities, while the Securities and Exchange Act of 1934 (SA'34) regulates matters pertaining to reporting antifraud and insider trading.

There are exceptions to the registration requirements that pertain to ESOPs of privately held corporations. If the employees are not asked to purchase stock of the sponsoring company either directly or by directing that funds be transferred from another qualified plan to the ESOP to be used to buy company stock, the shares would be exempted from registration requirements. Conversely, if the employees are given the opportunity to use cash that is in their qualified plan to buy stock, it might require that the stock become registered under SA'33. There are exceptions to the registration requirements that must be examined on a case by case basis.

Registration of the stock is not required where the corporation either contributes cash to the ESOP which is then used to purchase newly issued stock from the company, or where the corporation simply contributes cash to the plan. Nor is registration required in those situations wherein stockholders sell their shares to the ESOP.

In considering the applicability of federal and state law, it should be noted that the ESOP trust is a single stockholder, notwithstanding the number of participants in the ESOP.

48.1 SIMPLIFYING SECURITIES COMPLIANCE

Rule 701 of the Securities Act of 1933 was amended as of April 7, 1999, to simplify the compliance requirements that private issuing companies must meet when making offers to employees enabling them to buy stock through broad-based stock purchase plans, 401(k) plans, or in connection with stock option plans. The rules apply to a variety of compensatory benefit plans or written contracts in connection with certain offers and sales of securities, including ESOPs and 401(k) plans wherein employees are permitted to invest in employer securities.

Federal law allows corporations to make written offers to invest in these securities to directors, general partners, trustees, officers, consultants, or advisors without registering the stock. This can be treated as part of a compensation agreement.

48.2 ANTIFRAUD REGULATIONS

The issuing company must adhere only to the antifraud disclosure regulations if the amount of stock sold is less than $12 million. If the amount of stock sold exceeds $5 million, the issuer must also disclose copies of the plan under which they are making the offer, as well as the risk factors involved in the security being offered. Certain financial statements must also be disclosed.

48.3 REGISTRATION EXEMPTIONS

There is a formula for determining the amounts of securities that can be offered without being registered; the offering is exempt from federal registration requirements if the sale of stock in the offering during a 12-month period does not exceed the greater of:

- 15 percent of the assets of the issuer as of the last day of the company's fiscal year;

- An amount not exceeding 15 percent of the outstanding securities of that class, including stock options; or

- $1 million.

Use of this exemption from federal law does not relieve the issuer from complying with laws of the states wherein the offer is made.

There are safeguards related to ESOPs that preclude the possibility that the sponsoring company may create so many shareholders as a result of distributions of stock to ESOP participants that the stock may have to become registered.

The put option as well as a right of first refusal diminishes the opportunity of private company stock from reaching third party hands, as does a bylaw or charter amendment that restricts ownership of substantially all the stock to employees. Assuming that stock were distributed to the ESOP participants, stock distributed to participants of a private company's ESOP is generally subject to an investment letter that prevents resale of the securities to a third party.

In any event, if a company makes an offer to sell its stock only to residents of the home state of the sponsor's principal office and the sponsoring company derives 80 percent of its gross revenue as a result of business it conducts in that state, the offering is exempt from registering under federal law.

Irrespective of state boundaries, Rule 505 of the SEC's Regulation D permits a company to offer to sell its securities without registering them to up to 35 investors even if they are nonaccredited, so long as the offering does not exceed $5 million.

If the offering does not exceed $500,000, there is no restriction as to the number of buyers even if they are neither accredited nor sophisticated and SEC registration is not required (Reg D Rule 504).

48.4 STOCK OFFERINGS TO SOPHISTICATED OR ACCREDITED INVESTORS

Registration can generally be avoided if the issuing corporation offers to sell its securities only to sophisticated or accredited investors.

Sophisticated investors are considered to be those individuals who have the capability of assessing the merits and risks of investments and making informed investment decisions with or without the assistance of professional advisors.

The term *accredited investor* can comprise qualified Employee Retirement Income Security Act (ERISA) benefit plans, corporations and/or their officers, executives and directors, partners, partnerships, or individuals who, with or without their spouses, have a net worth of more than $1 million or an annual income for the preceding two-year period exceeding $200,000, or $300,000 including spousal income, with the likelihood of it continuing at that level in the years ahead.

48.5 PUBLIC COMPANY ESOPs

ESOPs of public companies are considered to be affiliates and the registered shares fall under Rule 144, which inhibits their tradeability unless an independent trustee acquires the stock and subsequently sells it. Registration of publicly traded stock that is distributed to individuals is not generally required because of the various applicable exemptions. This is also true of the stock distributions from ESOPs that hold registered shares. These shares can become freely tradable without restriction when distributed to plan participants.

48.6 BLUE SKY LAWS

Blue sky laws of the various states should be researched thoroughly for any possible application to ESOPs. These laws vary from state to state and should be reviewed carefully and irrespective of the exemptions from registration under federal law, certain states might require registration of the securities offering.

All aspects of the securities laws should, of course, be cleared with counsel.

CHAPTER FORTY-NINE

Fiduciary Considerations

All qualified plans under the Employee Retirement Income Security Act (ERISA) are required by the Department of Labor (DOL) to have a minimum of one fiduciary. The plan must actually name the fiduciary or prescribe the procedure whereby a fiduciary is named or otherwise identified.

A fiduciary, as defined by ERISA, is any person to the extent:

- He or she exercises any discretionary authority or control over the management of the plan;

- He or she exercises any discretionary authority or control regarding the management or disposition of plan assets;

- He or she renders investment advice for a fee with respect to any money or property of the plan; or

- He or she has any discretionary authority or responsibility in plan administration.

Prior to the ESOP's existence, those individuals who design the plan are not fiduciaries according to the DOL's Advisory Opinion document 76-65. The same document further stipulates that in the design phase prior to the ESOP's existence, those who render service are not parties in interest.

ERISA's definition places into a fiduciary role the following: plan trustees, those persons who are involved in plan administration, members of an ESOP investment or administrative committee, the sponsoring corporation, corporate officers and directors, investment advisers, and those who supervise those persons. This definition applies to all forms of tax-qualified plans. A person who exercises or has the power to exercise a fiduciary function is a fiduciary irrespective of the title. Fiduciary activities include the ESOP's management or administration of the acquisition or investment of the plan's assets, delegating or having the power to delegate such duties to other fiduciaries or having the ability to make decisions relating to the ESOP.

Prudence dictates that ESOP fiduciaries be represented by independent legal as well as financial counsel, since the fiduciary is responsible for all ESOP-related decisions.

49.1 THOSE WHO ARE NOT FIDUCIARIES

Department of Labor (DOL) Regulations Section 2509.75-8 notes that certain functions are not fiduciary duties because they are ministered in nature. They include the following:

- Application of rules to determine eligibility for participation or benefits

- Calculation of service and compensation for benefit purposes

- Preparing communications to employees

- Maintaining participants' service and employment records

- Preparing reports by government agencies

- Calculating benefits

- Explaining the plan to new participants and advising participants of their rights and options under the plan

- Collecting contributions and applying them as specified in the plan

- Preparing reports covering participants' benefits

- Processing claims

- Making recommendations to others for decisions with respect to plan administration.

49.2 INVESTMENT DIVERSIFICATION AND FAIR RETURN EXEMPTION

While pension and profit-sharing plans are required by ERISA to diversify plan investments and realize a fair return on them, considerable relief is given to the fiduciaries of ESOPs. ESOPs are mandated to invest primarily in qualifying employer securities and are exempt from the *fair return* and *diversified investments* rules that apply to other qualified plans.

49.3 EXCLUSIVE BENEFIT OF PARTICIPANTS

An ESOP is precluded from making a loan to anyone, although the reverse of such a transaction is sanctioned by ERISA, so long as the loan to the ESOP is for the exclusive benefit of the plan participants and their beneficiaries and at a reasonable interest rate. The ESOP can sell securities of the sponsor for adequate consideration (fair market value) provided that there is no commission involved in the transaction. It has been determined that a plan can be for the exclusive benefit of the participants and their beneficiaries while still benefiting the sponsoring corporation and its shareholders. The IRS observed that both seller and buyer can benefit from a leveraged ESOP transaction. Revenue Ruling 69-65 referred to the exclusive benefit of the employees rule as follows:

"This requirement, however, does not prevent others from also deriving some benefit from a transaction with the trust. For example, a sale of securities at a profit benefits the seller, but if the purchase price is not in excess of the fair market value of the securities at the time of the sale and the applicable investment requisites have also been met, the investment is consistent with the exclusive benefit retirement."

49.4 TRUSTEE SELECTION

It is the duty of the fiduciaries to make hard decisions within the nonprecise boundaries of fairness to the employees.

Choice of a trustee who is conversant with the issues concerning ESOPs is most important. It should also be noted that the ESOP lender should not serve as trustee to the plan according to a ruling by the Department of Labor. DOL Advisory Opinion 76-32 states that a bank that is a secured lender to the sponsoring corporation of the ESOP should not serve as ESOP trustee because of the possible conflict of interest.

49.5 ESOP AS A TAKEOVER DEFENSE

If an ESOP is to be used as a takeover defense, this fact must be disclosed in the proxy statement. If an ESOP is established and funded prior to the advent of a tender offer, this is undoubtedly an acceptable procedure. If the ESOP's implementation and funding occurs subsequent to a tender, a request for an injunction by the potential acquirer might very well be upheld. Unless the ESOP uses a totally independent trustee, it is possible that a conflict of interest might be perceived.

49.6 MULTI-INVESTOR LEVERAGED BUYOUTS

LBOs are those wherein management groups or outside investors invest hard cash for their share of the equity while the ESOP borrows to acquire stock for the employee participants. It is advisable that the ESOP hire an independent fiduciary as early in the transaction as possible and that the fiduciary should have independent legal and financial advisors. The independent fiduciary, usually the trustee, should opine prior to the closing of the transaction as to its fairness for the ESOP. While the independent fiduciary is concerned with getting the maximum return for the ESOP participants, they walk the tightrope because they know that the cash investors will do the deal only if they receive a rate of return that they feel is reasonable for them. Reasonable expenses that the committee incurs can be borne by either the corporation or the ESOP.

49.7 ADEQUATE CONSIDERATION

The principal duty of a fiduciary to the ESOP is to assure its participants at least as favorable a return on investment as other investors receive (i.e., adequate consideration), factoring in the relative levels of risk borne by each party. The use of different types of securities has a distinct bearing on the degree of risk. For example, convertible preferred stock has smaller downside risk than common stock that pays no dividends but relies on performance by management to achieve equity growth. Each class of stock must be valued separately in order to determine that the transaction will meet the standard of adequate consideration.

An ERISA violation by a fiduciary could trigger remedies as extreme as requiring him/her to repay the losses incurred by the plan or as mild as a 5 percent excise tax on the amount that was involved in the transaction. Corporate indemnification may prove adequate for this risk, however fiduciary liability insurance is available at a reasonable price and should be considered by the fiduciaries.

CHAPTER FIFTY

How to Communicate ESOP Benefits to Employees for Greater Public Relations

ESOPs can be left to gather dust in the bottom drawer or can be placed on a pedestal as a constant reminder that the employees own equity in the company. Some companies expend considerable effort to capitalize on this fact by proclaiming themselves to be ESOP companies or even employee-owned companies. This carries with it the implication of better quality control and the suggestion that, all things being equal, an ESOP company is better for the consumer. ESOP companies do give their employees the incentive to achieve perfection in their work, thereby becoming more competitive and more profitable and increasing the value of their shares.

If employees and the community at large are constantly reminded of the fact that they have a stake in the company, productivity should improve. This should be followed by an increase in the value of the stock allocated to participants' accounts as well as the stock owned by the stockholders outside of the ESOP.

The IRS and the DOL, underscoring the need to communicate benefits, have set forth minimum requirements for disclosure of key elements of the ESOP to employees. They can be capsulized as follows:

- Employees must be notified of the intent to adopt an ESOP;

- Notice to interested parties must be posted or distributed;

- A summary plan description (SPD) must be provided for each participant.

So much for the mandatory aspects of disclosure. Let's move on to the nonmandatory and equally important facets of communication—the meat of the program that brings on the fun part of ESOPs. The enjoyment comes when the employer begins to notice improved morale and greater productivity brought about by employees feeling that they have a piece of the action.

If the plan participants are uncertain as to what their *action* consists of—or indeed whether or not it really exists—a benefit plan can become counterproductive. By merely stopping at the SPD, the employer may be taking too much for granted. The corporate owner may be giving the employees too much credit for basic knowledge about mundane facts. One should note that very few employees have ever owned stocks. Many surprisingly simple questions have been brought up at employee meetings, such as:

- What is stock?

- What are dividends?

- How are profits determined?

- How does management decide how much to contribute to the plan?

- What if the value of the stock declines?

- How much do I get when I retire?

The first commandment among journalists is that a story responds to the questions that flash into every reader's mind—What? Who? When? Where? Why? Employees ask the same questions at meetings but add others to the list. How? What if? What is meant by?

The SPD does a fair job at getting communications on the proper track, but it falls short at the point where subjective thinking begins. There is just no substitute for eyeball-to-eyeball sessions, preferably at small gatherings, which tend to reduce inhibitions among the attendees. The larger the number of questions from employees, the greater the interest and appreciation of the program. A lack of questions at the meeting does not necessarily mean that they will not be asked somewhere else or at some other time. And when they are, those responding to such queries will lack the expertise that the well-informed conductor of an organized meeting will have. That's why careful consideration should be given to electing the meeting leader.

Bulletins relating to various areas of employee interest are always well received and well read if they are interesting. Employees enjoy being the first to hear about the new defense contract that was awarded to their firm, or about the public's response to the new product that has just been unveiled by the marketing division. A point of interest about the ESOP should be interspersed between items in the bulletin.

Posters are powerful instruments of communication. And while they are used with great success as brainwashing devices in dictatorial states, no inference of bad intent should be drawn here when it comes to using posters to convey the spirit of employee ownership. Perhaps a poster contest to kick off the ESOP might help get everyone off and running. The more involvement the better.

Slide and other audiovisual presentations are available—some being more effective than others. It is quite possible that the sponsoring company may wish to design its own slide show, or have a custom show created by an outside resource. The program should be made part of the indoctrination of new employees even though they may not yet be eligible to participate in the ESOP. It shows them what lies ahead.

An employee benefit booklet can range from being devoid of graphics to incorporating expensive layouts that run the cost through the roof. In any event, the booklet should be thoroughly informative; otherwise it might raise more questions than it answers.

An effective method of bringing into focus the meaning of the company's ESOP is to prepare a printout for each participant projecting the value of his or her account balance to the age of retirement. This would be based on certain conservative assumptions of annual contributions of stock and/or cash, forfeitures from turnover, salary growth rate, and stock growth rate.

Productivity improvement is likely to result if one or two alternate assumptions are made as to the rate of growth of the stock. Employees can see what a slight additional effort on their part can mean to them in dollars and cents.

An important side effect of broadcasting the fact on the letterhead and elsewhere that the company is employee owned is the fact that customers like to deal with owners. They anticipate the likelihood of receiving more reliable treatment, and they will experience it. Greater sales mean productivity gains.

Communications deserve time and thought. A well-conceived information program can more than pay its cost in improved productivity and employee morale. Management should factor in measuring devices to see what kind of feedback it is receiving. The tried-and-true suggestion box can tell a great deal. After all, with an ESOP, participants will gain by the company's overall progress and well-being.

50.1 BUILDING THE OWNERSHIP CULTURE

For a program of communicating the ESOP to be effective, the corporate objectives must first be clearly understood by top management. As obvious as this may seem, relatively few companies have defined, written, and disseminated a Roles and Missions statement among its hierarchy or employees at large.

The ESOP communications program gives the company a superlative opportunity to develop a relationship of mutual respect among senior managers, middle managers, and other employees. It should propel the employees to an awareness of ownership when they approach their duties so that they treat their job environment and attitude toward customers as owners rather than as renters.

The ESOP communications process can give employees a better understanding of the effect that such things as good customer relations, large market share, good service, and product innovation can have on the value of the stock in their ESOP accounts. A good ESOP communications program must be permanent and should blossom and develop a patina with age. It can and should infuse the employees with an ownership culture.

After a while, the process will be transformed from an "ESOP communications program" personified by memos, directives, and videos, to open participation. Communications should evolve from a one-way direction to a two-way street that will address employee concerns, an employee hot line to senior management, face-to-face meetings between senior managers and employees and calibrated awards for suggestions leading to efficiencies, quality-of-life enhancements, and greater profitability.

The ESOP can become the catalyst for improved profitability, corporate expansion, and enhanced employee relations and motivation. The better the communications and participative management, the greater the reward. It has been determined that the combined effect of participation and ownership leads to better employee performance than either component by itself.

CHAPTER FIFTY-ONE

ESOPs for Lending Institutions

Small or medium-sized banks or savings and loan institutions are often family controlled and possibly face succession planning issues. By installing an ESOP, the financial institution can create an internal tax-favored market for its stock but will find that the plan has other rewarding benefits that are uniquely beneficial for that form of business. This chapter will discuss some of these benefits.

51.1 WHY A BANK OR A SAVINGS AND LOAN SHOULD ADOPT AN ESOP

A bank or a savings and loan, whether public or private, whose ownership is concentrated in relatively few hands, family or otherwise, can dispose of large blocks of stock with little fanfare or publicity by selling the stock to its ESOP. A bank cannot redeem its own stock but an ESOP can buy it and do so with tax-deductible dollars. This makes it tailor-made for getting liquidity into the stockholders' hands and the stock into the employees' ESOP accounts. ESOPs are also often adopted by financial institutions to infuse working capital. Another bank or savings and loan (S&L) lends money to the ESOP and the funds are used to acquire newly issued stock in the sponsoring bank. The funds create capital that can generate a 10 or 20 to 1 lending capability. These leveraged transactions have also been used for financing the leveraged buyouts (LBOs) of other banks, thereby increasing the acquiring bank's scope of operations and lending ability. This, in turn, leads to greater earnings.

The multiple effect is probably more applicable to the banking industry than to any other. This leverage can be given great impetus by the adoption of an ESOP whether it borrows money or not. A bank or savings and loan can contribute newly issued stock to a nonleveraged ESOP or a stock bonus plan in an amount up to 15 percent of covered payroll. The contribution is tax deductible and the tax savings are achieved with no cash expenditure.

For a bank or S&L in the 40 percent combined state and federal tax bracket, an ESOP can create $1 of tax savings by making a deductible contribution of $1.66 of newly issued stock to the ESOP. Each dollar of increased working capital and cash flow, as noted above, lets the bank expand its lending ability as much as twenty-fold. If the bank has a qualified profit-sharing plan and converts it to an ESOP, this can provide even greater cash flow.

The assets of the profit-sharing plan could, within the realm of prudence, be used to purchase the bank's newly issued stock, thereby improving its lending power. These capital infusion factors can lead to greater earnings, which, in turn, tend to offset dilution. Another offset is the greater productivity that can result from equity participation among the employees.

The stock of many banks and S&Ls are thinly traded. Such institutions often consider going private. A bank is not permitted to redeem its own stock. If it were, it would have to do so with after-tax dollars. In any event, an ESOP offers an alternative to stock redemption by the bank. In order to go private, the number of stockholders must be reduced to below the 300 mark, thereby eliminating the need for meeting expensive disclosure requirements. The ESOP would provide a more certain market for the remaining shareholders. Finally, the bank holding company can use the ESOP for refinancing existing debt on a more favorable basis. If an ESOP owns as much as 25 percent of the bank's stock, it must register as a holding company. This is not an onerous problem, however.

The shares owned by the ESOP may become a major voting block on behalf of management since employees tend to vote in favor of management when a vote is passed through. This is useful in hostile takeover situations.

The fact that productivity would be expected to be enhanced by the equity ownership enjoyed by ESOP participants should have a salutary effect on earnings and lending capacity.

Stockholders of privately owned banks and S&Ls that have ESOPs would be afforded a marketplace for their shares without the need for the bank to go public. This would serve as an alternative to going public or selling to outsiders in order to provide liquidity for current stockholders.

The positive effect on employee morale should be significant since the shares held by the ESOP trustee in their accounts can become their retirement nest eggs.

As noted above, banks and S&Ls are often precluded by law from redeeming their own stock. This had proven to be an impediment to their establishing ESOPs since leveraged ESOPs had permitted employees to demand stock upon distribution. Banks are given an exception to the requirement that stock be distributed if state law prohibits banks from redeeming stock. They can distribute cash instead.

51.2 ESOPS AND BANKS AS ESTATE TRUSTEES

Banks are often trustees of the estates of recently deceased owners/chief executive officers (CEOs) of private corporations who left the controlling stock of the company in trust to the inexperienced spouse. The trust asset might consist of a majority block of closely held stock or thinly held public stock having no way of being cashed out other than at a distressed price. As executor and trustee of many estates, a bank finds itself in many can-of-worms situations that cause trust officers sleepless nights. On the one hand, there is no market for the nonpublic stock—on the other, offering a large block of thinly held public stock would tend to depress the price. The bank can be criticized if it holds onto a stagnant stock and subject to litigation if it sells at what might be a ridiculously low price. So it's damned if it does and damned if it doesn't.

Let's take the case of such a corporation that has a decent track record and is paying taxes in the top bracket. Here an ESOP might be just what the doctor ordered. Here is how the *bail out* of a widow's stock in a private corporation works:

1. The corporation installs an ESOP to which the bank, assuming it is not also serving as trustee to the ESOP, makes a loan that will let the ESOP purchase the widow's stock at fair market value. The corporation will make tax-deductible contributions to the ESOP to service principal and interest.

2. The ESOP purchases stock from the executor of the estate at a price determined by third-party appraisal, thereby avoiding criticism. This provides liquidity with which the executor can pay taxes or diversify holdings in the estate.

3. The executives and other employees become the new owners, and the bank's trust department breathes a sigh of relief.

In upholding its fiduciary role, the bank no longer needs to choose between two equally unappealing solutions, liquidating or selling to outsiders, to see that the widow's best interests are served.

Without a mechanism such as an ESOP, the business might be subject to liquidation to pay the estate taxes. ESOPs let the corporations maintain its executive staff, which might have drifted away because of the uncertain future of the control of companies. Chances are the bank will retain a corporate customer that might otherwise have been lost while at the same time avoiding a potentially festering problem.

51.3 ESOPS FOR FEDERAL SAVINGS AND LOANS

The ESOP incentives and regulations apply to S&L institutions just as they apply to other corporations. S&Ls must also adhere to regulations superimposed upon them by the bank board. That institution has given implied approval for the adoption of ESOPs by federally chartered S&Ls. This is true of state chartered S&Ls as well, subject to limitations that may exist in various states.

An ESOP is permitted to acquire as much as 25 percent of a class of securities of an S&L on its own or in conjunction with other companies or individuals. If the ESOP in concert with others acquires more than 25 percent, it will fall under the restrictions of the bank board.

51.4 S&L AS AN AFFILIATED PERSON

If an ESOP of a federally insured S&L holds 10 percent or more of the stock of the S&L, either by itself or aggregated with others, it is deemed to be an affiliated person of the S&L and, as such, would be precluded from making or guaranteeing a loan to an affiliated person. As such, it could not engage in a mirror loan transaction (i.e., the S&L borrows and relends to the S&L or guarantees the repayment of a loan to the ESOP). If the stock holdings of the ESOP remain below 10 percent, this restriction will not apply. In any event, the S&L would in all likelihood be permitted on a no-commitment basis to make contributions to the ESOP in order to service a loan even as an affiliated person.

A federally chartered S&L is not permitted to make loans to an unaffiliated ESOP if the funds are used to purchase stock of the S&L holding company or for the holding company's benefit. The holding company can guarantee a loan to its own ESOP under any circumstance of affiliation. A federally chartered S&L is not allowed to lend to an ESOP if the proceeds are to be used to purchase authorized but unissued shares of the S&L.

American Institute of Certified Public Accountants' (AICPA's) statement of position requires that an ESOP loan or the corporation's guarantee of such a loan must be carried on the financial statement as a reduction of capital. As touched upon in a previous chapter, this result does not occur in the case of a subordinated debt instrument, the maturity of which is for a period of seven or more years. For shorter subordinated security maturities, the percentage of the debt principal that can constitute regulatory capital is reduced from the 100 percent level.

51.5 EQUITY COMMITMENT NOTES AS REGULATORY CAPITAL

Equity commitment notes (ECNs) constitute a form of subordinated debt that has been used with great success in S&L ESOP transactions since they qualify as regulated capital. ECNs are exchanged for funds borrowed by the S&L. The S&L lends the proceeds to its ESOP and the S&L sells stock to the ESOP. The S&L

makes annual contributions to the ESOP, which the ESOP uses to repay the S&L. The S&L repays its lender who releases the ECN back to the S&L incrementally as the debt is paid down.

An ECN, while being a debt instrument, has certain equity-like characteristics in that it must be convertible into either authorized but unissued common or perpetual preferred stock. This occurs in the event of default on the part of the S&L. Its redemption by the S&L is in the form of a sale of the foregoing forms of stock. It is for this reason that ECNs are treated as regulatory capital. S&Ls are restricted to making loans for commercial purposes that are not secured by real estate to more than 10 percent of the S&L's assets. It is, therefore, of prime importance that S&Ls maximize their capital in order to create a greater lending capacity.

CHAPTER FIFTY-TWO

ESOP Disadvantages, Problems, and Solutions

Anything worthwhile is not without its problems. If the basic concept of an ESOP is appealing, it is important to see if there are solutions to those problems.

"There is neither good nor bad; our thinking makes it so." Shakespeare's observation is appropriate when considering the applicability of ESOPs to a given situation. One's perception of what is to be accomplished in a corporate environment will determine the viability of an ESOP for achieving a stated goal. If the ESOP can do what the owners want for their company, their employees, and themselves, then the upside potential of its use may more than compensate for any problem to be overcome as a result of implementing the ESOP.

A quip, "AESOP's Fables," is used frequently to characterize the too-good-to-be-true or free-lunch quality that, upon shallow analysis, might seem applicable to ESOPs. This is far from being an accurate characterization. Anything that is worthwhile does not come easily. Here are some ESOP problem areas that must be addressed.

52.1 PROBLEMS

(a) How to Get Current Tax Deduction Though Delaying Stock Sale

The ESOP could be adopted in the current year to secure a tax deduction for that year. However, if the company is growing, the company could fund the plan with cash for a few years, in which case no valuation would be needed.

Then, the ESOP trustee could use the cash to purchase employer stock. Only at that time would the stock have to be valued. The delay would give the stock a chance to appreciate and the cash in the ESOP would purchase fewer shares. This would mean less dilution to the owner's interest.

Alternatively, the ESOP could be installed in the current year but funding could be delayed until the corporate taxes are filed, including the automatic six-month extension as of which time the stock would be valued, reflecting the then higher value for the stock of this growing company.

From the owner's standpoint, contributions to an ESOP for a company whose value is very low can cause an adverse dilution of the stock. The employees, on the other hand, will benefit by having stock allocated to their accounts that has been valued on the low side if the upside potential for growth is destined to be realized. Assuming a given dollar value of the contribution, they will receive a greater number of shares that may be worth more in the future. Conversely, if little or no appreciation occurs, the ESOP could foster animosity rather than goodwill.

(b) How to Avoid Minority Discount

Minority discounts are often involved in ESOP transactions. This is true if the owner is selling less than control amounts of stock to the plan. There is some consolation in the fact that the owner is still receiving the salary, bonuses, and perks he or she had received prior to the sale.

It is important that a defensible valuation be arrived at and updated annually using consistent methodology. The ESOP fiduciaries must adhere to the requirement that the trustee purchase securities for no more than fair market value. If the trustee pays more than fair market value, the company could incur an excise tax. A worst-case circumstance could be disqualification of the plan. In actuality, this would happen only in rare cases. The subject of valuation is addressed in greater depth in Chapter 5. Valuation of the stock can be a problem, but one that independent valuation firms are accustomed to dealing with on a regular basis. Prevalent practice has it that the minority discount can be eliminated by giving the ESOP a binding option to acquire more than 50 percent of the outstanding stock within several years.

(c) How to Minimize Dilution

Dilution is a downside aspect of ESOPs that must be dealt with when considering such a plan. When a corporation issues new shares of stock, it cuts the corporate pie into additional slices. Upon contributing those shares to the ESOP for the benefit of its employees, the corporation reduces the size of the slices owned by the non-ESOP shareholders.

An in-depth examination of the dilution question can alter one's initial impression by pointing to various counterdilutionary aspects of ESOPs. There are two forms of dilution, namely, dilution of shares and dilution of equity. When a corporation pays taxes, the cash goes off the balance sheet and is lost forever. This is dilutionary of equity. The tax savings created by the contribution of stock to the ESOP can be considered an offset to the equity the outside owners would lose assuming the corporation is capable of using its newly created working capital productively. Doing so could increase the value of the stock of the ESOP participants as well as the outside owners. If a corporation in the 40 percent combined tax bracket generates a 15 percent return on invested capital, the tax savings will offset the dilutionary effect of the stock contribution in less than seven years. It is all gain thereafter.

In a growing company, the corporation can minimize dilution by contributing cash to the ESOP in one year and having the ESOP use the cash to purchase newly issued stock after the next valuation. Assuming the stock has appreciated, the cash will purchase fewer shares, thereby reducing the dilutionary effect still further.

52.2 DILUTIONARY EFFECT OF PENSIONS AND PROFIT-SHARING PLANS

A further offset to dilution that should be considered is the likelihood that the corporation would have another form of tax-qualified employee benefit plan such as a pension or a profit-sharing plan. Contributions to such plans go off the balance sheet, reducing the company's working capital and cash flow by the net after-tax expenditure. This is also dilutionary of equity and tends to reduce the value of each share of stock.

A strategy to reduce the equity dilution would be to convert the profit-sharing plan to an ESOP and use all contributions that would have gone off the balance sheet into the profit-sharing plan to be used instead for a corporate purpose such as for corporate expansion or for succession planning.

Another strategy for minimizing dilution would be to use preferred stock. In a nonleveraged ESOP, preferred stock can be a dilution retardant since it does not tend to grow in value as rapidly as does common stock in a growing company.

Another technique for reducing the effect of dilution is to have the corporation redeem the shares from those employees who are eligible for statutory distributions. Assuming that the corporation is growing, it would make its next deductible contribution of those redeemed shares to the ESOP after the subsequent valuation has occurred, at which time the stock will have risen in value. This would require a sale of a smaller number of shares to achieve a given tax deduction.

(a) Problem: How to Maintain Control

Control is an issue that should be well thought out but need not be a problem. The corporation's board of directors appoints the ESOP's administrative or management committee, which directs the trustee as to how to vote the stock. The major stockholder can hold all these positions, but he or she must be careful to wear different fiduciary hats. It is generally advisable to have an independent third party, such as a bank with a trust department or a trust company, serve as a directed trustee, serving under the direction of the administration committee.

Employee participants of ESOPs do not physically hold the stock and, indeed, may never see a share of stock in a private company ESOP. Plan assets are held by the trustee on behalf of the participants. Only on certain major corporate issues are the voting rights passed through to the ESOP participants. These issues include merger or consolidation, recapitalization, reclassification, liquidation, dissolution, or sale of substantially all the assets of the corporation. A sale of the company's stock to an outside buyer is not one of the issues on which the ESOP participants need to be given the opportunity to vote.

In a practical sense, on all other matters the control rests ultimately in the hands of the non-ESOP major shareholders who control the corporate board. Studies have shown that employees are not so much concerned with the question of voting as they are with their acquisition of equity.

Entrepreneurs are often apprehensive about the possibility of others interfering with the daily management of the company. Since the voting rights need not be passed through on other than the grave issues noted above, there is seldom any basis for concern. Some ESOP companies choose to pass the voting rights through to the participants on all matters and encourage participatory management. There are some outstanding examples of this among ESOP companies wherein productivity improvements are noteworthy.

In large leveraged buyout (LBO) transactions or takeover attempts of public corporations, some practitioners take the more conservative approach of passing the voting rights through on unallocated shares as well as on those shares that were allocated to the participants' accounts. Upon the employee's termination, the corporation can distribute cash or stock, subject, however, to the right of the employees to demand stock.

The corporation or the ESOP can have a right of first refusal to purchase stock from terminated employees. Moreover, the corporate charter or bylaws can be amended to restrict stock ownership of substantially all of the stock to current employees or to a trust. This would have the effect of making it mandatory that substantially all of the stock remain with the corporation or the ESOP.

ESOP participants are given a put option enabling them to look forward to cash rather than stock. Since the employees will be taxed upon distribution, they will tend to want cash rather than stock. This is an additional factor in recycling the stock back for further control by the non-ESOP stockholders.

(b) Problem: How to Cash Out ESOP Participants

There will come a time when the stock in a private company's ESOP must be repurchased by the corporation or by the ESOP. Employees want to know that when they become disabled, die, terminate employment, or retire, there will be a market for their stock.

The cash must be provided for this purpose. This is a problem, but one that can be solved quite satisfactorily by applying appropriate funding techniques in conjunction with actuarially sound repurchase liability studies. Public corporations whose stock is widely traded do not face this problem, since there is a ready market for the stock allocated to ESOP accounts. This subject was treated in greater depth in Chapter 42.

(c) Problem: How the ESOP Will Affect a Later Sale of the Company

Suppose the founding stockholder sold 40 percent of the outstanding stock to the company's ESOP and retains 60 percent. A few years later, an outsider offers to purchase all of the stock of the company. If the ESOP stock were sold within three years of a sale and if it causes the ESOP stock to fall below 30 percent of the outstanding stock, under section 1042 there is a 10 percent excise tax on the amount of stock sold. This would not be a problem if the stock left the ESOP as a result of a Section 368 merger.

If the offer is for less than fair market value, the ESOP cannot sell the shares because an ESOP cannot pay more than fair market value. If the offer is equal to or greater than fair market value, the ESOP can sell the shares and the vote need not be passed through to the employees although the vote can be passed through to them.

The buyer would simply write two checks for the outstanding stock—one to the founder for his or her remaining 60 percent interest and one to the ESOP trustee for the 40 percent block of stock owned by the ESOP.

The buyer could retain the ESOP or terminate it as deemed appropriate. The employees could roll the proceeds of the sale into an individual retirement account (IRA) or another qualified plan.

A merger requires that the vote be passed through to the ESOP participants on their vested shares, as does a sale of substantially all the company assets.

CHAPTER FIFTY-THREE

The ESOP Implementation Procedure

The question as to whether or not to adopt an ESOP involves a great deal of subjectivity on the part of the company owners. It would be useful to hold discussions with a firm that specializes in implementing ESOPs to see whether the founder's objectives can be achieved by such a plan. If it is determined that the concept should go forward, the ESOP practitioner can coordinate and facilitate the process.

53.1 FEASIBILITY STUDY

A feasibility study can help the corporate owners or management determine whether an ESOP would fit their needs. A feasibility study should consist of:

- A preliminary valuation of the company's stock, assuming the stock has no established readily tradeable market. If such a market exists, a valuation is not required.

- Structuring the transaction—whether it be a corporate acquisition, a buyout of stockholders, or simply a capital infusion

- A dilution study to determine the net dilutionary effect, if any, upon the holdings of existing shareholders

- A liquidity study to determine the cash requirements for repurchasing the stock pursuant to a put option. This is sometimes referred to as the emerging repurchase liability

- A study to determine whether the ESOP should work in tandem with or replace an existing pension, profit sharing, or 401(k) plan. The study should examine the advisability as to whether the present plan should be frozen and partially converted or fully converted, and how an ESOP would mesh with other employee benefit-qualified and nonqualified plans.

- The company should be positioned to achieve the financial objectives needed to service bank loans that may be sought in connection with a leveraged ESOP. The feasibility study will enhance the committee's ability to procure financing at the most favorable rate.

53.2 STEPS TO ADOPTING AN ESOP

If it is determined that an ESOP is to be adopted, the following steps should ensue, some simultaneously:

1. The structuring of the proposed ESOP transaction should be done.

2. A feasibility study should be performed.

3. Board counsel should prepare a resolution to adopt an ESOP. The board will call for the design and drafting of a plan and trust document by the ESOP specialist.

4. The board will name an administrative committee, which will select and subsequently direct a trustee in all appropriate ESOP matters.

5. The trustee and corporate officer would execute the plan and trust document prior to the end of the fiscal year for which a tax deduction is desired.

6. A bank account should be established for the ESOP trust preferably prior to the fiscal year's end.

7. The company should explore sources of financing if the ESOP is to be leveraged.

8. Consideration should be given to a new class of stock to be sold to the ESOP and it should be prepared.

9. The board will authorize a full-blown valuation (assuming the company is privately held) by an independent appraisal firm, most likely the one that did the preliminary valuation.

10. The ESOP practitioner should submit the plan to the Internal Revenue Service (IRS) for a Letter of Determination.

11. A repurchase liability report should be prepared.

12. The firm documents conforming to the ESOP values should be finalized by counsel.

13. A summary plan description should be prepared and possibly put into booklet form to be distributed to the employees.

14. Contribution by the sponsoring corporation of cash to repay the debt should be made.

15. Employee meetings should be held to develop the greatest amount of public relations in connection with the ESOP's installation.

Larger ESOP transactions can be more complex and can involve more steps and more players than can ESOPs that involve interfamily disputes.

53.3 THE ESOP AFTER YEAR ONE

An ESOP becomes part of the ongoing financial architecture of the corporation and should be used to solve many corporate and stockholder problems while serving as a marvelous employee fringe benefit. It is quite possible that it will be used as an integral part of a succession plan or used in connection with the acquisition of another company or possibly used in divesting the company of an unwanted subsidiary in order to streamline the company. In any event, a liquidity study should be made every several years in order to determine the emerging liabilities and uncover cash requirements in the event of death, retirement, or other turnover for exercising the put.

Updates of the stock valuation are fairly inexpensive, generally amounting to approximately one half of the first-year cost.

Annual administration fees are roughly equivalent to fees for administering profit-sharing plans. It is important that the administrator be equipped with the computer software to keep track of the base cost of the stock as it is allocated to the participant's accounts and layer it year after year, including the base cost of forfeitures as of the time they were allocated to the accounts. The system should be able to alert the committee and trustee as to the timing of the diversification required for the accounts of participants who reach certain ages.

Constant overview of the plan and its performance is essential to the well-being of the ESOP. The administrator must also be vigilant as to changes that may occur from time to time in the areas of legislation and legal interpretation of ESOP regulations.

The ESOP can prove to be a completely new and intriguing experience for a solid corporation that is well-suited to its adoption. It should not be installed for a marginal concern.

A plan of action that would include the allocation of stock to new employees should be implemented.

Because an ESOP, unlike other qualified plans, is an instrument of corporate finance rather than a retirement plan, it should be implemented only after taking into consideration the effect the ESOP might have on corporate financial goals, executive benefit planning, corporate ownership succession, and estate planning for major stockholders.

Structuring the ESOP properly should go a long way toward achieving the well thought out objectives. The corporation should be prepared for a possible positive culture change and the executives will become more alert to opportunities that present themselves. Studies show that ESOP companies do better than their counterparts.

CHAPTER FIFTY-FOUR

Accounting Basics

The American Institute of Certified Public Accountants (AICPA) issued its Statement of Position (SOP) 93-6 on November 22, 1993. SOP 93-6 governs the accounting for ESOPs. It supersedes ESOP 76-3, which the AICPA issued in December, 1976.

Although accounting for nonleveraged ESOPs is not changed by the new SOP, it does offer guidance for such plans. The SOP affects leveraged ESOPs and changes the way transactions are recorded on the financial statements effective for fiscal years that began after December 15, 1993. This applies to shares of stock that have not been committed to be released as of the beginning of the adoption year. The SOP 93-6 accounting is applicable to shares purchased by ESOPs after December 31, 1992, but employers have the option of applying the terms of SOP 93-6 to shares the ESOPs had purchased prior to December 31, 1992, so long as these shares of stock have not been committed to be released as of the first day of the adoption years.

The changes were deemed necessary because of the dramatic increase in the number of ESOPs since SOP 76-3 was issued in 1976 and by the complexity and diversity of many of the transactions that have occurred since that time.

54.1 HOW CONTRIBUTIONS TO A NONLEVERAGED ESOP ARE TREATED

Contribution of cash or newly-issued shares of stock to a nonleveraged ESOP are recorded as compensation expense. If stock is contributed, the spread between par value and the appraisal value of the stock is credited to paid-in capital.

54.2 ACCOUNTING FOR DIVIDENDS

Dividends could not be deducted until 1985, after which time dividends were permitted to be deducted if used to repay ESOP loans. This development was not contemplated in that early period of ESOP development. This alone has added to the sophistication associated with ESOP debt structuring. The accounting treatment associated with the use of dividends had been subject to controversy, but has now been clarified by SOP 93-6. Dividends that are paid on shares of stock that are allocated to the ESOP participants are charged to retained earnings. Those dividends that are paid on shares that are unallocated are charged on the income statement as compensation.

54.3 REPORTING ESOP LOANS ON THE FINANCIAL STATEMENT

Outside lenders, such as banks and insurance companies, can lend directly to the ESOP, in which case the sponsoring corporation generally guarantees the repayment of the loan. This is referred to as a direct loan.

Lenders usually feel more comfortable lending to the employer since they like to be closer to the source of repayment. This is an outside loan. The employer then lends the funds to the ESOP. This is an inside loan.

With greater frequency, the sponsoring employer lends to ESOP using funds it has accumulated in retained earnings. This is referred to as an employer loan. SOP 93-6 addresses the accounting treatment for each of these approaches.

Direct loans, indirect loans, and employer loans are all recorded on the balance sheet as a liability. A contra-equity account is created as an offsetting and separate entry. In the case of a direct loan to the ESOP by an outside lender, the employer contributions or dividends paid to the ESOP to service the loan reduces debt. Interest costs are accrued and interest is paid along with principal on the direct and indirect loans.

An outside loan to the employer and then a loan by the employer to the ESOP would be reflected on the balance sheet as debt. This liability is reduced as the loan is amortized. The contra-equity account that is created on the balance sheet's equity section is equal to the amount of the ESOP debt, thereby offsetting the debt. The loan amount borrowed by the ESOP is not reflected as in the asset section of the balance sheet as an asset.

An employer loan outside of retained earnings to the ESOP is recorded neither as a note receivable nor as a note payable and the interest is neither a cost nor income on the financial.

If the loan were used to purchase stock from the sponsoring corporation, the balance sheet would reflect the cash that was infused or the assets purchased by that cash. Contributions to the ESOP by the sponsoring employer that are used to repay ESOP debt are treated as compensation expense and interest repayment.

54.4 RECORDING THE PURCHASE AND RELEASE OF ESOP STOCK

ESOP debt is often collateralized by the shares of the sponsoring corporation and, if necessary, other collateral. The shares of stock are held by the ESOP in a suspense account and released to be allocated to the participants' accounts as of the fiscal year end. They are also released as collateral at that time. The shares can be allocated as principal is amortized or as principal and interest is paid. The former is the more commonly used methodology.

SOP 93-6 requires that the transactional charges be made as the date the shares are committed to be released from the suspense account rather than on the date they are actually released. The charge will be based on fair value of the shares.

Whether the company sells treasury stock or authorized but unissued stock to the ESOP, or if the ESOP purchases stock from a selling stockholder, the company should record an offset in the contra-equity account, a charge to unearned shares.

When the ESOP purchases outstanding stock using funds loaned to it by outside lenders, debt should be credited. If it is internally funded, cash would be credited. Where dividends are paid on unallocated shares to reduce ESOP debt, they are not reported as dividends on the financial statements, but they are designated as compensation. Dividends passed through to the ESOP participants or allocated to their accounts are also reported as compensation and charged to retained earnings.

54.5 EARNINGS PER SHARE

Shares held by the ESOP are considered for financial reporting purposes to be outstanding if they have been committed to be released. Conversely, shares are not outstanding if they have not been committed to be released. Convertible preferred stock is considered for this purpose to be the equivalent of common stock.

CHAPTER FIFTY-FIVE

Meet Some ESOP Companies

55.1 CASE HISTORY CAPSULES

(a) Bethlehem Steel Corporation

Bethlehem Steel Corporation, Allentown, Pennsylvania, achieved its first year of profitability in 1987 after suffering a string of losses during the preceding six years. The company, in accordance with a formula, distributed $1.5 million in cash to its United Steelworkers union employees. The company also contributed approximately 94 shares of preferred stock to be allocated to each employee's ESOP account. This was partial repayment for the wage and benefit reduction agreed to by the union employees in 1986. It was these wage concessions that made the company more competitive, profitable, and secure for its more than 24,000 employees at that time.

(b) Bostwick-Braun Company

Bostwick-Braun Company, Toledo, Ohio, founded in 1862, is 100 percent owned by the ESOP that was established in 1979. The company had been family owned but none of the younger generation was interested in the business as a vocation. Rather than risk the possibility of employee dislocations which frequently accompany sale of companies to outsiders, the chairman chose the ESOP route and did a partial conversion of the profit-sharing plan, using its assets to acquire stock from the family.

The company's more than 300 union and nonunion employees are eligible to participate after one year of service.

(c) Canterbury Press

Canterbury Press, Rome, New York, is a printing firm specializing in periodicals for the pharmaceutical and medical fields. The firm is 100 percent ESOP owned by its union and nonunion employees as ESOP participants. The plan, created in 1975 as a means of spreading ownership among its employees, accomplished this on a gradual basis until the sole stockholder retired in 1981, at which time the corporation loaned the ESOP an amount to buy the balance of his Canterbury stock.

The company feels that the ESOP has played a significant role in improving the quality of its product, which in turn has enhanced corporate growth and profitability.

(d) Channelock

Channelock, Meadville, Pennsylvania, is a fine example of a private company with an ESOP that includes its union employees. The ESOP, implemented in 1973, was designed as a means of involving employees in equity ownership of the company while at the same time providing a marketplace for stock in this family-owned company that was founded in 1886. The ESOP participants, comprising approximately 400 employees, own slightly less than half of the outstanding stock of the company. The United Steelworkers comprise approximately three quarters of the employee base. The firm is well known as a producer of quality pliers.

(e) Clay Equipment

Clay Equipment, Cedar Falls, Louisiana, a manufacturer of agricultural equipment, established its ESOP in 1984 as a 100 percent employee-owned company covering all union and nonunion employees. The union is the International Association of Machinists.

The company's profit-sharing plan's assets were frozen and the plan was converted to an ESOP that borrowed funds from the holding company to enable the ESOP to purchase the operating company subject to a 30-year note. As of the end of 1987, 25 percent of this stock had been allocated to the participants' accounts. The voting rights are passed through to the employees on their allocated shares and the trustee votes the unallocated shares. Until such time as the employee group reaches the control point, it is felt that the vote pass-through serves as a good training mechanism to prepare the employees to control the destiny of the company. The corporation keeps the employees well informed so as to enhance the decision process.

(f) ComSonics, Inc.

ComSonics, Inc., Harrisonburg, Virginia, a privately held company, has experienced rapid growth in the electronic equipment field. The company has a highly participatory approach to employee involvement. While top management establishes goals, second- and third-tier management evaluates progress toward achieving those objectives in monthly meetings. The company's stock is 100 percent owned by its ESOP.

(g) Delta Electronics

Delta Electronics, Alexandria, Virginia, founded in 1962, is a leading designer and manufacturer of products and systems related to the broadcasting and telecommunications industries. The ESOP purchased some of its shares from the corporation, which had just redeemed them from the retiring founders and other stockholders. The corporation made it possible for the ESOP to do this by borrowing funds from a bank and lending the proceeds to the ESOP with substantially similar terms. Of the stock that is owned by the employees, 53 percent was owned by the ESOP as a result of the initial purchase.

Productivity improvements have occurred since the advent of the ESOP and the employees have noticed an appreciable gain in their account balances as a result of substantial annual employer contributions and share value growth.

(h) Home Depot

This rapidly growing company has an ESOP. It has been listed as one of the "Best 100 Companies to Work for in America." The company also has a merit-based bonus plan for hourly employees and a stock option program for management starting at the assistant manager level.

(i) Kerotest Manufacturing Corporation

Kerotest Manufacturing Corporation, Pittsburgh, Pennsylvania, a manufacturer of valves for the petroleum and chemical industry, created its ESOP in 1983 covering its more than 200 union and nonunion employees.

The company was a division of Control Data, which wanted to divest itself of this successful division that did not fit synergistically with corporate development goals. Management proposed a leveraged buyout on the basis of a $5 million loan to enable the ESOP to own all the class A stock. The class B stock was structured so as to have a negative value (which moved in tandem with the class A securities if certain growth objectives were realized). The class B stock would increase in value as the class A stock did, but starting at a lower basis and showing greater proportionate growth in value. This made it possible for the management group's investment to reap a reward commensurate with its investment and production achievements.

(j) Leslie Paper

Leslie Paper, Minneapolis, Minnesota, a wholesale paper distributor founded in 1894, established an ESOP in 1976. The ESOP owns between 60 percent and 70 percent of the outstanding shares with the balance being owned by many of the more than 300 employees through direct purchases. Members of collective bargaining units are precluded from ESOP participation.

Productivity is extraordinarily high, and this has translated into an annual compound stock appreciation rate of 18 percent to 20 percent since the ESOP's inception. Employee participation in operations is emphasized, and each employee has business cards that call him or her *partner.*

(k) Lowe's Companies, Inc.

Lowe's Companies, Inc., North Wilkesboro, North Carolina, a six-store retailer and wholesaler of building materials and related products, established its ESOP in 1978 after having had a profit-sharing plan for the prior 21 years. The company now has hundreds of stores with sales approximating $2.5 billion dollars, making it the largest firm of its type in the country.

The company has in excess of 15,000 employees, all of whom are ESOP participants and, as such, own approximately 25 percent of the company stock.

(l) North Coast Brass and Copper

North Coast Brass and Copper, Cleveland, Ohio, was acquired in January 1988 by the 535 employees of what had been a division of British Petroleum of America (H.P.). The division, Chase Brass Sheet, was on the verge of being closed by H. P., but the unions negotiated a below-liquidation purchase price and an ESOP was established to finance a $10 million bank loan. The total debt package comprised an $8 million loan and $22 million as a revolving line of credit. The company was renamed North Coast Brass and Copper.

The International Association of Machinists and the Professional Employees Union have a deep involvement in the workings of the ESOP, and each has representation on the board. The union employees made wage concessions to enhance the company's ability to service the debt. An intricate educational and participation program has been implemented.

(m) Oregon Steel Mills, Inc.

Oregon Steel Mills, Inc., Portland, Oregon, made a Securities and Exchange Commission (SEC) public offering of $1.62 million shares. Its ESOP sold $1.24 million shares and other shareholders offered and sold 137,312 shares to the public. The company used the $30 million to retire an $8.5 million loan and infuse the balance into the company for working capital and improvements.

(n) Quad Graphics, Inc.

Quad Graphics, Inc., Pewaukee, Wisconsin, prints well-known magazines, including *Newsweek, U.S. News and World Report, Ms,* and many others. Its ESOP, covering roughly 3,000 employees, has about 39 percent of the stock in the company. Its involvement in the printing business has given the firm a predisposition to communicating the benefits of equity ownership to its employees most effectively. The firm gives the employees broad authority coupled with responsibility in defining and running their respective areas of operations. The company has been experiencing growth in sales and profitability in the area of 40 percent to 50 percent annually.

(o) Rural/Metro Corporation

Rural/Metro Corporation, Scottsdale, Arizona, is an employee-owned company, its ESOP having been instituted in 1979. The company is the nation's largest private fire protection and medical care provider, having grown at an annual rate of 33 percent since 1981. In 1988, the company had revenues exceeding $50 million. It operates units that are the equivalent to 15 ambulance companies and 25 fire departments in five states. Its customers include municipalities as well as corporations and individuals. The company attributes a great deal of its employee's motivation to the company's ESOP.

(p) Science Applications International Corporation

Science Applications International Corporation, San Diego, California, is a defense contractor, the majority control of which lies in the hands of its ESOP participants. The voting rights are passed through the ESOP to its participants, who also elect the 18-member board, of which six are employees. The corporation has an intricate participative management system composed of a large number of committees. The committee system (coupled with employee ownership) works, as evidenced by the rapid growth enjoyed by the corporation and its employee owners.

(q) United Airlines

The company's employees now own a majority of the company's stock as a result of the implementation of an ESOP in mid-1994. As of this writing, United is the largest employee-owned company in the United States. Making the transition come together was a tremendous feat of negotiation and financial engineering. The various unions, pension plan and mutual fund investors, investment bankers, and other factions, each with its own set of interests, became unified in its determination to make the ESOP work.

The employees took wage reductions of 25 percent and made other work-related concessions. The airline industry is extremely competitive, and it is believed that employee ownership can make a huge difference in the ability of United to maintain a good market share and profitability.

(r) Viking Engineering and Development, Inc.

Viking Engineering and Development, Inc., Fridley, Minnesota, placed its ESOP in effect in 1981 and leveraged it in 1985 in order to purchase 30 percent of the outstanding stock from the majority owner. The ESOP was given an option to acquire additional shares to bring its holdings to 51 percent.

Viking has a significant market share of an automated wooden pallet assembly system that it developed and manufactures. The company employs between 85 and 95 people, all of whom are eligible to become ESOP participants.

CHAPTER FIFTY-SIX

Driving Share Value for Small to Medium-Sized Companies

To maximize the benefits ESOPs can afford the corporation, the shareholders, the employees, and the economy, it is imperative that the employees perceive the advantages of the ESOP. This awareness does not come without careful planning on the part of management. The ability of the sponsoring corporation to provide incentives for the employees—while at the same time benefiting the company—has been legislated with the inherent nature and capabilities of the ESOP.

56.1 TURNING TURKEYS INTO IMPROVED ORGANIZATIONAL PERFORMANCE AND INCREASED SHARE VALUE

ESOPs have many obvious applications, particularly as they relate to forms of ownership transfer, stockholder buyouts, acquisitions, and capital formation. There are also many situations in which the owners of a privately held company are still young and entertain no thought of cashing in presently or in the foreseeable future. Why would an ESOP be worthy of consideration in this situation?

There still exists today the benevolent autocratic business owner who desires to do good things for his or her employees. Say the company has installed a profit-sharing plan, perhaps a 401(k), and turkeys are given to employees at Thanksgiving and hams at Christmas. Although a nice gesture, these "passive" approaches do very little to build employee commitment and motivation toward improved organizational performance, increased profitability, and a corresponding increase in the company's share value.

The typical profit-sharing plan is a *passive* program because the payoff is generally too far in the future to excite most employees. Employees in their 20s and 30s are thinking not about retirement, but rather how to get some incremental income so they can afford to buy something today. Why, then, should the company consider converting its profit-sharing program into an ESOP? Isn't the ESOP also designed as a long-term event? Not necessarily. Armed with the facts that (1) ESOPs can pay dividends that are tax-deductible to the company and (2) there are also no FICA or workers' compensation deductions associated with dividends, an "active" program may be designed that contributes to employee commitment, motivation, and overall improved organizational performance.

56.2 DRIVING SHARE VALUE—AN EXAMPLE

Let's take a typical company with 75 employees, annual revenues of $10 million, pretax profits of $750,000, and an annual payroll of $2 million. The company in our example also has a profit-sharing plan to which it typically contributes 5 percent of total compensation, $100,000 to the plan each year, depending on company performance. The following describes how we can convert this typical "passive" situation into an "active" program that will drive share value.

(a) Step One: Fair Market Valuation

The first step in our "Driving Share Value Program" is to have a valuation of the company performed by a certified business appraiser (CBA) to determine the fair market value of the company and the value of its shares of stock. Assume this is done and the shares are valued at $800 each.

(b) Step Two: Recapitalization

Typically, there are a limited number of shares in a privately held company such that if purchased by an ESOP would result in an individual employee receiving a fraction of a share during any contribution period. Owning .05 share from a psychological point of view is not as meaningful as owning 50 or 100 shares, although the account balance might be the same.

In order to overcome this situation, the company in our example undergoes a recapitalization resulting in a share value of $5.00 each. It creates a convertible preferred or a super common class of stock that pays dividends. The company also authorizes more shares.

In establishing the ESOP, the "vesting schedule" would be comparable to that of the profit-sharing plan in order that all employees would receive credit for their years of service with respect to their vesting status.

(c) Step Three: Establish an ESOP and Freeze the Profit-Sharing Plan

Using an ESOP professional services firm, the company now establishes an ESOP and freezes the company's existing profit-sharing plan. That is to say, no further contributions will be made to the profit-sharing plan, and the assets of the plan will continue to be invested in the portfolio that presently exists.

(d) Step Four—Contribute Shares of Stock to the ESOP

Since this is a nonleveraged ESOP, the company can contribute stock or cash, on a tax-deductible basis, up to 15 percent of annual payroll which, in this case, is $300,000 in stock rather than cash. A foundation is now established for the payment of dividends.

The cost to the company of doing this is zero and taxable profits are immediately reduced by $300,000 for the contribution to the ESOP, reducing the company's taxes and increasing cash flow by the taxes that are saved, an important benefit of the program that should not be overlooked.

At $5.00 per share, we have now contributed 60,000 shares to the ESOP with each employee, on average, receiving 800 shares.

(e) Step Five: Communication of Program to Employee Owners

As previously discussed, the ESOP Plan should be communicated to the company's new employee owners. In conjunction with the communications, the Driving Share Value Program would also be introduced, focusing on the long-term benefits of the ESOP as well as on the short-term objectives of the program, namely, to improve organizational performance and profitability and drive share value. Most important is the fact that each employee owner will immediately receive a payoff in the form of cash dividends if performance goals are attained.

(f) Step Six: The Management/Employee Owner Driving Share Value Committee

Participation and involvement, as noted earlier, are the keys to developing an ownership culture and a successful ESOP company. In our example, a joint management/employee owner committee is formed. Employee owner representatives on the committee would be elected by their peers and serve for a designated period of time, such as a year, after which time other employee owners would be provided with an opportunity to serve on the committee. Management representation should consist of the company's owner(s) and senior executives in order to emphasize the importance of the program and establish credibility.

(g) Step Seven: Identification of High-Performance Impact Areas

The first task of the committee is for its members to agree on areas of the company where, if improvements were made, such as increasing gross profits by 2.5 percent, reducing costs, minimizing scrap, or improving customer service, it would have an immediate high impact on improving company profitability and increasing share value.

Once these areas are identified, short-term goals/objectives would be established, such as achieving an increase in gross profit by 2.5 percent over the next quarter.

This task might not be completed in one committee meeting. It would therefore be useful for the employee owner representatives to consult with their constituents to gain additional involvement and input relative to potential high-impact performance areas.

(h) Step Eight: Determining the Payoff

The next task of the committee would be to agree on the "payoff." As an example, if gross profit is increased by 2.5 percent over the next quarter, resulting in a contribution of $100,000, how will this be shared? For illustrative purposes, assume the committee agrees that this will be shared 50–50, the company retaining $50,000 and the other $50,000 being passed through to the employee owners in the form of a quarterly dividend. Payoff ranges might also be established for partial goal/objective attainments. For example, if gross profit were increased by 2.0 percent instead of 2.5 percent, a smaller dividend would be paid than if the 100 percent goal were met.

(i) Step Nine: The Quarterly Shareholders Meeting

At the end of the quarter, a meeting would be held with all of the employee owners, at which time financial performance and high-impact area objectives would be reviewed and the quarterly dividend checks issued. Assuming the gross profit objectives as outlined above were attained, each employee owner would receive a dividend check on an average of approximately $660.00. Obviously, the attainment of some goals might not lead to a payoff to this extent. However, even a small payoff of $25 or $50 begins to lay the foundation and connection to improved company performance and immediate rewards. The company has now converted a "passive" employee benefit plan into an "active" program in which the company, its owners, and employee owners benefit.

Most important, the value of the company should be considerably higher as a result of the Driving Share Value Program. By receiving dividends on the stock that is allocated to their accounts, the employees relate to the value and the meaning of stock ownership.

56.3 REVIVING THE MATURE ESOP

Many existing ESOPs were established years ago with the primary objective of acquiring the owner's stock under the Section 1042 provision. Few of these companies recognized the benefits of the development of an ownership culture at the time, so these ESOPs have become passive programs.

A major opportunity exists to revive these dormant programs through the establishment of a Driving Share Value Program. The obvious benefit would be to increase share value and allow the shareholders to sell additional shares to the ESOP at a significantly higher value compared to their first 30 percent sale.

CHAPTER FIFTY-SEVEN

The Driving Share Value Program for Larger ESOP Companies

Many larger private and public companies have a great deal of interest in ESOPs; many of them have adopted ESOPs; and many more are exploring the feasibility of adopting such a plan.

57.1 THE LARGER COMPANY

Chapter 56 discussed an example of how the Driving Share Value Program can work in a smaller company. What about the larger company, which may have several hundreds or thousands of employees and also operates from multiple locations? Obviously, one management/employee owner driving share value committee taps the creativity of the entire organization.

One should consider the establishment of a formal process extending or "cascading" the Driving Share Value Program. The following describes how this might be structured.

57.2 EMPLOYEE OWNER DRIVING SHARE VALUE GROUPS (DSVGs)

The DSVG is a formal organization comprising designated representatives of the employee owners and management. A number of DSVGs can be established in the company, depending on its size, degree of functionalization, and number of locations.

The role of the DSVG is to meet on a regular basis to identify issues, problems, and opportunities that deal with improving overall organizational performance, profitability, and that will drive share value. The DSVG also develops the recommendations for their resolution and consideration by the senior DSV committee as previously discussed.

In addition, the DSVG may review overall organizational performance versus established DSVG goals/objectives on a regular basis with their constituencies to continually reinforce the importance of the program. The DSVG also serves as the upward communications link between management and the employee owners, creating a process whereby individual ideas, suggestions, problems, and other pertinent topics can be addressed in a controlled forum instead of the general solicitation of ideas (the old suggestion box) on a random basis. Also, unlike previous suggestion programs—because there is a direct and immediate reward for improved organizational performance—the program will not die because of lack of interest or management feedback and/or management's unresponsiveness to the employee's suggestion.

57.3 ESTABLISHING DSVGs

Careful planning should take place relative to the establishment of DSVGs. Members of the DSVG should be trained in problem analysis and decision making, basic finance, as well as how to conduct an effective DSVG meeting. Guidelines should also be developed outlining how the DSVG will function, how representatives of the employee owners will be selected, how long they will serve on the DSVG, what information (performance and financial) will be made available to them, and, finally, what authority and responsibility the DSVG will have.

57.4 DSVGs—NOT A REPLACEMENT FOR MANAGEMENT

It is important to emphasize that a DSVG is not meant to replace management's authority, accountability, and responsibility for results. The DSVG should *not* make decisions relative to operations, nor bypass any level of management responsible for the area or issues they are addressing. The DSVG should be viewed as an *advisory* body, composed of management and employee owners, who may address any issue relative to improving organizational performance. The outcome of their regular meetings should result in recommendations for management's consideration (via the senior management/employee owners driving share value committee) rather than making the decisions themselves. Organizational conflict can occur too readily if the DSVG assumes power not in its charter and makes decisions which management, regardless of level, should be making. Once again, the DSVG's role should be spelled out in advance and carefully monitored so that it does not encroach on management's responsibility for results.

The DSVG can be a powerful vehicle for employee owner involvement, resulting in improved organizational performance and profitability. The organization should address the preceding issues first and should not rush into forming DSVGs without careful planning.

Following is a checklist covering the issues that should be addressed in the formation of DSVGs.

57.5 DRIVING SHARE VALUE GROUPS FORMATION CHECKLIST

The following items should be reviewed prior to forming a DSVG:

1. **How many members should we have?** The answer depends on the size of the company, number of departments, locations, and so on. A smaller company may have only one group, but a number of DSVGs would be appropriate in a larger company.

2. **How many levels of groups should we have?** Again, this depends on the size of the company in terms of the number of levels that separate the chief executive officer (CEO) from the employee owners at the operational level. Larger companies with regional, district, and local organizational structures might want to consider a DSVG for each level.

3. **What should the size of the group be?** Unless the company has elected to form DSVGs by function or department, the DSVG should be composed of employee owners from each of the company's key functional areas.

4. **How many management representatives should there be?** As a general guideline, the group should be composed of approximately one third management and two thirds employee owners. Also, the level of management representation should be such that they are understanding of operational issues and are close to the day-to-day operations of the business. Depending on the size of the organization, middle management would make appropriate representatives on the group.

5. **How should members be selected?** Employee owners from the company's key functional or geographic areas should elect a representative from their area(s) to serve on the group. Management representation should be appointed by the CEO or other high-level functional or geographic executives of the company, such as regional vice presidents, vice president of manufacturing, and so on.

6. **How long should members serve?** Members should serve on the group for at least six months and no longer than a year. Rotating members provides other employee owners with an opportunity to participate and grow

as a result of the experience. One third of the group's members should remain for an additional partial term in order to maintain group continuity.

7. **How often, when, and where should the group meet?** The group should meet at least once a month among themselves with another optional meeting to present issues, recommendations, etc., to the authority they report to (senior management/employee owner driving share value committee, etc.). Meetings should be held on company time and in a meeting facility/conference room where they will be free from interruptions.

8. **What is the group's role?** The group's role is to explore issues, problems, opportunities, and the like, and to develop recommendations for senior management consideration that can lead to improved organizational performance, profitability, and increased share value. The group's role is also that of a vehicle for two-way communications. Employee owners should be encouraged to discuss their thoughts, suggestions, problems, and so on with their representative for presentation at group meetings. Because everyone will share in the successful implementation of an idea, suggestion, and resultant dividends for goal/objective achievement, "pride of authorship" issues associated with typical suggestion programs are eliminated. Group members should also provide feedback to the employee owners they represent relative to the outcome of issues and problems suggested to them and discussed by the group.

9. **What is the group's relationship with line management?** The group is an advisory body and should be allowed to explore and discuss issues with line management as appropriate, but not to make decisions relative to the day-to-day operations of the business. In addition, issues that are typically of a management–employee relationship, such as compensation, performance, and the like, are outside the scope of the group's consideration.

10. **How much and what kind of information should the group have access to?** In the case of privately held companies whose financial information has not been generally shared in the past, the decision rests with the CEO/owner in terms of how much information to share with the groups. Obviously, the employee owners are interested in how the company is performing, particularly as it relates to the driving share value goals and objectives. The company should share as much performance-related information with the groups as they feel comfortable with. If a concern exists in terms of sensitive information being leaked outside the company, the company should consider having all group members endorse confidentiality/nondisclosure agreements.

11. **What is the skill level of the group members?** Do the group members, managers, and employee owners alike have good problem-solving skills? Can they conduct an effective and productive meeting? Do they understand

the financial implications of reducing expenses on improved profitability? If the members have not been used to participating in this type of environment in the past, consideration should be given to providing group members training in these areas before the group begins to function.

12. **What kind of support will the group receive?** The group should be provided with the necessary administrative and logistical support to operate effectively (typing and copying support for agenda's meeting, minutes, recommendations, and proposal presentations, etc.).

13. **Group charter.** The groups should have a charter under which to operate. The charter should be published so that everyone in the company understands how the Driving Share Value Program works, its authorities and responsibilities, and how it will function. The charter should address all of the items contained in this checklist.

14. **The senior management/employee owner DSVG committee.** Whether the company is small or large, there is a need for a senior committee. As discussed previously, this committee would include senior management, perhaps members of the company's ESOP administrative committee, and representative employee owners. In the case of large companies, recommendations made by the company's DSVGs would be reviewed eventually by this committee.

- *Purpose.* The purpose of this committee is to establish the formal reporting relationships between the DSVGs and a body that has the power and authority to review and implement recommendations made by the DSVGs. In addition, this committee would establish the high-impact performance objectives and eventual dividend payoffs. Also, the committee should monitor progress of the other DSVGs and provide support and guidance to the groups when necessary. This might include the committee identifying issues or areas they desire the groups to study and submit recommendations accordingly.

- *Responsibilities.* The following is a list of suggested responsibilities of the committee. An implementation checklist is also provided for use in the committee's planning of the company's Driving Share Value Program.

  (a) *DSVG charter and guidelines.* Develop and publish a charter and guidelines for the DSVGs. This describes the group's purpose, role, relationships with management, and the like, similar to the information described previously.

  (b) *Company mission and values.* Provide the group with a copy of the company missions and governing values that the company desires to operate under now that it is employee owned.

(c) *Establish DSVGs.* Take the lead in the establishment and implementation of the company's DSVGs, including assistance in the selection process of group chairpersons, management, and employee owner representatives.

(d) *Review, approve, reject proposals and recommendations.* Review proposals and recommendations on a timely basis when presented upward by the groups. Provide fair and objective reviews of the proposals and recommendations and provide feedback as to their acceptance and implementation, or reasons for their rejection.

(e) *Establish objectives and payoff.* Establish the objectives and the payoff in terms of dividends for objective accomplishment. In the case of a one-time recommendation which does not fit the establishment of an objective (if the backside roller bearings were replaced on the production machine, scrap could be reduced by 20 percent), determine a one-time dividend payoff if the recommendation is implemented.

(f) *Review and monitor DSVG progress.* Review and monitor the progress of the groups. This can be accomplished by reviewing minutes of group meetings, projects in progress, and the quality and quantity of proposals and recommendations submitted to the committee. Occasional use of outside observers at group meetings may also be appropriate, particularly where a group may be experiencing some difficulty.

(g) *Provide recognition.* Provide recognition and rewards for a group's efforts and accomplishments. Recognition can be provided after the acceptance of proposals submitted to the committee in the form of letters of appreciation to the group's members, notice in the company's publications, bulletin boards, and at company functions and meetings. Obviously, announcing what the payoff was or will be in the form of cash dividends as a result of a particular group's efforts goes a long way in reinforcing the efforts of all the groups continually.

(h) *Administrative and other support.* The committee should ensure that each group receives the necessary administrative and other support required to operate effectively. This would include providing notebooks, stationery, pencils, and other necessary supplies to group members. Development of group logos and other forms of group identification should also be considered.

(i) *Communications with line management.* The committee should ensure that all company management is totally informed of the establishment of DSVGs and provided with copies of the group's charter.

This is critical, as line management's support and understanding of the group's role is necessary to avoid potential conflict.

(j) *Policies and procedures.* Policies and procedures may be necessary to account for a group member's time away from the job in group meetings or training if it affects unit financial reporting and other performance measurements. This helps to ensure line management's cooperation with the program.

57.6 THE SENIOR MANAGEMENT/EMPLOYEE OWNER DSVG COMMITTEE IMPLEMENTATION CHECKLIST

One of the first tasks of planning for driving share value groups is to ask strategic questions that will help guide the structure and participative process. After these questions are answered, and using the other information contained in this guide, the senior committee can move forward to establish and implement the program.

Following are some of the key questions that should be answered.

1. Communications

- How will members of the senior committee receive information from the groups?
- How will information be reported to the sponsoring individual or department?
- How will groups access organizational records and files? What records and files will be available to the groups? What records will *not* be made available?

2. Decision making

- What is the scope of power and authority of individual groups?
- How will decisions be made on the implementation of group proposals and recommendations?
- How will conflicts and disagreements among groups, leaders, or facilitators be mediated and resolved?
- How will decisions be made regarding formation of new *groups* and the status of inactive groups?

3. Evaluation

- What criteria will be used to evaluate the success of the program?
- What are the standards for the approval and implementation of recommendations?

- How will the progress and the development of the groups be monitored?
- Who will be responsible for evaluation?

4. Resources and support systems

- What internal resources and support systems are available to the groups?
- What external resources will be required (consultants, training materials, etc.)?
- How much company time will be used for information gathering, training, and group meetings?
- How much time will employee owners spend on group projects?
- How much time will be required from supervisors and managers?
- What other organizational resources (facilities, equipment, supplies, administrative support) will be available for the groups?

5. Finances

- What is the overall cost estimate, both direct and indirect, of implementing the program?
- Which budget will cover the expenses, such as outside resources, training materials, and printing?
- What funds are available in the current budget and what funds will be required in the future to maintain the program?
- What is a reasonable expectation of the cost-to-savings ratio in the first year of the program?

6. Orientation

- How will employee owners be informed about the program (discussion, meetings, printed materials, video, etc.)?
- How will the call for volunteers be handled?
- What role will the line supervisor play in orientation?
- How will new group members be oriented in the future?

57.7 SUMMARY

Although this checklist does not include all the questions that might arise, the major areas for discussion are covered here. The senior committee should spend sufficient time to answer these questions, as well as review the other material in this guide as they plan the company's driving share value program. Time spent in careful planning of the program can prevent difficulties later.

Finally, the senior committee should assess the company's present management and leadership style and attitudes toward participation and information sharing. If participation and information sharing have not been encouraged in the past, it may be necessary to train all those who will be responsible for the program's success in participative management techniques; this effort might start with senior management personnel.

Obviously, considerable work is involved in establishing and maintaining a driving share value program. Properly implemented, the benefits for everyone can be substantial, including:

- Increased employee owner commitment and motivation

- Reduced costs and improved productivity

- Increased profitability and higher share value

- Immediate rewards (cash dividends) for goal achievement; and

- The conversion of a *passive* retirement plan into an *active program,* which can produce meaningful results.

CHAPTER FIFTY-EIGHT

Participative Management

Through the years, a relatively small number of employees owned stock in the privately held corporations where they were employed. The employees simply were not given the opportunity to buy shares due to the reluctance of the owners to allow employees to own stock in their companies. This reticence was brought about by various perceptions of such things as interference in operations and the specter of dilution.

Many of these entrepreneurs were apprehensive about the potential for employee stockholders telling them how to run the company, possibly creating derivative action suits and sharing in the equity of the company. Owners often perceived employee stock ownership as a threat. The founders often equated equity ownership with rights to manage.

ESOPs have had a major impact on getting entrepreneurs to share ownership with their employees due in great measure to the tax incentives and the continuity of control afforded the founders of private corporations. The ESOP lets the founder effectively retain voting rights over the shares, even after they have been allocated to the employees' accounts.

Once the barrier of employee trust ownership has been traversed, a strange phenomenon occurs. Major stockholders find that employees who have a beneficial stake in the trust-held equity of their companies are not a threat. Often, the entrepreneur gradually develops a realization that ESOP-participant employees become more interested in the same issues that the founder had thought was his or her sole domain, that is, sales improvement, production efficiency, cost reduction, customer goodwill, market share, and retained earnings growth.

It soon becomes apparent that the greater the amount of stock that is allocated to the employees' ESOP accounts along with greater participative management, the more pronounced is the effect on productivity. Productivity enhancement, in turn, leads to greater profitability.

Employees, in effect, become owners when stock is allocated to their ESOP accounts. The question is, do they feel and act like owners? Probably not immediately—that is, unless there is a well conceived strategy on the part of top management to communicate the purpose and workings of the ESOP to the employee participants.

The corporate sponsor should not assume that the employees will, through an osmosis effect, become endowed with an ownership culture concurrent with the ESOP's announcement. The transformation from a nonowner mentality to an owner mentality does not come without careful orchestration.

Owners of privately held corporations are motivated to install ESOPs for a variety of reasons, including the owners' desire to diversify their assets, achieve corporate growth through increased working capital, succession planning, acquisitions, reward of loyalty, and greater productivity.

All of these reasons for implementing ESOPs are beneficial for both the owners and the employees. Unless the benefits are conveyed to the employee participants in a meaningful way, employees may tend to read into the program something other than the sponsor's true intent.

Stock ownership, coupled with participative management, has been shown to be far more effective in achieving productivity gains than either component on a stand-alone basis. Productivity improvement, by increasing profits, will add stock value, thereby yielding rewards to stock owners.

Participative management does not come easily to most entrepreneurs. Typically, they are independent creatures who do not cater to interference, real or perceived. Corporate founders traditionally have felt comfortable with the fact that their mistakes are their own, as are their achievements.

58.1 THE TRANSITION TO THE OWNERSHIP CULTURE

It is not uncommon for founders of small to medium-sized privately held companies to restrict decision making to a relatively small echelon at the top, rather than bringing the lowest level of employees into the decision-making loop. The employees at that lower level typically have relatively little motivation to put themselves out on a limb by making changes in their daily operations.

Yet, that is where the expertise in specific operations lies. ESOP ownership can afford all employees from the top on down the incentive to effectuate efficiencies, because the stock that is allocated to their ESOP accounts will reflect these enhancements of profitability. A participative environment will benefit the non-ESOP stockholders as well as the participants.

Studies have demonstrated a correlation between the amounts of stock allocated to employees' ESOP accounts and productivity enhancements. Small amounts tend to produce little noticeable change, but as the value of the account balances increases, the productivity factor rises.

There is more profound change in those companies that couple meaningful levels of stock ownership with participative management style.

The old saw "Lease an acre of desert land to a farmer and you will have a desert; give an acre of land to a farmer and you will have an oasis" applies to ESOPs, but only if employees are made to feel like owners.

Founders who share ownership of their companies with employees are indeed generous, notwithstanding tax advantages. For the major stockholder to be motivated to provide more meaningful amounts of stock to the employees, he or she would like to see positive signs that the employees begin to act like stockholders and share the same concerns about the business that the founder has.

This arrangement is not likely to occur without a concerted effort. Although the founder feels that he or she is offering gold on a silver platter to the employees, the "gift" is not necessarily appreciated automatically by the employees. It is important to explain to them *why* this is "gold on a silver platter."

58.2 CREATING AN OWNERSHIP CULTURE

To create an ownership culture among the ESOP participants, it is essential that a well-conceived communications program be implemented at the very outset. The owner should convey his or her motivation for making stock ownership available to the employees, whether it be for estate liquidity, succession planning, capital formation, acquisitions, to reward loyalty, or simply to get the employees more involved with the company's fortunes (for better or for worse).

The corporate board will achieve its objectives more assuredly if it strives to make employees feel like owners by creating an ownership culture that is pervasive throughout the company.

Placards and payroll stuffers proclaiming employee stock ownership is only part of the window dressing for an ESOP company. To create a *real* sense of ownership, the employees should be given a clear understanding of the financial workings of the company. They should be given a basic understanding of what stock is, how it is valued, and how it is affected by profitability. Employees should be trained as to the relationship of expenses to revenue and how the efficiencies of each department affect profitability and share value.

An ownership culture can best be achieved by giving employees the knowledge that their voices are being heard at the top level of the company. Award programs for production efficiencies and marketing improvements can be adopted that will encourage employees to put forth their ideas. An ESOP "employee of the month" is a useful approach to adopt.

Employee advisory committees can be established to serve as advisors to the ESOP committee. The results of these committee meetings should be publicized throughout the company. Top management should be mandated to consider in a detailed manner the ESOP committee reports and act upon the recommendations, either positively or negatively, but in all instances advising the committee of management's intents. Monthly newsletters have a valuable place in helping to maintain a stream of information to the employees at all levels relating to stock ownership.

Participative management can lead to the development of an ownership culture among the employees. With it comes a greater understanding and appreciation for the ESOP, and the effect on productivity and profitability rewards for all are a likely outcome.

58.3 COMPONENTS OF THE OWNERSHIP CULTURE

(a) Knowledge about the ESOP

The summary plan description (SPD) is the first step in conveying the workings of the ESOP. The SPD is a legal requirement that must be given to all of the employees within 90 days of their becoming eligible to participate in the ESOP. It tells them the eligibility requirements and how stock is allocated to their accounts and the vesting schedule, as well as where to get other information that essentially parallels the key elements of the plan and trust documents.

It is good practice to supplement the ESOP and provide the employees with an even more basic booklet or handbook for a more user-friendly information source that refers back to the SPD, which, in turn, refers back to the plan and trust documents as the final authority.

(b) Business Knowledge

In order for ESOP participants to *act* like owners, they must *think* like owners. For this to occur, they must possess a significant amount of knowledge about the company that had heretofore been the domain of the top management.

The participants must learn about the owner's motivation for creating the ESOP. Unless this information is imparted to the employees, rumors will abound as to the owner's intent. Some employees may even harbor suspicions as to the "real" reason for creating the plan. Employees must also become conversant with how the plan works. It is important that they understand how stock is transferred from selling stockholders or from the company to their accounts, what forces drive the value of the stock up or down, and how they get cashed out of the plan.

A number of successful ESOP companies have conducted "minicourses" in basic accounting for all of the employees, from the top to the janitorial level. The emphasis here is to instruct the ESOP participants as to how profits and losses are derived and factors that affect profitability. Participants are made to understand how the employees' actions in their own departments can affect the price of the stock that is in their ESOP account.

Although an open-book approach is not mandated by ESOP law, it is becoming more and more apparent to corporate owners that sharing information with employees is beneficial. In fact, the more employees learn about gross sales, costs of doing business, market share, profit margins, and how these factors affect the employees' security, the more employees tend to pitch in and help the company achieve a better bottom line.

(c) Communicating Knowledge

It is wise to encourage a flow of knowledge throughout the company. This should be done vertically as well as horizontally on a "cross-fertilization" basis. Departments should communicate with each other as to how each can help the other maximize cooperative synergies between the departments. Information, ideas, and feedback should be the everyday rule.

All employees should be brought into the decision-making process and be recognized for having contributed ideas that will increase efficiency at their department level. This strategy will result in employees becoming more creative and more adept at solving everyday problems. The prevailing atmosphere of the company should be conducive to expressing ideas without fear of being "put down" and without superiors feeling threatened from below. The goal of all should be to create profits for the company which, in turn, reaches their pockets through the ESOP.

(d) Inducing Employee Participation

The more employees are encouraged to participate in the decision-making process, the greater the effect on productivity. Employees who are given the opportunity and the responsibility to make decisions should be held accountable for the results that follow. Participative groups of inter- or intradepartment employees can be an effective means of ensuring greater employee participation. In each of these groups, constant reminders should be made that will reinforce the employees' self-image as owners. The individual talents of each employee should be recognized by their peers at the participative management group meetings. The employees will blossom and will tend to enlarge on their unique talents for the betterment of all. The ownership culture will begin to permeate the total corporate environment.

58.4 SUMMARY

To capitalize on the value of participative management, it is imperative that a company should set forth its business objectives and define its vision to create an ownership culture among all employees. Strategies should be designed that will improve work flow, quality, sales, cost controls, and administration.

A program of communication and education should be established for ESOP participants at all department levels as it pertains to developing ownership culture. It would be effective as well to define productivity benchmarks and measures of progress for the purpose of assessing the effectiveness of the participative management effort.

The strategy should be long term but must be implemented with short-term checkpoints. Employees should be reminded often that they *are* owners and they must *think* like owners.

The company's advertising effort should proclaim to customers and suppliers that they are dealing with decision-making owners. The rewards will soon become apparent.

CHAPTER FIFTY-NINE

Governance Issues in ESOP Companies

59.1 INTRODUCTION

Corporations that implement ESOPs do so for a wide variety of purposes. ESOPs may be used to implement programs that, for all practical purposes, seem to be for the benefit of the shareholder that is selling stock to the ESOP under Internal Revenue Code (IRC) Section 1042, or for the benefit of the corporation that is using the ESOP to finance growth.

Irrespective of the fact that an ESOP can benefit shareholders or the corporation itself, the regulations that govern ESOPs state very clearly that ESOPs—and all other qualified retirement plans—must be for the exclusive benefit of the employees. One must walk a fine line to serve working entities while doing so for the exclusive benefit of only one entity.

The ESOP is not only a retirement plan but is also ownership of stock in the sponsoring company. Good corporate governance thus demands that the trustee be treated in a way that benefits stockholders.

59.2 IMPACT ON EMPLOYEES OF THE FIRST ESOP TRANSACTION

Corporate governance should also give thorough consideration to techniques that will help develop an ownership culture among the ESOP participants. Many corporate sponsors of ESOPs that have been in force for a decade or more have arrived at a phase of their existence when the initial financing for the transaction that provided the impetus to adopt the ESOP has been paid off.

The first transaction might have involved the sale of a block of stock by a founding sole shareholder who took advantage of the tax deferral under IRC Section 1042. This might have been a sale representing 30 percent of the outstanding shares. Now the loan to the ESOP has been fully amortized and the stock completely allocated to the accounts of the ESOP participants. At the time the loan was initiated, the value of the stock declined by the amount of the loan. The participants may not have fully comprehended why this occurred—after all, the company was having its best year. Their lack of understanding may have been due to the inadequacy of the original communication program.

As the principal of the loan started to be paid down, the shares were released for allocation to the employees' ESOP accounts. The process started to make more sense to them because they experienced the ESOP beginning to work for them. Real value was being added to their accounts. It is often at this point that a quantum leap occurs in employees' understanding of the relevance of the ESOP to their future well-being. As stock continues to be allocated year after year, the employee ownership culture becomes ever more visible.

During the early stage of an ESOP, while the loan is being paid down, the decision process is entirely in the hands of the management, particularly as to important financial matters and advice to the trustee on ESOP-related decisions. As time goes on, it often becomes apparent to management that the employees should become more involved.

Neither the Internal Revenue Service (IRS) nor the Department of Labor (DOL) requires that the employees/participants participate in the management and operational aspects of the employer. Experience has demonstrated, however, that greater participative management practices can be rewarding. This is particularly true as more stock is allocated to the employees' ESOP accounts. The combination of these two elements in ESOP companies has resulted in greater productivity, according to various studies. Advisory committees of ESOP participants have been formed at a number of companies. Although they have no fiduciary power or legal responsibility in connection with the ESOP, they are often effective in strengthening the lines of communication among the various levels of employees.

Open-book management is becoming more widespread as a technique to educate employees as to ways in which they can impact profitability and share value. Quarterly meetings, forums, and various other techniques to encourage employees to lend their input can have a positive effect on productivity and create a happier work force.

Mature ESOP companies are good at finding the best ways to govern themselves. There seems to be no common denominator among the companies that have ESOPs any more than there is with those that have no ESOP, other than the fact that they are individualistic.

59.3 HOW TO AVOID CREATING TWO CLASSES OF EMPLOYEES

The loan has been fully amortized and the stock that was sold in the Code Section 1042 transaction has all been allocated to the accounts of the employees. What about new employees who have since been brought into the company? Will there be two classes of employees, namely, those who own equity in the company and those who do not? Let's discuss some of the ways that this can be avoided.

The loan from the corporation to the ESOP, the inside loan, can be designed with a longer term of years than the loan from the bank to the corporation. This will stretch out the period during which stock will be allocated to the employees' accounts. By so doing, an employee who becomes eligible for participation in the ESOP after the bank has been paid in full can still receive allocations of stock in his or her ESOP account.

The newer employees can also receive allocations if the selling shareholder sells another traunch of stock after having sold one earlier.

If no further stock is to be sold, the company can begin to make contributions of stock to the ESOP. Alternatively, it might contribute cash to the ESOP, which would be used to cash out the accounts of terminating ESOP participants. The stock of those ex-participants will be recycled within the ESOP and reallocated among all of the participants, including the newer ones.

If a participant terminates before being fully vested, the forfeitures from their accounts will be reallocated among those employees who are still with the company, including the newcomers.

CHAPTER SIXTY

Succession Planning Case Histories

60.1 INTRODUCTION

Founders of private corporations who have more than one heir usually face a fairness dilemma as to the apportionment of equity among their children. There is no common denominator as to the myriad of circumstances among such families, as evidenced by some of the situations with which this author has been involved from a consulting perspective.

60.2 CASE 1: THE PARENTS WHO WANTED TO BE FAIR

(a) The Facts

Richard Thompson, age 63, is 100 percent owner of a manufacturing firm, Thompson, Inc. Richard is ready to start easing out of the business to pursue his various personal interests, not the least of which is travel. He and his wife have one son, Mark, who has been working in the family business in various capacities for the past few years. Mark graduated from college with a major in business and is attending night classes in a technical school that offers a program in an aspect of his father's trade. He aspires to sit in his dad's chief executive officer (CEO) chair someday and his parents are hopeful and confident that he will do so. The parents have a married daughter, Judy, who is employed as a general manager of a distribution firm. She has evidenced no desire to work in her father's business, but Judy has expressed a strong desire to have her own distribution firm someday.

The great preponderance of Richard's assets is stock in this nonpublic C corporation. Corporate earnings are healthy and the company's accountant estimates that the stock of the company would have a fair market value of $20 million. The stock is appreciating at a 15 percent compounded annual rate. The corporation's annual payroll is $4 million. The firm contributes about $300,000 per year to its profit-sharing plan.

(b) The Parent's Objectives

Richard wants to transfer stock and eventual control of his corporation to Mark; therefore, selling the company to outside investors is not an option. Richard would like to start diversifying his assets and moving away from his nonliquid position to one that is highly liquid and able to provide him and his wife with an income so that he will not require a salary from the business during his son's tenure at the helm.

Dad and Mom do not want to give company stock to their daughter because her position as a minority shareholder in her brother's company would not be in anyone's best interest. They love their daughter just as much as they do their son, but they have no other assets to speak of that they could give to her at this time.

Richard, as founder of the company, has always had a feeling of loyalty toward the managers and other employees who helped bring the company to its current state of success. He would like to have them share in the future success of the company.

(c) Course of Action

Mr. and Mrs. Thompson formed a family limited partnership (FLP) to which they transferred the stock of Thompson, Inc. This was without tax consequence. They also created a new corporation, NEWCO. Mr. Thompson owned 51 percent of NEWCO's stock, Mrs. Thompson owned 48 percent, and Mark owned one percent. NEWCO became the general partner (GP) of the FLP. The GP unit comprised one percent of the value of the partnership.

Mr. and Mrs. Thompson owned all of the limited partnership (LP) units, which comprised 99 percent of the value of the FLP. The one percent GP had 100 percent voting control of the FLP and the 99 percent LP units had zero rights as to voting or transferability.

An independent appraiser was engaged to determine the value of the corporation's stock from two perspectives, namely from the perspective of the parents making minority gifts of stock to an FLP and from the perspective of selling a minority share of Thompson, Inc. stock to the ESOP.

The appraiser assigned a larger valuation discount for purposes of making gifts of LP units than for purposes of selling a minority stock interest to the ESOP. The logic of his thinking lay in the fact that the holder of an LP unit in the FLP has no market at all for the stock and no power to vote or to transfer it in any way. The stock that is allocated to the accounts of the ESOP participants, by contrast, does have a guaranteed market. Holders have an option that allows them to put the stock to the corporation when they terminate, retire, die, or become disabled. The discount placed on the LP units for gifting purposes was 45 percent.

Mr. and Mrs. Thompson made a combined one-time gift of LP units to Mark equal to their gift exemption at the time, of $1.3 million. This was equivalent to a nondiscounted value of $2.36 million. And the FLP sold 30 percent to the ESOP, the loan being repaid with pretax dollars.

(d) ESOP

We converted the company's profit-sharing plan to an employee stock ownership trust, keeping the profit-sharing plan assets invested as they had been. All new corporate contributions would be used to service the leveraged ESOP. We procured senior debt financing to enable the ESOP to purchase stock from the FLP in an amount that represented 49 percent of the outstanding shares of the corporation.

(e) Section 1042

By adhering to the provisions of Internal Revenue Code (IRC) Section 1042, which involved investing the proceeds of the sale in qualified replacement securities within a year after the sale, the partnership would be able to defer or possibly ultimately avoid capital gains tax on the appreciation of the stock. Because Richard started the company in his garage, his basis in the company was, for all practical purposes, nearly zero.

(f) Investing the Proceeds

Mr. Thompson had a strong desire to gradually shift ownership of the business to Mark, who would devote his future to building the company. At the same time, Richard intended to be fair to his daughter by helping her along in the career of her choosing.

An opportunity seemed to present itself when his daughter told him that the owner of the distribution firm that employed her was considering retiring and had indicated that he might soon seek a buyer for the firm. She told her employer that she was interested in acquiring the company.

We arranged for the partnership to invest the proceeds of the sale of its Thompson, Inc. stock in a specially designed long-term note, a floating rate note (FRN) that is suitable as qualified replacement property under Section 1042. The FLP borrowed 90 percent of the value of the FRN without fear of triggering the capital gains tax. The FLP used $1.9 million of the amount it borrowed from the long-term note to make an equity investment for a minority interest as a coinvestor with daughter Judy so as to make it possible for her to acquire the distributing company from the owner. The selling shareholder took a note for the balance of the purchase price based upon the projected restructured cash flow. Judy acquired control of the company and was off and running in her new capacity as CEO of the distribution company, the fulfillment of her dream. This transaction did not constitute a gift and therefore did not use up any of the parents' lifetime gift tax exemption.

Their daughter was not to have any ownership in the family business, so the parents made gifts of LP units to her in the amount of $20,000 annually. They also planned to give Judy LP units in amounts that corresponded with the increases in the lifetime gift exemption as they become available.

The parents will leave any remaining balance of Thompson, Inc. stock to Mark that had not been sold to the ESOP during their lifetimes.

(g) Control

Mr. Thompson will be able to maintain effective control of Thompson, Inc. for as long as he wishes. He not only controls NEWCO, the GP that controls the assets that are in the FLP, but he holds the stock that had not been transferred to the FLP or sold to the ESOP.

Effective control of the ESOP lies in the hands of the individual who owns more stock than anyone outside of the ESOP. If, for example, Richard sold his remaining shares to the ESOP, the son's shares comprising all of the shares outside of the ESOP would have effective voting control over all of the ESOP shares. Any company stock left in the estates of Dad and Mom would be left by will to the son as would the GP unit. Any nonemployer stock or other assets in the estates could be divided equitably between the children at the time of the death of the surviving parent.

(h) Income Transition

Richard had been pulling a well-deserved substantial salary and bonus out of the company. For the succession plan to be successful, it had to take into consideration income continuity. Richard made it clear to his advisors that he did not intend to continue to derive any compensation from the company after his son became qualified to be CEO.

He wanted to give his son every opportunity to make the company continue its sterling growth pattern and even improve upon it. Obviously, this would be thwarted were Richard to drain earnings out of the company. The income that the parents would receive from their qualified replacement securities would provide more than ample income to let them do what they wished during their retirement years. It should be noted that the full proceeds of the sale went to work for the parents, because they were not eroded by capital gains tax under IRC Section 1042. Richard agreed to serve his son as a consultant for a reasonable period of time (i.e., until the ESOP loan was retired). He would also retain voting control during that period.

(i) Providing the New CEO with Additional Equity

The son would not be able to be an ongoing participant in the ESOP, because his father sold his stock under Section 1042. We advised Richard to structure a program whereby the son would be granted performance stock options so that he could reap the benefits of any future growth in the value of the stock. This would allow him to increase his percentage ownership in the company.

(j) Buy–Sell Agreement

The father entered into a cross-purchase buy–sell agreement with his son, which provided that upon Richard's death, if it occurred prior to his wife's death, the shares he still owned at that time would be sold to his son. This was funded by a life insurance policy on Richard's life, with the son as owner and beneficiary. The corporation would pay the premium under a reverse split-dollar structure, with Mark owning the unencumbered cash value of the policy. The effect of this is to let the corporation absorb the major cost of the insurance while providing Mark with a tax-favored retirement plan.

(k) Summary

The succession planning permitted Richard to turn the company reins over to his son and covered all the required bases in conforming with the parent's objectives. Here is what the program achieved:

- The plan satisfied the fairness issue of providing adequately for the child who was not to be involved in the business while she was still young enough to make something of the opportunity. Fair does not necessarily mean equal.

- It provided a means for Richard and his wife to step out of the company gracefully, without being forced to continue to take income from the company after relinquishing control to their son.

- The ESOP was the enabling vehicle of succession plan. It provided the means whereby the parents' nonliquid assets could be transformed to liquid assets with no capital gains tax erosion.

- The IRS would pay about 41 cents on the dollar toward the ownership transfer by allowing the corporation to deduct the principal and interest payments on the portion of the stock that Richard sold to the ESOP.

- The $300,000 annual contribution the company had been making to the profit-sharing plan was diverted to debt service to put liquidity into Richard's hands and provide him with the means to diversify his estate and achieve succession planning.

- The ESOP gave Richard the opportunity to say "thanks" to his valuable employees who had stood by him for many years. The ESOP would provide them with equity tax free, with no outlay on their parts.

- The ESOP provided all of the employees with the incentive to increase productivity and profitability.

- The ESOP accelerated the son's timetable for assuming a significant equity stake in the company.

- The family limited partnership allowed Richard to transfer a greater amount of stock to Mark than would normally be the case, because of the larger discount assigned to the gift. The amount he gave to his son would, of course, not grow in Richard's estate and would ultimately reduce his taxable estate.

- The irrevocable trust, funded by life insurance, will transfer large blocks of tax-free cash to the children.

- The implementation of the succession plan gave credence to Mark that there was light at the end of the tunnel. He would be able to assume the title of CEO and, eventually, control of the company.

60.3 CASE 2: TRANSITION PLAN FOR OWNERS WITH DIFFERENT GOALS

(a) The Facts

Bill, age 55, and Phil, age 70, each own 50 percent of the stock of Manuco, Inc., a machine shop that they founded 25 years earlier. Bill is president and CEO. Phil is chairman and chief operating officer (COO). Phil has been sharing more and more of his daily operational duties with his son, Paul, age 40, who has worked in the company for 12 years.

Bill has a son, Frank, age 24, who has been working in the business in various capacities for the past three years. The company operates as a C corporation. Bill and Phil have current annual salaries of $200,000. Pretax annual earnings, currently running at $1.5 million, have been growing over the past five years at 18 percent annually. Bill and Phil recently rejected an offer of $9 million from a potential buyer.

Aside from his stock in Manuco, Inc., Phil has an investment rental property that carries itself but little more. In a nutshell, he is very illiquid. Phil has depended on his salary from Manuco, Inc., to maintain his standard of living. He had considered trying to get his co-owner, Bill, to agree to selling the company to an outside buyer, but this would deprive Phil's son of a potentially lucrative future with the company. He would also like to know that the company that he co-founded will be perpetuated. Phil had been looking into the idea of selling some of his stock to an ESOP and diversifying his assets into a form that would provide a livable income. He wanted to get some company stock into Paul's hands as well. Phil really wanted to retire from the business.

(b) Bill's Objectives

Bill has no desire to retire in the foreseeable future but might be ready to start easing out in about 10 years. His son, Frank, has not shown the aptitude for becoming CEO that Paul has. Bill feels that Frank might be too inexperienced to provide a clue as to his potential at this early stage. Perhaps, as Frank develops, he might be equipped to succeed Paul.

(c) The Game Plan

Phil and Bill concurred with the result of the feasibility study we performed, which showed that the company could comfortably service $4.5 million of debt to counterlend to an ESOP for purchase of that amount of stock from the stockholder.

A valuation firm determined that the minority value of the company for ESOP purposes was $7.5 million, but that a control premium would bring it to a value of $9 million. The independent valuation determined the total value of the stock of the company to be $9 million on an enterprise or control basis. Phil decided that he would sell 40 percent of the outstanding stock of the company to the ESOP and would sell the remaining 10 percent to his son, Paul.

To be eligible for the control premium or enterprise price for his shares, it was agreed that Bill would sell 10.1 percent of his stock to the ESOP in addition to that sold by Phil under Section 1042. This brought the ESOP into a position of owning 50.1 percent, a percentage that justified the selling shareholders receiving a control price rather than a minority discounted price for their stock. Phil worked out an agreement with Paul whereby Paul would pay his dad for the 10 percent portion of the company stock over a period of 10 years, principally through the means of a corporate bonus. Phil would pay capital gains tax on that increment of the sale.

(d) Recapitalization

We suggested that the company be recapitalized prior to the sale of stock by the shareholders. A new class of convertible preferred stock was created that paid a 10 percent annual dividend. Dividends paid by the corporation on the convertible preferred stock in the ESOP would be tax deductible by the company if used to pay down ESOP debt. The stock would convert into the common stock at the end of the term period of the loan.

We designed the stock so that upon conversion, the conversion premium would result in a reallocation of equity to the benefit of Bill and, to a proportionately lesser extent, Paul, because they would own all of the common stock at that point in time.

Their equity gain to the holders of the common stock was fair because the employees had dividends allocated to their ESOP stock accounts; the owners of the common stock did not receive dividends because they would not have been tax deductible by the corporation.

(e) Financing the Sale

The transactional price for the purchase of 50.1 percent of the outstanding shares by the ESOP from Phil and Bill amounted to $4,509,000. We were successful in procuring that amount of senior debt from a commercial bank, due in great measure to the fact that the ESOP created major tax deductions which resulted in increasing the cash flow of the company significantly for debt service.

The corporation was permitted to make tax-deductible contributions of 25 percent of its $3 million of covered payroll ($750,000) plus unlimited interest. It was also allowed to deduct the 10 percent dividend ($450,000) on the $4.5 million of stock that was sold to the ESOP.

The deduction for the payment of principal was $1.2 million, saving $492,000 in taxes (41 percent tax bracket). Interest is tax deductible over and beyond this amount.

(f) Reinvesting the Sales Proceeds

Both Phil and Bill reinvested the proceeds of the sale in qualified replacement property within the prescribed 12-month period after the transaction, thereby deferring or possibly avoiding recognition of capital gains tax on the sale.

(g) Results

Phil achieved his objective of retiring on a timely basis and diversifying his assets without experiencing any erosion on the proceeds due to capital gains tax. He also put his son, Paul, into an equity position and enabled him to move into Phil's position as COO. Bill, while selling some of his stock representing 10.1 percent of the outstanding shares of the company, was actually able to increase his net equity position because he was able to benefit from the conversion ratio reallocation of equity. Paul also increased his equity share, though to a proportionately lesser extent.

Bill maintained effective control of the corporation, inasmuch as he retained the majority of the stock outside of that owned by the ESOP trust.

The employees became beneficial owners of the equity as participants of the ESOP, without contributing a dime or being taxed on the shares that were allocated to their accounts. They will gain equity as stock appreciates in value.

The government contributed tax savings valued at 41 percent of the value of the transaction.

60.4 CASE 3: TRANSITION USING A CHESOP

Robert Gage, age 65, founded Gage Company, Inc. He became a graduate mechanical engineer 30 years ago. His wife, Anne, age 64, worked in the firm for the first 20 years but then returned to college to earn a master's degree in American literature, a subject in which she has a passionate interest. The company is a manufacturer of high-precision medical equipment. Rob is an inventor and literally started the company by producing his first product by hand in his garage.

The first year's sales amounted to $50,000 but grew rapidly when Robert hired his first salesman. Robert invented several additional products that were sold successfully in the same market. Most of the company's revenue now comes from manufacturing according to customers' specifications that require close tolerance work.

Robert hired a young engineer, Gordon, away from a competitor 10 years earlier and agreed to give him an option to purchase 25 percent of the stock of the corporation. Gordon was to exercise the options over time using the performance bonuses that Robert would pay him.

(a) The Objective

Robert had the foresight to groom Gordon as his eventual successor. In the precise manner of a true engineer, Robert had long ago targeted age 60 as the date he would start reducing the time he spent at work and planned to retire completely at age 65. Gordon would assume the title of CEO at that time.

(b) The Exit Vehicle

Robert had a number of approaches to dispose of his 75 percent interest in the corporation. His sense of loyalty to the company's 75 employees and particularly to Gordon eliminated the thought of selling the company to an outside buyer. He had received overtures from many tire-kickers, one of whom had recently made a serious offer of $12 million for the business, which he rejected.

Robert was a frequent guest lecturer at the engineering school at his alma mater. He supported the school's building fund drives and wanted to continue his financial support as well as his lecturing activity in the years ahead.

From our description of the CHESOP (charitable ESOP), Robert felt that it would be ideal for allowing him to fulfill his objectives: to have the company in Gordon's hands and have a lifetime income that would allow him and Anne to pursue their interests with financial security.

(c) The Mechanics

Robert had us implement an ESOP for the company. The ESOP engaged an independent valuation firm to establish fair market value for the company stock; the value for the company was determined to be $14 million. We were able to procure financing from a commercial senior debt lender in the amount of $7 million based upon ESOP financing. The purpose of the loan was to acquire stock for the ESOP from Robert.

Although this amount was less than the $10.5 million that would be needed to acquire all of Robert's 75 percent interest in the company, it was felt that deductible debt service for the $7 million loan was well within the company's cash flow capacity and would still allow the company to continue the growth it had been experiencing for many years.

Robert gave the ESOP a four-year option to acquire his remaining shares at the current value of $3.5 million, based upon the presumption that a successful refinancing could occur at that time. Robert elected to sell his shares in accordance with IRC Section 1042. He purchased qualified replacement property (QRP) well within 12 months after the sale of his company stock. He then donated his QRP to his charitable remainder unitrust (CRUT) over a period of years so that he could continue to spread his tax deductions for the gifts over a greater number of years. He would deduct 30 percent of his adjusted gross income annually. The amount of the gift deduction was calculated by determining the amount of the assets of the CRUT that would remain for charity when Robert and his wife died. Meanwhile, the CRUT would have paid them a lifetime income based on a percentage of the trust assets. Robert and his wife were trustees of the CRUT and had absolute control over the choice of investments.

Aside from the donor's tax deduction, the earnings of the CRUT accumulate tax-free, and at the end of the line the CRUT assets will go to charities of the donor's choice and are not includable in the donor's taxable estate. The CRUT, however, deprives the children of their inheritance. Robert and his wife remedied this by creating an irrevocable trust whose sole purpose was to purchase life insurance on the donors' lives.

The children are the beneficiaries. The insurance death benefits are received income tax-free and estate tax-free. The parents make gifts of the annual premium to the CRUT out of the tax savings and the income stream they receive from the CRUT.

(d) Result

- Robert provided for the orderly transition of the company with control vested in Gordon, because he, as the only stockholder outside of the ESOP, had effective control over the ESOP shares.

- Robert and his wife maximized their retirement income by arranging to have their selected investments build up tax-free inside the CRUT.

- Robert departed from the company with a clear conscience, because his loyal employees would not only be more secure, in the sense that they would not be displaced as a result of a merger or sale, but they would also actually own the company to which they were devoting their working careers.

- Robert and Anne can continue to make donations to the engineering school from time to time out of the CRUT assets. They can endow a chair at the college upon their death if this is their desire.

- Robert ended up with a greater amount to invest after the sale than he would have had he sold the corporation to an outside buyer.

- By transferring the QRP into the CRUT, his assets became creditor-proof.

- The assets escaped being subject to estate taxes.

- The donor's child was not disinherited because of the funded irrevocable trust.

(e) Summary

The ESOP made it possible for Robert to provide for succession planning that was humane to the employees while providing a more secure retirement for him and for Anne.

60.5 CASE 4: THE MULTISTOCKHOLDER BUYOUT

(a) The Facts

Weldo, Inc. is a 50-year-old company in a rural community. The company was purchased from its ailing founder 15 years ago by the four current officers and 13 other local investors who, though not employed by the company, felt that the community could not afford to allow the company to go into liquidation or lose the company through acquisition. At that time, the company had 15 employees. Now it has 70 employees from the area and is very profitable.

The current stockholders who have the greatest number of shares have reached ages at which they would like to start ridding their estates of illiquid investments other than their residences. They quickly discarded the obvious choice of selling the company to a strategic buyer, because that would undoubtedly mean a relocation of the company away from their community. We were brought in to consider the feasibility of doing an ESOP buyout. It was important to determine the number of shareholders that wanted to sell, because a tender offer would have to be made to all of the stockholders. As it turned out, all of the shareholders wanted to liquidate at least some of their holdings using a Section 1042 election and engaged us to implement an ESOP for the firm.

An independent valuation determined the fair market value to be $10 million.

(b) Obtaining Financing

We put together a compelling presentation for the state's Economic Development Authority (EDA), showing the economic impact that a loss of jobs of this magnitude would have on the community and on the state itself. The EDA pointed out that it would be far more enthusiastic about our prospects for procuring the financing if the employees themselves put up some cash as an indication of their faith in, and commitment to, the buyout.

The employees had a negligible amount of cash equity other than in the corporation's defined contribution plan. As a group, they had approximately $2 million allocated to their pension accounts. We pointed out that the pension funds could not be used by the employees directly to invest in the company's stock. It would be technically feasible if the company were to terminate the pension plan. All plan participants would become fully vested. The employees could either take their cash and be taxed or, as a better alternative, they could roll the assets from their pension accounts into an individual retirement account (IRA) within 60 days after the distribution of the assets occurred. An employee could then, on a purely voluntary basis, use the assets in his or her IRA to purchase stock of the employer company as an investment of the IRA. Before these funds could be used for the purpose at hand, an offering memorandum had to be prepared and possible securities law issues had to be considered. The employees opted to use $1 million of their qualified plan money to acquire Weldco stock. We were able to procure EDA-backed funding for $9 million at a favorable interest rate, the funding for enabling the ESOP to acquire all of the remaining shares of the company.

The $1 million of employee cash was earmarked as operating capital. The selling shareholders sold 100 percent of their stock to the ESOP electing under Section 1042. They took back a subordinated note from the ESOP with payments deferred until the bank was repaid.

Weldo, Inc. then began servicing the debt by making tax-deductible contributions to the ESOP in an amount equal to principal and interest, and the employees were transformed into employee owners.

(c) Summary

The company is very important to the welfare of the local community in that it represents a large tax base and is an employer of a large percentage of the heads of households in the area. The ESOP turned out to be the key to keeping the firm in the community. It is expected that the employees, as owners, will have a new spark that will enhance their creativity and productivity. Within one month after the buyout, the company's letterhead and trucks carried the message, "This is an employee-owned company."

The selling shareholders were pleased that a market had been created for their stock. The fact that they could sell their shares with no recognition of capital gains tax was frosting on the cake.

60.6 CASE 5: THE MANAGEMENT BUYOUT OF A DIVISION

(a) The Facts

Mr. Beam, the founder of Traico, Inc., a privately held corporation, wanted to start becoming more liquid. He made a decision to divest his company of a division that could operate successfully on a stand-alone basis. He had planned on seeking a buyer, such as, perhaps, a venture capital firm.

Mr. Johnson, the division's general manager, at the behest of Mr. Beam, contacted a management buyout firm to see if they were interested in acquiring the division from Traico, Inc., but encountered little interest in such an acquisition. Mr. Johnson then asked the owner of Traico if he could put his hat in the ring to compete with this or other potential suitors for acquiring the division. Mr. Beam had fond feelings toward the general manager, who had worked his way up the ladder over his 15-year tenure with the company. Moreover, he was doing a great job of running the division. If he did not go along with the deal, there would be no deal. With these thoughts in mind, Mr. Beam recognized that the general manager and the division's employees should probably be given preferential consideration over other potential buyers.

The division was in a highly specialized field that required a great deal of expertise. The general manager and some of the other talented employees would be hard to replace. If several of them were to leave the company, the division would not be nearly as valuable to a buyer as it would were they to become part of a management group to remain with the company. The general manager was not operating under any noncompetition agreement, and the mere suggestion that he and possibly other key employees might want to do other things with their lives could be quite dampening to the enthusiasm of potential acquirers.

(b) The Financial Analysis

Analysis showed that on a stand-alone basis, the earnings of the division could be used to service sufficient debt in an ESOP structure to enable the general manager to make a good offer to acquire the division from the parent.

By using an ESOP to purchase shares in addition to the amount that the general manager would purchase, the deal could be sweetened considerably—ESOP financing would permit the deal to be done on a pretax rather than after-tax basis.

(c) Structuring the Buyout

Our structure for the purchase seemed logical and doable to both Mr. Beam and Mr. Johnson. We suggested that a new corporation be created (NEWCO).

NEWCO's capital structure was comprised of common stock representing 10 percent of the value of the corporation and a super common, dividend-paying stock. The dividend would be used to help pay the ESOP debt and no further dividends would be paid after the end of the loan term of years. An independent valuation determined fair market value to be $8 million. We implemented an ESOP for NEWCO. The general manager invested $800,000 for the common stock (i.e. 10 percent of the purchase price).

The ESOP would invest its borrowed funds to acquire the super common stock of NEWCO.

(d) Capitalization

We procured $6 million of senior debt from an out-of-state bank and mezzanine or subordinate debt financing for another 15 percent of the purchase price. The company was projected to be in the 41 percent state and federal tax bracket. This meant that the government was providing 41 percent of the buyout cost, because principal as well as interest was fully tax deductible.

We suggested the use of various classes of stock, along with stock options, thereby making it possible for the management group to gain a significant amount of additional equity. The valuation firm had the degree of sophistication required to value the forms of securities that were to be used.

(e) Use of Dividends

We designed the ESOP to exclude members of collective bargaining units. The nonunion employees constituted *only* about 25 percent of the total employee population.

The payroll of the nonunion employees was too small to do the ESOP transaction; in a leveraged ESOP, 25 percent of the covered payroll was the maximum amount that could be contributed *and* deducted by the corporation for the payment of principal.

The super common stock was designed to pay a 9 percent dividend. The corporation could deduct the dividend it paid on the stock in the ESOP for the purpose of acquiring stock from NEWCO. Therefore, for every $1 million of funds borrowed by the ESOP, NEWCO could pay $90,000 of tax-deductible dividends to the stock in the ESOP. For the $7.2 million block of super common stock that the ESOP purchased, the dividend was $648,000 that would be used to service the ESOP and be totally tax deductible by NEWCO. This is in addition to the deductible contributions based upon payroll. The company could deduct an unlimited amount of interest over and beyond this amount. Therefore, although the covered payroll was too small for the amount of financing that was to be involved in the transaction, we made up the shortfall through the use of dividends.

(f) Summary

NEWCO is prospering. Earnings that were being used to enhance the consolidated financials are being used to pay down the acquisition debt, with some left over to build the company.

None of the employees faced dislocation in the management buyout scenario, as they likely would have had the division been sold to an outside acquirer. NEWCO is now a thriving enterprise, and the tax savings are helping to retire the acquisition debt.

CHAPTER SIXTY-ONE

Companies That Should Not Have an ESOP

61.1 ESOP NONCANDIDATES—RULES OF THUMB

Corporations with a poor track record of earnings and whose prospects are not likely to improve are not logical candidates for an ESOP. It is important that a company be in a position to demonstrate historical and sustainable stability for purposes of valuing its stock.

Many corporations, though well endowed with assets and profitability, may be lacking in payroll intensity. Such companies might be unable to generate sufficient tax savings through an ESOP to make such a plan worthwhile. A nonleveraged ESOP permits a maximum annual contribution of 15 percent of covered payroll. If the corporation is in a 40 percent combined state and federal tax bracket, and has a covered annual payroll of $200,000, a 15 percent corporate contribution (i.e., $30,000) would give the company a $12,000 tax savings. This may not be worth the effort and cost to install an ESOP.

Companies whose prospects for growth are limited due to a decline in demand for their products or because of the deterioration of the firm's geographic location should not adopt an ESOP.

Companies whose revenues are volatile are not very well suited to have an ESOP.

An owner of a firm that is likely to experience extraordinary growth may feel that an ESOP is too dilutionary in the early years unless the owner likes the idea of giving his or her loyal employees the joy of early equity gains.

A corporation that has not formulated its objectives as to what it would like to accomplish with respect to future equity ownership in the company should not implement an ESOP until that decision has been made.

Corporations whose owners have no desire to permit rank-and-file employees to share in the harvest of equity appreciation are certainly not candidates for an ESOP, irrespective of how the owners themselves might benefit. They would never consider their own rewards to be sufficiently adequate to offset their anguish at relinquishing any equity to the employees.

Corporations whose employees are not located in the United States cannot include them in an ESOP and are therefore not ESOP candidates.

Owners whose sole motivation in considering an ESOP is to bail out of the company, possibly using the firm's profit-sharing plan assets to purchase stock from the owner and leave the employees holding the bag, are not candidates for adopting an ESOP because their objectives cannot be met. The reason for this is that there are too many safeguards and penalties for usurping one's fiduciary responsibilities.

Limited liability companies (LLCs) are ineligible as ESOP sponsors, but the employees of LLCs that are owned by C or S corporations can be participants.

CHAPTER SIXTY-TWO

The Perfect Exit—Maximize Tax Benefit to Selling Shareholder and to the Corporation

Mr. Robert Walsh (not his real name), age 71, was the 100 percent stockholder of Walshco Enterprises (not its real name), a C corporation that he founded 25 years ago. The company is now valued at $20 million and its stock constitutes about 75 percent of his estate. He and his wife have two adult children, neither of whom are interested in being involved with the business.

Mr. Walsh has developed a good group of managers, one of whom has served as general manager for several years and has been doing a good job of actually running the company, allowing Mr. Walsh to allocate more and more of his time pursuing other personal interests.

Bob Walsh had considered some unsolicited offers from would-be buyers but he did not want his loyal employees to face an uncertain future and be left high and dry from an equity standpoint. Yet he felt that he was ready to retire from the company.

62.1 EXIT STRATEGY

We asked Bob, "Would you be interested in a way whereby you could sell your stock tax-free and perpetuate your company, letting it operate totally tax-free?" Bob's comment: "Sounds too good to be true."

We thereupon suggested an exit strategy that Bob found too attractive to pass up. He asked us to implement the plan of action. We created an ESOP for the company and had Mr. Walsh sell 100 percent of his stock to the ESOP under Code Section 1042, which permitted him to defer his taxes or possibly avoid them permanently.

To do this, the transaction had to result in the ESOP's owning 30 percent or more of the outstanding stock within 12 months of the sale.

The bank was willing to lend the company only $9 million, or about 45 percent of the value of the company stock. The corporation then loaned the $9 million to the ESOP.

Bob took back a note from the ESOP for the remaining $11 million. This note was subordinated to the bank loan with a moratorium on repaying principal and interest until the bank note was fully amortized. The ESOP purchased $20 million of stock from Bob Walsh.

A problem had to be addressed with respect to Bob's ability to purchase qualified replacement property within 12 months after the date of the sale, the prerequisite for being able to defer the taxes on the sale of his stock to the ESOP. The reason for this is that although Bob had sold $20 million of stock to the ESOP, he received only $9 million as a result of the bank loan, far short of the $20 million that he had needed to invest in qualified replacement property (QRP).

62.2 FLOATING RATE NOTE

To solve this problem, Bob invested the $9 million in a 60-year floating rate note (FRN), essentially a long-term noncallable bond, which was issued by a triple-A domestic corporation and which was designed to qualify as QRP.

The FRN pays a rate of interest that is adjusted quarterly. It is considered to be virtually perfect collateral, such that various banks will lend up to 90 percent or more against the note and at a constant spread of somewhere near one percent. Therefore, by borrowing 90 percent, there is essentially no spread between the amount of interest that is credited and the interest that is charged.

Bob then arranged a bridge loan for $11 million. This transaction was arranged simultaneously so that the $9 million that the bank loaned to the corporation plus the $11 million bridge loan enabled Bob to purchase a $20 million FRN. He then borrowed $11 million against the value of the FRN and repaid the bridge loan.

Mr. Walsh was able to use most of the cash he put down on the FRN to have an actively traded portfolio without triggering the capital gains tax down to his original basis in the stock of the company he founded.

After the bank loan was fully paid, it was time for Bob to start collecting on the $11 million note he took back from the company. The corporation continued to make tax-deductible contributions to the ESOP in an amount that was equal to principal and interest. Instead of paying this to the bank, the ESOP trustee began making the payments to Bob.

The principal payments he received were income tax-free since he had already met the requirements of Code Section 1042 by purchasing the FRN. Those payments were a return of his principal. The interest payments were taxable. He enjoyed being in the role of banker since he received the interest payments rather than the bank getting them.

He could invest the principal and interest payments freely just as he could with the earlier proceeds he had received from the bank loan.

62.3 HOW THE COMPANY CAN OPERATE TAX-FREE

In order to take advantage of the Section 1042 election, the company had to be a C corporation. At the beginning of the following year, after selling his stock to the ESOP under Section 1042, the corporation changed from being a C corporation and elected to be taxed as a Subchapter S corporation.

In a Subchapter S corporation, there is no tax at the corporate level. The tax flows through to the stockholder(s). The ESOP now owned 100 percent of the outstanding stock of the company, and since the sole shareholder was a tax-exempt entity, neither the company nor its stockholder paid any taxes. The company operated in a totally tax-free environment.

Because the corporation no longer had to divert a large percentage of its earnings to pay taxes, it was easier for the company to service the ESOP debt. As the corporation made distributions to its shareholder, the ESOP used the portion of the distributions that was not allocated to the ESOP participants' accounts toward debt repayment in addition to the contributions it received from the company to service the debt. This enabled the company to accelerate its debt repayment to the bank and later to Bob Walsh.

62.4 SUMMARY

Bob Walsh was able to achieve his objectives of perpetuating the company while putting himself into a liquid position without any tax erosion.

The ESOP also enabled the corporation to get large tax deductions and indeed avoid paying any taxes. The employees, rather than facing an uncertain future, will own and share in the growth of the company.

The corporation will continue to operate in a totally tax-free environment, thereby enhancing its ability to remain robust and have a major advantage over its competitors that must pay taxes.

Bob was able to receive an income from his invested securities, enhanced by the interest income he received on the note he had taken back from the ESOP.

The ESOP made all of this possible.

CHAPTER SIXTY-THREE

Administrative Policy Regarding Self-Correction— A Reprieve for Past Errors

63.1 INTRODUCTION

The administrative policy regarding self-correction (APRSC) was made available to enable sponsors of qualified plans to cure certain administrative defects in their plans without involving the Internal Revenue Service in the procedure.

APRSC was introduced publicly by the IRS Employee Plans Division on January 7, 1997, to allow plan sponsors and administrators to correct certain operational errors without running the risk of disqualifying the plan and thereby creating costly problems. APRSC is designed to allow plan operations to cure the problems that arise when the terms of a qualified plan or trust document are not adhered to. These must be errors or oversights that would cause the plan to be disqualified under IRC Section 401(a). The IRS created this new policy of self-correction of certain errors because the agency realizes that qualified plans have become very complex, and believes that when plan administrators make unintentional mistakes from time to time, they should be given a fair chance to correct these problems before they are forced by the IRS to comply with the rules. More specifically, here are the key elements of the changes brought about by APRSC:

1. It gives plan sponsors a period of one year for the timely correction of disqualifying defects that are operational by nature. This will avoid any IRS sanction or need to file under the Closing Agreement Program (CAP) or the Voluntary Compliance Resolution (VCR) Program for voluntary compliance of defects.

2. It clarifies the criteria for determining whether a mistake is sufficiently insignificant as not to warrant disqualification, whether or not the defect has been self-corrected (if, for example, certain benefits were not made available to eligible employees on a timely basis.)

APRSC cannot be used for the following:

1. Correcting errors that require the sponsor to file a plan amendment with the IRS.

2. Correcting operational defects that are demographic in nature, such as a shift in the makeup of the employer's work force and which would be in violation of IRC Section 401(a)(26) or Code Section 410(a).

3. Curing violations of the rule requiring that the plan be for the exclusive benefit of the employees, if there is diversion or other misuse of plan assets. This form of violation might also fall under the jurisdiction of the Department of Labor as well.

Nor is it applicable to a situation such as not adhering to the specific rules governing a sale of stock to an ESOP. On a tax-deferred basis under IRC Section 1042, it cannot be used.

APRSC is not available to correct prohibited transactions that may have occurred. For errors that are curable under APRSC, the sponsor of the qualified plan must not only remedy the specific problem at hand but must also implement systems designed to keep such errors from reoccurring. The plan sponsor must restore the plan and the status of all employees who were affected by the error or oversight to the position they would have been in if the error had not occurred. For APRSC to work, the plan sponsor must remedy the error in operation of the plan no later than the end of the plan year that follows the plan year in which the operational error occurred.

It is good practice for plan sponsors to uncover errors that might be applicable through their own self-audits, rather than having them uncovered by an IRS audit, which would preclude using the APRSC amnesty. Because of the popularity of this procedure, district IRS offices have scrutinized the use of APRSC and whether it can apply to each situation in question.

This program is available in addition to the Voluntary Compliance Resolution program. VCR sets forth guidelines for enabling plan sponsors to correct plan qualification defects. The IRS will issue a compliance letter pertaining to each specific request for cure that is brought before the IRS under the VCR program. This may be the better route if there is any question as to whether a given defect falls under the APRSC program.

63.2 ELIGIBILITY TO USE APRSC

For the plan sponsor or administrator to take advantage of APRSC, it must demonstrate that procedures and practices were in place that were designed to allow complete compliance, and that the rules were violated only because of an error or oversight on the part of the sponsor or administrator in applying the procedures. The IRS provides, as a specific example of an established practice designed to permit compliance treatment under APRSC, a check sheet to track allocations and key employee status for determining whether a plan is top-heavy.

For APRSC to be available, the plan must be operating under a consent letter of determination, including such a letter of all amendments.

Under APRSC, the sponsor or administrator must make complete corrections of errors for all of the plan years, irrespective of statutes of limitations. A correction that is inadequate can invalidate the self-correction.

The APRSC procedure cannot be used if the plan is under audit or if the plan sponsor has been notified that the plan is to be audited. An exception to this is if the defect is considered "insignificant" under APRSC.

If the sponsor corrects the operational defect by the end of the plan year that follows the plan year in which the error occurred, the problem will not be considered a disqualifying error or defect. If the operational defects are deemed "insignificant," they will not cause the plan to become disqualified. The IRS uses seven criteria in determining whether an operational defect is insignificant and thereby nondisqualifying even if it is not corrected within one year following the year in which the defect or error occurred. These criteria are:

1. The number of violations during the period under examination

2. The percentage of plan assets and contributions involved

3. The number of years in which the violation occurred

4. The number of participants affected relative to the number in the plan

5. The number of participants affected relative to the number that could have been affected

6. Whether correction was made prior to examination

7. The reason for the violation (such as date errors)

63.3 SUMMARY

APRSC CAP or VCR are welcome procedures in that they can save plan fiduciaries a great deal of concern and time in disposing of less serious defects.

CHAPTER SIXTY-FOUR

The Free ESOP Information Hotline 800-422-ESOP (3767)

There is a tremendous information gap pertaining to ESOPs. If this were not so, the vast majority of profitable and growing corporations with an annual payroll of approximately $700,000 or more would have such a plan.

- Why wouldn't a private company owner want to establish a private trading center for the stock of his or her corporation?

- Why wouldn't the owner want to be able to sell some or essentially all of his or her stock tax-deferred, or possibly tax-free, and still vote and control the stock he or she sold?

- Why wouldn't a company want to finance growth with pretax dollars? Why wouldn't the chief executive officer (CEO) want to accelerate the repayment of existing loans by deducting principal and payments?

- Why wouldn't the major or minor stockholder want to buy out a co-stockholder's interest with pretax rather than after-tax dollars and tax-free to the seller?

- Why wouldn't a company want to gain market share by using tax savings to reduce prices?

- Why wouldn't a corporation want to recover taxes in two prior years?

- Why wouldn't the corporate decision maker want to replace costly pension and profit-sharing plans with the most cost-effective employee benefit plan?

- Why wouldn't the corporation want to match its employees' 401(k) plan contributions with stock rather than cash?

- Why wouldn't the company want to reward loyalty while increasing productivity?

- Why wouldn't the majority stockholder want to establish a proven, practical business succession plan?

- Why wouldn't the owner want to sell stock tax-free and have the company operate in a totally tax-free environment?

Why? I'll tell you why. It is generally because of an information gap. This often manifests itself in the form of erroneous perceptions. For example, "I don't want the employees to tell me how to run my company" or "I don't want to dilute my stock" or "I don't want to lose control."

Perhaps a trusted advisor responds to the CEO's query by offering the well meaning, deathless nonscientific discussion-ending comment, "ESOPs? They've got problems."

The author's response to this often-heard observation is "Gosh, everything that is worthwhile has problems. Being married has problems, having kids has problems, yes, and running a corporation has problems. You still do these things, nonetheless."

We have observed over the years that it is common for owners of private corporations to want information concerning ESOPs but not to know where to obtain it. Moreover, quite often, they do not even know what questions to ask.

In order to help ESOPs proliferate by providing a resource for those who are interested in receiving specific information, the author's firm has established a free *ESOP Information Hotline.*

From past experience, we know that CEOs, chief financial officers (CFOs), certified public accountants (CPAs), financial planners, and life insurance advisors will find this service to be of particular value. If you have a profitable company with 25 or more employees and do not have an ESOP, we will prepare a free preliminary feasibility study for you.

THE FREE ESOP INFORMATION HOTLINE IS 800-422-ESOP (3767), or e-mail the author at *bob@esotgroup.com.*

Index

401(k) plan:
    administration of, 228–229
    employer match and, 227
    ESOP conversion to, 87, 209
    KSOP and, 227–228

A

Accounting, 279–281
    for contributions to nonleveraged
        ESOP, 279
    for dividends, 280
    for earnings per share, 281
    for loans, 280–281
    for stock purchase and release, 281
Accredited investors, 253
Acquisitions, 145–160
    appeal of, to seller, 159–160
    choice of target for, 155–156
    to diversify, 203–204
    structuring of, 157–159
    techniques for, 145–153
        asset purchase, 146–147, 148
        post-transaction ESOP, 147–149
        with pre-tax dollars, 149–151, 152
        with tax-free dollars, 151, 153
Adequate consideration, 46–47, 258

Administration fees, 277
Affiliated person, S&L as, 266
Allocation parameters, 65–69. *See also*
        Contribution parameters
    benefits, 65–66
    exclusions, 62
    family members, 67
    over 25 percent ownership, 68–69
American Institute of Certified Public
        Accountants, statement of
        position 93-6, 279–281
Appraiser, of stock:
    independence of, 45–46, 191
    information needs of, 52–53
    selection of, 191–193
Asset method of valuation, 48–49

B

Bankruptcy, 179
Banks:
    document analysis by, 178
    ESOPs for, 263–267
        banks and S&Ls, 263–265
        federal S&Ls, 265–266
    as estate trustees, 265
    fraudulent conveyance and, 179

knowledge of ESOP and, 183
lending criteria of, 177–178, 182–183
put option exception for, 95, 96
repurchase liability study and, 179–180
Benefits, *see* Distribution, of benefits;
    Vesting, of benefits
Bethlehem Steel, 283
Blasi, Joseph, 15
Blue sky laws, 254
Bostwick-Braun Company, 283
Buy-sell agreements, 96

C
Canterbury Press, 284
Case histories:
  of specific companies
    Bethlehem Steel, 283
    Bostwick-Braun Company, 283
    Canterbury Press, 284
    Channelock, 284
    Clay Equipment, 284
    ComSonics, Inc, 284–285
    Delta Electronics, 285
    Home Depot, 285
    Kerotest Manufacturing
        Corporation, 285
    Leslie Paper, 286
    Lowe's Companies, Inc., 286
    North Coast Brass and Copper, 286
    Oregon Steel Mills, Inc., 286–287
    Quad Graphics, Inc., 287
    Rural/Metro Corporation, 287
    Science Applications International
        Corporation, 287
    United Airlines, 287–288
    Viking Engineering and
        Development, Inc., 288
  of succession planning options,
    315–329
    with CHESOP, 323–325
    fairness to heirs, 315–320
    management buyout of division,
      327–329
    multistockholder buyout, 325–327
    owners with differing goals,
      320–322

Cash flow, increasing, 145
  with contribution of stock, 79–80
  with partial plan conversions, 80–82
  with profit-sharing plan conversions,
    82–85
Cashing out, 174–175, 195–197,
    272–273. *See also* Repurchase
    liability
C Corporation:
  conversion to S Corporation, 74–75
  leveraged ESOP, 63
Channelock, 284
Charitable ESOP (CHESOP), 217–223
  charitable lead trust and, 223
  charitable remainder trust and,
    221–222
  example of, 323–325
  in general, 217–220
  gift annuity and, 222
  pooled income fund buyout and,
    222–223
  tax effects of
    on corporation, 220–221
    on donor, 220
Charitable lead trust, 223
Charitable remainder trust (CRT),
    162–163, 221–222
Charitable remainder unitrust (CRUT),
    130–131
  in example, 324–325
Chrysler Corporation Loan Guarantee
    Act, 3
Clay Equipment, 284
Collateral, 178, 180, 182
Collective bargaining unit, eligibility
    of, 55
Combination ESOP, 63
  S Corporations and, 75–76
Commitment fee, for loan, 181
Communication, with employees,
    259–262
  about ownership culture, 307–309
  DSVGs and, 301
  in example, 291
Comparability with public companies
    method of valuation, 49

Comparable sales method of valuation, 49
Compensation, eligible, 62
Compensation plan, ESOP as, 237–238
ComSonics, Inc, 284–285
Conglomerate, *see* Acquisitions
Conrail, 2
Conte, Michael, 15
Contribution parameters, 61–65. *See also*
    Allocation parameters
  combined ESOP, 63
  dividends, 64–65
  eligible compensation, 62
  employer limits, 61, 62–63
  leveraged ESOP, 63–64
  with other qualified plans, 65
Control, maintaining, 173–176, 271–272
Controlled group, eligibility of, 56–57
Control premium, 50–52
  appraiser and, 192
Conversion, of ESOP, 87
Corporation:
  charitable ESOP's effect on, 220–221
  consents to nontax recognition, 37–39
  credit worthiness of, 177–178
  divestiture of divisions by, 111–113,
    139–144
    example of, 139–141
    succession planning and, 141–142
  ESOP benefits to, 8–9
  governance issues of, 204–206
  increasing value of, 121–122
  options for mature, 203–204
  purchase of stock from, 134–135, 136
  tax-free sale of, retaining control,
    173–176
Costs:
  administration fee, 277
  to implement ESOPs, 11
  loan commitment fee, 181

D
Debt service, *see* Leveraged ESOP;
  Loans
Deductible dividends, 101–104
Deficit Reduction Act of 1984, 3, 13,
  31, 101

Defined-benefit pension plan, 7
  contribution limits to, 226
Defined-contribution pension plan, 7
  contribution limits to, 225–226
  stock investment of, 226
Delaware and Hudson Railroad, 2
Delta Electronics, 285
De minimis rule, 36, 94, 106
Department of Labor (DOL)
  adequate consideration and, 46–47
  fiduciary and, 255
  nonfiduciary duties and, 256
  valuation and, 193
Dilution:
  contribution of stock to ESOP and,
    79–80
  minimizing of, 168–169, 270–271
  offsets to, 114
Direct loan, 280
Direct stock purchase programs, 244–245
Discounted cash flow valuation method, 49
Distribution, of benefits, 91–100
  bank analysis of, 179
  buy-sell agreements, 96
  diversification rules/methods, 92,
    93–94, 99
  dividends, 94
  as liability, 179
  liberal practice, 93
  nonleveraged rules, 92–93
  put options, 95–96, 107
  repurchase liability and, 215
  tax on, 97–98, 100
  withholding and, 95, 99–100
  written policy on, 98–99
Diversification:
  fiduciary and, 256–257
  repurchase liability and, 215
  rules of, 93–94, 99, 105–108
    implementation of, 106–108
Divestiture, 111–113, 139–144
  example of, 139–141
  succession planning and, 141–142
Dividends:
  accounting for, 280
  contribution parameters, 64–65

deductible, 101–104
distribution of, 94
exempt from withholding, 95
to repay loan, 133, 175–176
S Corporations and, 72
Division, of company:
divestiture of, 111–113, 139–144
management buyout example, 327–329
Driving share value group (DSVG),
295–297
formation checklist for, 297–301
implementation checklist for, 301–302

E

Earnings per share, 281
Economic Growth and Tax Relief
Reconciliation Act of 2001,
4, 103
Economic Recovery Tax Act of 1981, 3
Economy, ESOP benefits to, 10
Eligibility:
for ESOP participation, 55–57
for nonrecognition allocation, 36–37
for nonrecognition sale, 32
Emerson, Ralph Waldo, 115
Employee Retirement Income Security
Act of 1974 (ERISA), 2, 7, 13
fair market value and, 189, 191
fiduciary and, 255–256
repurchase liability and, 180
Employees:
allocating stock to new, 202–203, 313
avoiding two classes of, 313
communication with, 259–262
in example, 291
driving share value groups (DVSGs)
and, 295–297
eligibility of, 55–57, 62
ESOP benefits to, 9–10, 176
increasing share value for
in large companies, 295–303
in small to medium companies,
289–293
participative management and,
305–310
passing dividend through to, 102–104

profit-sharing conversion to ESOP and,
82–83
terminated, 73
Employee stock ownership trusts
(ESOTs), 6
Employer loan, 280
Equity:
increasing with ESOP, 121–122
management buyout and, 20
Equity commitment notes (ECNs),
266–267
Equity financing, 113
Equity participation planning, 239–248
under Code Section 423, 245
direct stock purchase programs,
244–245
ESOPs, 248
in general, 239–240
nonqualified stock bonus plan,
246–247
restricted stock plan, 247
stock options, 240
advantages of, 242
in closely held companies, 243
incentive plan, 241–242
nonqualified plan, 242
in private companies, 243–244
vesting of, 243
ESOPs:
advantages of, 5–10, 201–202, 208,
248, 333–335
candidates likely for, 249–250
candidates unlikely for, 331–332
case histories of, 283–288
combination, 63, 75–76
conversions to, 87
costs to implement, 11
defined/described, 7, 13–14
disadvantages/problems/solutions,
269–273
current tax deduction, 269–270
dilution minimization, 270–271
minority discount avoidance, 270
early skepticism about, 14
as exit alternative, 20–21, 25
freezing of, 207, 208

historical/regulatory background of, 1–4, 10–11, 13
implementation procedure for, 275–278
  after one year, 277–278
  feasibility study, 275–276
  steps in, 276–277
information hotline for, 337–338
options for mature, 203–204, 293
selling stock to, 29
termination of, 209
Estate taxes, 116
Estate trustees, ESOPs and banks as, 265
Excise tax:
  on ESOP's stock disposal, 32, 37
  on over 25 percent owners, 69
  on pre-59½ distributions, 98
Exit strategies, 125–127. *See* IPO; Management leveraged buyout; Outside buyer, sale to with ESOP, 165–170
  cashless tax deduction/minimum dilution, 168–169
  cashless transaction, 167–168
  contribution of redeemed shares/ minimum dilution, 169
  deducting loan principal, 169–170
  prefunding, 165
  self-banking, 166
  stock sale without leverage, 166

F

Fair market value, *see* Valuation, of stock
Fairness opinion, 50, 190
Fair return exemption, 256–257
Fair-return-on-investment rule, 59
Family limited partnership (FLP), 128
  example of, 315–320
Family members:
  allocation eligibility of, 67
  defined, 36
Federal Insurance Contribution Act (FICA), 103
Federal savings and loans, 265–266
Fiduciary:
  adequate consideration, 258
  defined by ERISA/DOL, 255–256

and ESOP as takeover defense, 257
exclusive benefit of participants, 257
exemption diversification/fair return exemption and, 256–257
multi-investor leveraged buyouts, 258
trustee selection, 257
Financial Accounting Standards Board (FASB) No. 96, 102
Financing options, 113, 181
  leveraged, 38–39
  seller financing techniques, 35–36
  zero net outlay, 59–60
Five-year averaging, 97
Floating-rate note (FRN), 33–34, 161
  in example, 334–335
Forfeitures, allocation of, 65–66
Founders, *see* Owners
Fraudulent conveyance, 179
Freezing, of ESOP, 207, 208

G

Gift annuities, 222
Going-concern asset method of valuation, 48–49
Golden handcuff, 237, 240
Governance issues, 204–206, 311–313

H

Highly compensated employees, limits on tax-deferred contributions, 227–228. *See also* Nonqualified non-equity incentive plans
Home Depot, 285

I

Implementation procedure, 275–278
  after one year, 277–278
  feasibility study, 275–276
  steps in, 276–277
Incentive plans, *see* Equity participation planning; Nonqualified non-equity incentive plans
Incentive stock option plan, 240–242
Independent contractors, excluded, 62
Information hotline, 337–338
Inside loan, 280

Installment sale, tax nonrecognition on, 39
Installments distribution, 92–93
Insurance, to fund SERP, 236–237
Internal Revenue Service (IRS):
 Advanced Notice 88-56, 94
 Code Section 133, 3, 4
 Code Section 267(b), 67
 Code Section 318(a), 68
 Code Section 351, 171–172
 Code Section 401(a), 55–57
 Code Section 401(a)(28), 93, 105
 Code Section 404, 61, 62, 225
 Code Section 404(a)(3), 62, 65
 Code Section 404(a)(9), 63
 Code Section 404(a)(9)(A), 101
 Code Section 404(k), 64
 Code Section 404(k)(2)(A)(i), 102
 Code Section 409(k)(1), 91
 Code Section 409(n), 40
 Code Section 415, 61, 62
 Code Section 415(c), 101
 Code Section 423, 245
 Code Section 501(c)(3), 217
 Code Section 1042, 31–40, 56, 127
 Code Section 1043, 223
 Code Section 4975(e)(7), 7, 63
 Code Section 4978, 32
 ISO requirements of, 241–242
 Private Letter Ruling 8828009,
  228–229
 Private Letter Ruling 9102017, 39
 Revenue Ruling 46, 2
 Revenue Ruling 59-60, 47–48
 Revenue Ruling 69-65, 257
 Technical Advice Memorandum
  9304003, 102
Investment tax credit (ITC), 2
IPO (initial public offering), 19–20, 127
 ESOP vs., 27–29
IRA (individual retirement account):
 ESOP conversion to, 87
 rollover to, 97, 209
 terminated S Corporation employees
  and, 73
Irrevocable life insurance trust
  (ILIT), 131

J
Jobs, saving of, 16

K
Kerotest Manufacturing Corporation, 285
KPMG Peat Marwick survey, 124
Kruse, Douglas, 15
KSOP, 227–228
 administration of, 228–229

L
Last in-first out (LIFO), 75
Lenders, *see* Banks
Leslie Paper, 286
Leverage, nonrecognition with less,
  38–39
Leveraged buyout (LBO), in general,
  109–111. *See also* Leveraged
  ESOP
Leveraged ESOP, 109–114, 133–137. *See
  also* Management leveraged buyout
  (MBO); Nonleveraged ESOP
 acquisition and, 155
 advantages to corporate value,
  121–122
 contribution parameters, 63–64
 deductible contributions of, 228
 deducting principal of, 169–170
 dilutionary offsets, 114
 distribution and, 92
 divisional divestiture and, 111–113
 mechanics of, 113–114
 non-ESOP loan compared to, 136–137
 options at maturity, 202–203
 to save jobs, 16
 S Corporations and, 72
 succession and, 115–119
  example of, 117–119
 tax leverage of, 110
 transaction basics of, 134–135, 136
 vs. public equity financing, 28–29
Limited liability companies (LLCs),
  ineligibility of, 332
Loans, 187–190. *See also* Leveraged ESOP
 commitment fee for, 181
 cutting cost of, 7

deductible dividends and, 101–102
reporting of, 280–281
Long, Russell E., 13
Loss carry forwards (NOLs), 185
Losses, corporate, 185
Lowe's Companies, Inc., 286

M

Management, *see also* Driving share
value groups (DVSGs)
equity of, 181
participative, 305–310
Management leveraged buyout (MBO),
20, 139–144
disadvantages of, 24
example of, 139–141
mechanics of, 113–114
spinoffs and, 113
as a succession planning aide, 141–142
Marketability discounts, 52, 130
Market value, *see* Valuation, of stock
Marx, Karl, 1
Michigan, University of, Survey
Research Center, 15
Miniconglomerate, *see* Acquisitions
Minority discount, 50–52, 130
appraiser and, 192
avoiding, 270
Miscellaneous Revenue Act of 1980, 3
Money-purchase pension plan, 7, 63
contribution limits to, 225
increasing deductible contribution
with, 196
stock investment of, 226
Multi-investor leveraged buyout, 258
Multiple-investor ESOP buyouts, 189–190

N

National Employee Ownership Council
study, 15
Net income makeup charitable unitrust
(NUMCRUT), 221
Net investment return, maximizing,
130–131
Noncallable preferred stock, 7
Non-ESOP loan, 136–137

Nonleveraged ESOP, *see also* Leveraged
ESOP
accounting for contributions to, 279
acquisition and, 155
cashing out through, 195–197
distribution rules for, 92–93
employer contribution limits to, 62–63
Nonqualified non-equity incentive plans,
231–238
design of plan, 231–234
participating units plan, 235
performance share plan, 235
phantom stock plan, 233, 234
stock appreciation rights plan
(SAR), 233, 234
supplemental executive retirement
plans (SERPs), 236–237
Nonqualified stock bonus plan,
246–247
Nonqualified stock option plan, 242
Nonrecognition sale, allocation rules, 67.
See also Tax-deferred stock
rollover
Nonresident alien employees, eligibility
of, 55
North Coast Brass and Copper, 286

O

Oregon Steel Mills, Inc., 286–287
Outside buyer, sale to, 41, 43, 127
disadvantages of, 18–19, 24
ESOP and, 21
ESOP vs., 29
strategies for, 199–200
Outside loan, 280
Owner(s), 195–197. *See also* Driving
share value groups (DVSGs)
diversification needs of, 127
as financer of ESOP, 35–36
liquidity needs of, 115–117, 173–176
portfolio of, 33–34
retirement of, 17–18
succession planning difficulties of,
23–24, 123–124
transition plan for different goals,
320–322

Ownership culture:
  components of, 308–309
  creating of, 307–308
  transition to, 306–307

P

Partial conversion, 81–82
Participating units plan, 235
Participative management, 204,
      305–310
  governance and, 311–313
  ownership culture
    components of, 308–309
    creating of, 307–308
    transition to, 306–307
Part-time employees, eligibility of, 55
Payroll ESOP (PAYSOP), 3
Peninsula Newspaper, Inc., 2
Per capita allocation, 65
Performance share plan, 235
Phantom stock plan, 233, 234
  ESOP to fund, 237–238
Pooled income fund buyout, 222–223
Prefunding, 127–128, 165
Pretax earnings:
  acquisition with, 149–151, 152
  incentive compensation and, 232
Principal, deducting, 169–170
Productivity, improved, 15–16
Profit-sharing pension plan:
  contribution limits to, 226
  conversion to ESOP, 81–85
  ESOP conversion to, 87, 209
  exempt from put option, 226
  freezing of, 291
  as passive program, 290
  stock investment of, 226
Public offering, *see* IPO(s)
Put option, 95–96, 107
  effect on repurchase liability,
      211–212
  profit-sharing plans exempt from, 226

Q

Quad Graphics, Inc., 287
Qualified plans, *see specific plans*

Qualified replacement property (QRP):
  as collateral, 178
  defined, 33
  FRNs as, 33–34
  installment sale and, 39
  portfolio makeup and, 161–162
  reporting of, 37
  tax on sale of, 33, 39–40
Qualifying employer securities, 7

R

Rabbi Trust, 236
Real estate, change to stock, 171–172
Recirculation, of shares, 213
Redemption, of shares, 213
Regional Rail Reorganization Act, 2
  1978 amendments to, 2
Relocation, preventing, 16
Repurchase liability, 182–183, 211–216
  effect on valuation, 212, 215
  funding programs for, 214–216
  of mature ESOP, 203
  put option's effect on, 211–212
  redeeming vs. recycling, 213
  study of, 206
Restricted stock plan, 247
Revenue Act of 1978, 2
Revenue Reconciliation Act 1989, 3–4
Rock Island Transition and Employee
      Assistance Act, 2
Rollovers, *see also* Tax-deferred stock
      rollover
  charitable remainder trust and, 162–163
  portfolio selection and, 162
  strategies for, 161–163
    floating rate note, 161
  tax on, 97–98, 100
Rural/Metro Corporation, 287

S

Safe harbor vesting schedules, 89–90
Salary increases, 231
Savings and loan institutions:
  as affiliated person, 266
  ESOPs for, 263–264
    federal, 265–266

Science Applications International
    Corporation, 287
Securities and Exchange Acts of 1933/
    1944, 251–252
Security law, 241–250
    antifraud regulations, 252
    blue sky laws, 254
    public company ESOPs, 253–254
    registration exemptions, 252–253
    simplifying compliance under, 252
    for sophisticated/accredited
        investors, 253
Self-banking, 166
Seller, see Owner
Senior debt, 113, 181
Share value, driving of:
    for large companies, 295–303
    for small to medium-sized companies,
        289–293
        example, 290–293
        reviving matured ESOP, 293
SLOB rules, 56
Small Business Development Act, 3
Small Business Job Protection Act of
    1996, 4
Social Security, 15
Sophisticated investors, 253
Spin-offs, 111–113, 139–144
    example of, 139–141
    succession planning and, 141–142
Stock, see also Distribution, of benefits;
        Share value, driving of; Stock
        options; Valuation, of stock
    changing real estate to, 171–172
    contributing to ESOP, 79–80
    creating market for, 6
    eligible for tax-deferred rollover, 32
    exchanging for cash while retaining
        control, 173–176
    gifts of appreciated, 217–223
    as liability, 115, 197
    purchased and release of, 281
    purchase of from corporation,
        134–135, 136
Stock appreciation rights plan (SAR),
    233, 234

Stock bonus plan, 63
Stockholders:
    cashing out with leveraged ESOP, 135
    ESOP benefits to, 9
Stock options, as incentive, 240
    advantages of, 242
    in closely held companies, 243
    incentive plan, 241–242
    nonqualified plan, 242
    in private companies, 243–244
    vesting of, 243
Subchapter S corporations, 71–77
    conversion to C Corporation, 74–75
    distribution not required, 95–96
    dividends deductible, 72
    dividends not deductible, 103
    ESOPs as employee benefit, 73–74
    leveraged ESOP, 63–64, 72
    prohibited transactions, 73
    strategies for, 75–77
    tax-deferred rollover unavailable to, 72
    tax flowthrough attributes of, 71
    terminated participants and, 73
Subordinated debt, 113, 181
Succession planning, 23–25
    advantages of ESOP for, 5–10,
        20–21, 25
    case histories of, 315–329
        with CHESOP, 323–325
        fairness to heirs, 315–320
        management buyout of division,
            327–329
        multistockholder buyout, 325–327
        owners with differing goals,
            320–322
    difficulties of, 123–126
    ESOP and, 126–128
        case study of, 129–131
    leveraged ESOP and, 115–119
        example of, 117–119
    reluctance of owners to address, 23–24
Summary plan description (SPD), 308
Supplemental executive retirement plans
    (SERPs), 236–237
Survey Research Center, University of
    Michigan, 15

T

Takeover defense, ESOP as, 257
Tax-deductible dividends, 101–104
Tax-deferred stock rollover, 31–43
  allocation eligibility, 36–37
  corporation's consent needed, 37
  holding requirements, 32–33
  of installment sale, 39
  with less leverage, 38–39
  qualified replacement property and,
      33–34, 39–40
  seller financing techniques, 35–36
  specific tax requirements of, 39–41
  stock eligibility, 32
  30 percent rule, 31–32
  unavailable to S corporations, 72
Taxes, *see also* Withholding
  deductions for charitable gifts, 217–223
  as discouraging of corporate
      perpetuation, 123–124
  recovering of, 185–186
Tax-free dollars, acquisition with, 151, 153
Taxpayer Relief Act of 1997, 4, 71
Tax Reduction Act ESOP (TRASOP), 2
Tax Reduction Act of 1975, 2
Tax Reform Act of 1976, 2
Tax Reform Act of 1986, 3, 13, 45, 89,
    91, 93, 98, 99, 191
Tax Revision Act of 1942, 1
Tax-sheltered retirement plans, 1
Technical Corrections Act of 1979, 2
Termination:
  of employee's tenure, 73
  of ESOP, 87, 209
Thin market, 19–20, 27
3-20 vesting schedule, 89–90
Total Succession Planning™, 126
Trade Act of 1974, 2
Triple-A account, 71
Trustees, 205
  selection of, 257
Twenty-five percent ownership,
    exceeding, 68

U

U.S. Congress, backing of ESOPs, 1–4,
    10–11, 13
U.S. Railway Association Authorization
    of 1979, 2
Unemployment Compensation
    Amendments Act of 1992, 95
United Airlines, 287–288

V

Valuation, of stock, 45–53. *See also*
    Share value, driving
  of adequate consideration, 46–47
  appraisers and
    independence of, 45–46, 191
    information needs of, 52–53
    selection of, 191–193
  control premium/minority discounts,
      50–52
  in example, 290
  fairness opinion, 50
  leveraged stock, 187–190
  marketability discounts, 52
  methods of, 48–50
    asset, 48–49
    comparability with public
        companies, 49
    comparable sales, 49
    discounted cash flow, 49
  report contents, 47–48, 193–194
  repurchase liability effect on,
      212, 215
  selecting firm for, 191–193
Valuation firm, selecting, 191–193
Venture capital, 110, 181
Vesting, of benefits, 89–90. *See also*
    Distribution, of benefits
  of stock options, 243
  at termination, 209
Viking Engineering and Development,
    Inc., 288
Von Thunen, Johann Henrich, 1

W

Wealth replacement trust (WRT), 131
Withholding:
    distribution and, 95, 99–100
    not required on tax-deductible
        dividends, 103
Working capital, increasing:
    with contribution of stock, 79–80
    with partial plan conversions, 80–82

    with profit-sharing plan conversions,
        82–85
    with purchase of stock, 134–135, 136

Z

Zero net outlay funding, 59–60